PRAISE FOR *A Chance in the Wo*

"*A Chance in the World* is a *must* read. Steve Pemberton's beautifully
is a rags to riches journey—beginning in a place and with a jari
experiences that could have destroyed his life. But Steve's refusal to give in to
those forces, and his resolve to create a better life, shows a courage and resilience that is an example for many of us to follow. He makes us all proud."

—STEDMAN GRAHAM, AUTHOR, EDUCATOR, ENTREPRENEUR

"Pages into this beautifully written story of Steve's early years, my heart
began to sing. I was profoundly moved by his amazing ability, despite his circumstances, to understand and forgive; redeem and reconcile; see possibilities not dead-ends; and begin a-new. Steve's triumph is a lesson for all of us."

—JOHNNETTA BETSCH COLE, PH.D, PRESIDENT EMERITA,
SPELMAN COLLEGE AND BENNETT COLLEGE FOR WOMEN

"*A Chance in the World* is a fantastic book. As a narrative, it tells the story of a
boy who found in books the imaginative ability to see a new, different, and
better world. As a history, it unearths a painful and abusive past that, against
all odds, forged the character of the wonderful man Steve Pemberton has
become. But, most important, the book affirms a set of values central to
all of humanity—love, hope, faith, and perseverance. *A Chance in the World*
reminds us of a universal truth: the human spirit is enduring."

—RONALD S. SULLIVAN JR., EDWARD R. JOHNSON
CLINICAL PROFESSOR OF LAW, HARVARD LAW SCHOOL

"Unfortunately like so many, Steve Pemberton endured more than his share
of hardship as a young child. Yet through true grit and unyielding hard
work with a high standard of dignity, Steve has not only become a leader in
the business world but also an inspiration to those of all walks of life. Steve's
book *A Chance in the World* will open one's heart and leave no doubt on the
unconquerable human spirit."

—DAVE PELZER, # 1 NEW YORK TIMES BEST SELLER *A CHILD
CALLED "IT,"* NATIONAL JEFFERSON AWARD RECIPIENT

"Steve Pemberton tells the story of an orphan who would not allow the tragedy of his childhood to destroy his spirit or his hope for a happy future. It is his own story and he tells it with honesty and without a trace of self-pity. As he follows the faint and fading trail back to his family, we are given a glimpse of a remarkable young man, uncomplaining and determined. Though horrified by what he was made to endure, in the end we are uplifted by his purity of heart, and rewarded by his success. *A Chance in the World* teaches us that from bad beginnings can come happy endings."

—LARRY LUCCHINO, PRESIDENT AND CHIEF
EXECUTIVE OFFICER, BOSTON RED SOX

"This is a remarkable story of pain, hope and most of all resilience. It is a powerful reminder of the complexity and urgency of the work we must do to keep our children safe, healthy and happy. It is an important book for service providers, policy makers, parents and community leaders concerned about making sure that all children enjoy the safety, security, normality and renewed sense of identity that Steve found."

—CHRISTINE L. JAMES-BROWN, CHIEF EXECUTIVE
OFFICER, CHILD WELFARE LEAGUE OF AMERICA

A

CHANCE

IN THE

WORLD

A
CHANCE
IN THE
WORLD

An Orphan Boy,
a Mysterious Past,
and How
He Found a Place
Called Home

STEVE PEMBERTON

THOMAS NELSON
Since 1798

NASHVILLE   DALLAS   MEXICO CITY   RIO DE JANEIRO

Published in Nashville, Tennessee, by Thomas Nelson. Thomas Nelson is a registered trademark of Thomas Nelson, Inc.

Thomas Nelson, Inc., titles may be purchased in bulk for educational, business, fund-raising, or sales promotional use. For information, please e-mail SpecialMarkets@ThomasNelson.com.

This story is based on true events, but certain names, persons, characters, places, and dates have been changed so that the persons and characters portrayed bear no resemblance to persons actually living or dead.

Page design by Mandi Cofer.

ISBN 978-1-4041-8355-1 (IE)

Library of Congress Cataloging-in-Publication Data

Pemberton, Stephen J., 1967-
A chance in the world : an orphan boy, a hidden past, and how he found a place called home / Stephen J. Pemberton.
p. cm.
Includes bibliographical references and index.
ISBN 978-1-59555-263-1 (alk. paper)
1. Orphans—New England—Biography. 2. Foster children—New England—Biography. I. Title.
HV983.P46 2012
362.73'3092—dc23
[B]
2011017143

Printed in the United States of America

13 14 15 QG 0 9 8 7 6 5 4

For Tonya, Quinn, Vaughn, and Kennedy
For being greater than my dreams

For Marian and Kenny
May this story, and this life, finally bring you peace

The fullness of life is in the hazards of life. And, at the worst, there is that within us, which can turn defeat into victory.

—EDITH HAMILTON, REFERRING TO
THE GREEK DRAMATIST AESCHYLUS

Contents

Contents

Part 3: The Journey Home

PART 1

AN ORPHAN BOY

CHAPTER 1

For decades a recurring memory haunted me. Or was it a dream? It's early evening, and I am in the backseat of a moving car, on the right-hand side. Another child sits beside me, on my left. Is this child a boy or girl? How old is he? What is her name? I am cold, hungry, and disoriented. In front sit two people, but I cannot tell what they look like. Are they men or women? They are asking me questions, and I am answering them. I sense they are trying to reassure me.

The car lurches to a stop. We get out and walk into a large brick building. It is incredibly clean, and my feet squeak when I walk. I think I am in a hospital. Why have I been brought here? The other child remains next to me. The two of us stand against the wall while my front-seat companions (who exited the car with us) talk in hushed tones to a woman dressed in white and a strange-looking hat. The three of them then approach us, and the other child is led away by the woman dressed in white. This child looks over his or her shoulder one last time at me. I don't know why, but I do not want the white-clad woman to take the child. Still, there is nothing I can do to stop her. I feel a hand on my shoulder holding me in place as they walk out of sight.

Now we are in the car again, driving. The streetlights whip by, fascinating me. Where am I going? We stop again, and I am hustled into another building whose features I can't discern. Someone carries me into a room and places me on a bed with a pillow. I have never been warmer and more comfortable in my life. Another woman appears, and the three of them keep saying, "You're going to be okay now." I drift off into a peaceful sleep.

For years these events lived in the gray area between memories and dreams. There were times when I accepted that I was never to know what these images meant and still other times when I believed that if I unpacked them one more time, I would finally unlock their meaning. The sheer persistence of these images haunted me as much as the images themselves. These events have always been with me, part of the poetry of my life, interwoven with first kisses, high school graduation day, college finals, first days on the job, and Lamaze classes.

One day I learned the truth. These memories were from the day I was taken from my mother.

I would never see her again.

CHAPTER 2

GRUMPY: Ask her who she is, and what she's doing here!
DOC: Ah, yes. What are you, and who are you doing here?

—Snow White and the Seven Dwarfs (Walt Disney)

As a young boy, and then well into my teens, I would stare long and hard in the mirror, drinking in every detail of my features. I went into the bathroom, locked the door, and turned on the water so the house's other occupants would believe I was busy. Then, with dramatic anticipation, I would pick up my head from its bowed state and peer into the mirror.

I started with my curly brown hair that I wore in an Afro. The crowns carried blond tints that would brighten noticeably during the summer. I skipped over my eyes, saving them for last, and proceeded to my strong and prominent forehead. My eyebrows held no real interest for me, although I got distracted from my inspection by trying to raise the right one as well as I could the left. (I still can't do it.) My nose was straight with no hooks or curves, and my nostrils were flared slightly. My lips were of average size, and on the rare occasions that I smiled, I noticed that the right side of my mouth would turn up ever so slightly. I had brown freckles of various shades under my eyes and on my nose. I also had a habit of tilting my head when I was listening to someone, almost as if I were asking them to pour the information into my ears. My skin was very fair—not white, but close.

On the fifth finger of my left hand was a small nub, and I held it up to the mirror, turning it this way and that, hoping that a new viewing angle would tell me what it was and where it had come from. On that same hand, I found a circular scar on the tip of my third finger, almost as if my fingerprint had been sliced off and then reattached. More scars appeared on my rib cage and on my left foot. A story had been written on me, and a violent one at that, but it was a tale I neither knew nor understood.

I ended my regular inspection with my eyes, since these did not seem to match the rest of me at all. They were a deep blue, and I leaned even closer to the mirror to get a better look, my nose nearly touching the glass, my breath leaving a temporary fog. I could discern gold flecks around the pupils with little rivers of blue running from them. I would stare so long and hard into my own eyes that it appeared as if I were observing another person. The effect dizzied me, so I looked away and shook my head to clear the cobwebs.

This type of examination was not borne of vanity. I was too young to try to determine whether I was handsome or not, or even to care. Nor was I all that interested in determining if I was black or white. I was trying to discover much more important things: Who did I look like? Where had I come from? And most important, where were my mother and father?

Further compounding the mystery was my last name: Klakowicz. This jumble of vowels and consonants felt alien to me. How had I gotten this name? Where did it come from?

I stared into that magnificent piece of glass—asking, probing, and demanding. But the mirror always kept its secrets.

CHAPTER 3

M y only memory of the Andrades, the people who took me in after I was removed from my mother, is not pleasant.

Several members of the Andrade family are preparing to go somewhere important. People shout, "Are you ready?" and "Let's go!" Finally, after much hustle and bustle, we stroll out onto the porch. A metal walkway extends from the porch to the sidewalk, and as we begin to move down it, I realize that we are approaching a car.

I stop dead in my tracks. *No way*, I think to myself. *I am not going.* In my four-year-old mind, cars are dangerous because when you get in them, your whole world changes. Unfortunately, I am too young to articulate these fears, and the only way I am going to get in the car is if someone picks me up and carries me.

They do not do that, though. They do something worse. They leave me on the back porch of the house and drive off. At first I think my ears have betrayed me and that I did not hear the doors slam, the engine start, and the car pull away from the curb. I leave the porch, walk down to where the car had been parked, and an empty space greets me.

I do not entirely believe that they have left me. I think they are coming right back—that they are just trying to scare me. I stand there on the walkway, listening, turning my head this way and that, hoping the wind will bring the sound of their approaching car, but there is nothing. I cry and yell for help. I beg them to come back. I promise to be a good boy.

Nothing I say brings them back.

I walk back down the path to the back porch and sit at the top of the stairs. The porch is not big; it is close to the ground and only has three steps. Yet its familiarity offers a safe haven. Beyond it is something less comforting: a forest of trees that stretches for miles. In that hostile place, shadows lurk and strange sounds echo. I do not dare leave the porch.

At some point I try the back door, but it is locked. As minutes pass and then hours, anxiety yields to a new emotion: terror. I have been left here—alone. They are not going to return. Daylight turns to dusk. It becomes completely dark. The night birds settle in, and crickets chirp. Additional night sounds ring, surrounding me. I jump at each one and cast furtive glances. I put my fingers in my ears, draw my knees to my chest, and rock back and forth.

Many hours later, car lights come down the road. A door slams, and I hear footsteps. I stand up.

A voice off in the distance asks, "Is he still there?"

The reply comes back, closer to me now, almost chuckling: "He sure is. Never moved from the spot."

CHAPTER 4

In August 1972, eighteen months after I had been placed in the Andrades' care, the family made a call to the Department of Social Services, requesting that the state take me from their home as soon as possible. When asked why, Mrs. Andrade, the family matriarch, said that she could not arrange for me to go to kindergarten. The social worker assigned to my case doubted this story, believing that Mrs. Andrade simply "did not want to be bothered [with me] anymore." There was another boy in the home whom she planned to adopt, and he had become the primary source of her attention.

When the social worker came to get me, I had no belongings and was dressed in shabby clothing. I also had a long list of untreated medical ailments, including an acute case of impetigo and an equally serious ear infection that had impaired my hearing and speech. I was perilously underweight and my nose had been broken. The Department of Social Services had paid only one visit to the home during the past eighteen months. After seeing my physical condition, the department shut down the Andrade home, removing the other boy chosen over me, and forbidding them from taking any more children. I have no memory of leaving the Andrades, and I doubt they shed any tears over my departure.

CHAPTER 5

I do not recall where I went after I left the Andrades, nor can I remember how much time had passed. But one warm summer afternoon when I was five, I found myself in a car with Patti Southworth, my latest social worker. We drove for a while before the car pulled up to a curb. She shut off the car, turned to me, and said, "Now, Steve, we are going to visit the Robinson family. I think you are going to like this place."

"Will this be a real home with a real daddy?" I asked.

"We'll see," Patti said, stepping out of the vehicle.

I yearned for a new home, a place where the family actually wanted to keep me. I also wanted to know about my original family, particularly my mother. Where was she? When was she coming to get me? The myriad social workers responsible for my case knew the answer, but they never told me. Several mentioned in my case file that I still felt a strong emotional connection to my family. One observed that, despite my quiet demeanor, I had some "very deep thoughts about my future."

I stepped out of the car and gazed up at the largest building I had ever seen. It was white with green trim on the outside. It seemed to stretch up forever. An iron fence surrounded the house, and a screened-in porch wrapped around the first level.

We walked up a small flight of cement stairs. Patti rapped on the white door and was greeted by a sweet, melodic voice: "Come in."

We walked into a very small kitchen and then into a larger room. Standing there to greet us was Betty Robinson, a short, heavyset, caramel-brown-complexioned African American woman with big brown eyes, perfect teeth, and a blinding smile that warmed my soul.

"What is your name?" Betty asked, bending down so that she was near eye level with me.

"Steve."

"Now, that is a nice name," she said, stepping back. I said nothing to this, but inside I was glowing.

"Do you like toys?" Betty asked.

I nodded my head yes, and Betty, who never seemed to stop smiling, pointed me to a plastic set of cowboys and Indians laid out on the carpet. I bent down and began playing while Patti sat in a chair opposite Betty. They talked in quiet tones. My ears perked up when I heard Patti say, "Still asks a lot about his mother . . . not ready to tell him about that yet."

I pretended not to hear and continued to play. Then a man strode into the living room. He was a big bear of a man, with a long mustache that went down to his chin. He was dressed all in blue, including his hat. He walked over to Betty and pecked her on the cheek.

"Having a good day at work, Willie?" she asked.

"Same as usual," he said in a deep voice. He nodded at me. "So, who is this?"

"This is Steve," Betty said, "although I like Stevie better." She winked at me, and again I glowed.

"Well, does he like basketball?" Willie asked, pulling out a small red ball from behind his back. He showed me how to dribble the ball. I'm not sure what amazed me more, watching the ball bounce up and down in perfect rhythm or his enormous, paint-flecked hands that nearly engulfed the ball.

A few minutes later, Willie announced that he had to go back to work. Before leaving, he leaned over to shake my hand. I watched my little hand disappear into his. "Nice to meetcha," he said. He walked away, but then, pausing in the doorway, he said, "By the way, you can keep that." His finger pointed at the red ball that I hadn't stopped bouncing since he first showed me how.

A short time later, Patti told me that it was time to go. As we were walking out the door, Betty stopped me. "Would you like a cookie?" she asked.

I bobbed my head yes.

She handed me two small cookies. I started to munch on one; the other I stuck in my pocket, crumbs falling to the bottom of the inside lining. Betty and Patti exchanged looks but said nothing.

I was too busy enjoying my cookie to figure out what their looks meant. Climbing into Patti's car, holding my precious cargo, I felt certain of something: This was the place. I had found a home.

CHAPTER 6

August 1972 left many footprints in history. On August 1, reports emerged that a $25,000 cashier's check—designated for President Richard Nixon's reelection bid—had found its way into the bank account of one of the Watergate burglars, formally linking the break-in to the Nixon campaign for the first time. That same day, National Security Adviser Henry Kissinger met with North Vietnamese diplomat Le Duc Tho in Paris to broker what would ultimately be a rather temporary cease-fire in Vietnam. Both stories were buried by the formal withdrawal of Democratic vice presidential nominee Thomas Eagleton, after weeks of rumor and speculation that he had been the recipient of shock therapy.

The Summer Olympics in Munich, intended to showcase a new and more democratic Germany but remembered for something far more sinister, started later that month. Gasoline was fifty-five cents a gallon, and the dark brilliance of *The Godfather* reigned at the box office.

Locally, New Bedford was abuzz over the tragic murder of a young prizefighter. And I arrived at the house on Arnold Street to live.

The house stood close to the corner of Arnold and Chancery streets in the western end of New Bedford, Massachusetts. As Patti and I stepped out of the car, I took a longer look at the neighborhood I would soon call mine. It was awash in colors and sounds that I had failed to notice on my first visit. Across the street sat a bright-red brick building that ran the length of the block. A large, red-white-and-blue sign outside read "Benjamin Fuller Paint Store." On the opposite corner stood Sunnybrook Farms, a local grocery store whose sign featured a perfectly painted picture of the sun. Right next door to the Robinson home, on Chancery Street, was a low-slung, white brick building with a green roof and no sign. It piqued my curiosity, now in overdrive. On the corner was a bright-orange fire hydrant, and on the opposite corner a bright-red stop sign. Farther down stood several homes of varying colors and designs.

Patti Southworth watched as I took it all in. "Ready?" she asked.

Betty was sitting on the back porch, wearing a pretty flowered shirt and blue shorts. Again she greeted me with that magnificent smile: "Welcome to your new home. We've been looking forward to having you." At her feet was a small tricycle with an orange frame, bright-yellow handlebars and seat, and blue pedals. The two small wheels in back and one big one in front sparkled in the sun. I gawked at it, fascinated.

"That," she said, "is called a Big Wheel. And it's yours!"

"Really?" I asked. I'd never received anything like this.

"Would you like to try it?"

I nodded.

She opened the back door of the porch and set the Big Wheel down on the ground. Off in the distance I could hear dogs barking and children playing. It was a stiflingly hot summer day. "You can ride it," she said, "but you have to stay right here on the sidewalk where I can see you." Again I felt that warm rush because, as best I could recall, no one had ever seemed concerned enough about me to care where I was going.

I had never ridden a bicycle or anything like it, but it didn't take me long to figure out the Big Wheel. I put my tiny feet on those blue pedals and roared up and down the sidewalk, my legs moving like pistons, the wind rushing through my ears. Betty and Patti watched with amusement.

I continued pedaling down the block until I saw Patti standing by the front door. "Bye, Steve," she said, waving her hand. "I'll be coming back to see you soon." I waved back and then sped off again on my Big Wheel, trying to impress her with my newfound toy. When I turned around for another circuit toward the house on Arnold Street, she was already in her car and driving away.

Betty was standing there, her hand on the white screen door, holding it open. "It's time to come inside," she said. "Make sure you bring the Big Wheel with you." I pedaled up to the front porch, stopping abruptly. I had hoped to impress her, too, with my skill, but her expression did not change. *Where is her smile?*

I grabbed the Big Wheel and mounted the stairs. The toy was cumbersome and clunky; I banged my shin against the cement stair and yelped. I glanced at her, expecting her to help me, but she did not. Finally, I reached the top of the stairs. "You can put it over there," she said, pointing to the spot where I'd first seen it. "And then come over here."

I did as she asked. She was sitting down now, in a tan wicker chair with a high back that only seemed to heighten her stature. "There are rules we have for living here," she said. "And one of them is that you are going to have chores around the house, starting with the dishes in the pantry. My son Reggie will show you where they are."

Who is Reggie? I had no sooner posed the question to myself than a large figure appeared in the doorway. Reggie Robinson was about sixteen years old at the time, with round features and a perfectly combed Afro, the spitting image of his mother, except taller. He wore a sleeveless T-shirt, gray shorts, and flip-flops. "That way," he said, pointing inside the house, past the doorway.

I began walking where he'd said. Then I felt a shove in my back, propelling me forward faster than my feet could take me. I nearly fell but caught my balance. I looked back at him, bewildered. *What was that for?*

He grinned back, and a bolt of fear rifled through me. Though I hadn't seen a look like his before, I understood it immediately. *He's making sure I know my place,* I thought. Then I felt another emotion, arresting and frightful. *There is something not quite right here.*

The pantry was right off the kitchen and only big enough for one person to pass through. Several shelves extended above my head on the left and right. At the pantry's far end was a large sink. "See these dishes?" he said, pointing to a mountain of glasses, plates, and silverware piled in the sink.

I nodded my head yes.

"You have to wash and dry all of them."

I looked at the sink and then back at him, completely confused by what he wanted me to do. I'd never washed dishes before and didn't have a clue how. The first problem was that the faucet was set far back in the sink, and I wasn't tall enough to reach it. "I can't reach that high," I said.

He pointed to a small wooden step stool right in front of the sink. "That's what the step stool is for, stupid."

I am not stupid, I thought.

When I stepped up on the stool, it wobbled, and I hung in that precarious place between balance and free fall before shifting my weight to steady myself. I could feel Reggie's shadow and malevolent grin beating into my back. Still, I wanted to perform my chores correctly. This was my new home, and I didn't want to do anything to jeopardize it. I surveyed the mountain of dishes again and turned on the water. Grabbing the first dish, I ran it under the faucet and then placed it on the counter.

"No!" Reggie said.

I turned my head at the sound of his voice, and he dealt me a thunderous smack across my face. It sent me flying off the step stool and caused me to bang my head against the pantry wall. "You're doing it wrong!" he said again, but this time his voice was low and guttural.

I felt tiny spikes of pain in the place where he had hit me, but I was too angry to pay much attention. I scrambled to my feet. "I'm going to tell on you," I said.

Reggie smiled—a wicked grin telling me to go right ahead.

I walked back to the front porch where Betty was sitting and drinking a can of Tab, the diet soft drink. "He hit me!" I said, pointing in the direction of the pantry.

The glowing eyes and beautiful smile that I had come to expect

16

were gone. In their place were coldness and indifference. "Get back in there and do those dishes," she said.

Reggie, who had followed me to the back porch, laughed. I didn't move. A swirl of thoughts flooded my mind: *There must be a mistake... I am not supposed to be here, am I?... This is not the same kind woman I met on my previous trip... This is not the place I am supposed to be... Why have I been left here?*

"Now!" Betty said.

I jumped at the savagery of her voice and began to cry. Walking back to the pantry, I noticed that the tires on the Big Wheel weren't as shiny and new as I had thought.

Reggie was waiting in the pantry. During the next half hour, through a brutal process of trial and error, I learned how to wash dishes. I also learned how to be afraid.

CHAPTER 7

Robinson Rule #1: You are never to tell anyone outside this house about what goes on here. If you do, you will go right back to that terrible home you were in.

Robinson Rule #2: We aren't your mother and father. You call us ma'am and sir.

Robinson Rule #3: You don't speak unless spoken to.

Robinson Rule #4: You are dumb and ugly. Something about you isn't right. Everybody knows this.

Robinson Rule #5: No one will ever take your word over ours.

Robinson Rule #6: You will eat what we give you, when we give it to you. When you're hungry, it's your tough luck. Do not open the refrigerator—ever.

Robinson Rule #7: We can beat you at any moment, in any place, at any time, with whatever is in arm's reach. We don't need a reason.

Robinson Rule #8: No one wants you, especially your own mother and father.

Robinson Rule #9: You are here to wait on us hand and foot. You're only as good as what you can do for us.

CHAPTER 8

To the outside world, the Robinsons appeared to be a loving family. Beneath the surface, however, tension, paranoia, violence, and deception reigned. There were Willie and Betty and their two sons, Eddie and Reggie. Eddie, the near-spitting image of famed Red Sox pitcher Luis Tiant, was older than Reggie and did not live at the house on Arnold Street. The Robinsons were known, too, for taking in foster children throughout the years, thirty-nine to be exact, a number Betty would tell anyone who doubted her charitable heart. What she never said was that none of them stayed until they were eighteen. The one exception was a girl, Lisa, who was four years younger than me and also lived at the house.

My new home was a "three-decker"—a three-story apartment building—common in the New England region. We lived in the first-floor apartment, and the Robinsons rented out the other two. The house had been poorly constructed—the five rooms were small and tight, the floors warped and slanted. Willie and Betty had one bedroom and Lisa another. I shared the last bedroom with Reggie, where I occupied the top bunk.

The Robinsons were African American. Willie was from the South, and Betty was from New Bedford. Food was plentiful—for the Robinsons—and the refrigerator and freezer were always well stocked. They had big appetites and were overweight. Dental care was not important, and they all had dentures. I escaped this fate only because I listened to my teachers and school nurses who told me to brush regularly and provided toothpaste and toothbrushes to make sure I did. The Robinsons never took me to a dentist.

The family dynamic was anything but warm. Eddie was treated as an outsider. On the Robinson meter, he was only slightly better than a foster child—an alienation I never fully understood. This was strangely comforting; I realized it was not just me who had to live by the Robinson Rules. He had moved out at his earliest opportunity, but whenever he came by to see his parents, they would attack and criticize him. He would leave the house in a huff, disappearing for weeks or months at a time. His absences were always crushing for me because I had come to adore him. Unlike Eddie, I did not have the luxury of simply leaving.

Reggie's calling in life, as best I could understand it, was to smoke reefer, shoplift, listen to Diana Ross, stay out until two or three o'clock in the morning, and sleep until noon. He also flat out refused to look for work of any kind. This always ignited Willie's anger, but Betty doted on Reggie and protected her youngest son, making excuses for him at every turn. Most times she succeeded, but one memorable time when I was about ten years old, Willie had had enough. He gathered all of Reggie's clothes in a bag and put the bag—and Reggie—out on the street. Betty went into hysterics, grabbed her heart Fred Sanford–style, slid off the couch, and begged for her nitroglycerine tablets. When the dust finally settled, Betty's heart attack had miraculously passed, and Reggie was safe and sound in his bed. A week later, I overheard Reggie and Betty laughing and joking about how they had pulled a fast one over on Willie.

That was Betty at her vilest—shrewd, manipulative, and feral in instinct. Over the years, I watched her exploit almost everyone around her. When guile didn't succeed, her tongue—acidic, cutting, and repulsive—would step in to fill the void. Words were like weapons to her, and she would hurl them at you, poisoned-tipped barbs aimed right for things you cared about the most. Far too often, she would hit her mark.

Lisa looked like a biological member of the Robinson clan. Not too long after she had arrived as a foster child, the Robinsons took the necessary legal steps to formally adopt her, something they never even considered for me. From the very beginning, it was clear to me that she was the daughter Betty never had. Not only was Lisa exempt from the rules of the Robinson home, but they also made up new ones just for her. When she failed third grade, largely because of a lack of effort, Betty bought her a new bike, justifying the purchase by saying that if Lisa were going to stay back, Betty was glad it had happened now rather than later. Meanwhile my straight A's and acceptance into the city's Talented and Gifted program went unrecognized and unrewarded.

Willie worked as a painter at the Polaroid film factory on the outskirts of New Bedford. Of no formal education (he couldn't read or write), Willie was a violent man, a human Mount Vesuvius, and like any volcano, you knew it was simply a matter of time before he blew. The only questions were (1) when and (2) whether any of that molten rock of rage and fury would flow over you. When it did, watch out.

Throughout the house were his tools of violence: rifles and pistols, knives and brass knuckles, even grenades and old artillery shells that he kept from his days in the military. Willie's chosen instrument of discipline for me was a brown leather strap, about as wide as an adult hand. It hung on the wall between the kitchen and the living room, along with his car keys and the flyswatter. Willie had cut the top of the strap into thin strips, and he would often oil it to make sure it did not become dry and brittle. He bared his teeth as he performed this task, his tongue lolling from his mouth as he concentrated. The only things that received more meticulous care from him were his guns.

Corporal punishment in the African American community, or "whoopins" as they are frequently called, have long been accepted as a cultural norm. Much of the use of corporal punishment stems from the widely held belief that to "spare the rod is to spoil the child." It is not uncommon for those raised under this system of punishment to recount those experiences, usually with lighthearted banter. You can hear the stories at family reunions and it is a favorite subject of African American comedians. Some preachers refer to it from the pulpit on

Sunday mornings, citing Scripture and the belief that if you love your child you will discipline him or her when necessary.

But Willie's beatings did not come from biblical Scripture or from love. He wanted to wield that strap and would use any opportunity to do so. A dirty dish, a light left on, or a door left open was enough to send the strap swooshing through the air. On one occasion, I came home from school, quite satisfied with the straight A's I received on my report card, only to find myself on the receiving end of the strap. He justified it by saying that I hadn't received a beating in a while and there must have been something I had done wrong.

His beatings were often carefully planned affairs, and he went about preparing for them as if they were family vacations. He particularly enjoyed telling me before I went to school in the morning that I was to receive a beating in the evening, knowing full well that it would dominate my day. I became quiet and withdrawn at school as I tried to find the courage to face what would happen when I got back to Arnold Street. There were times, though, when the pressure of the moment would get to me and I would burst into tears, mystifying my elementary school teachers. I came to live not just in fear but abject terror, the kind that rises up and takes over every sense of your being. Years later, long after the hunger and beatings were no longer residents of my mind, it would be that fear that would be the last to leave.

No matter how many cars came down Chancery Street or up Arnold Street, I knew the sound of Willie's station wagon. It had a loud rattle, like a giant who was gargling bowling balls. When I heard it, my throat got tight and my heart raced. There were times when I prayed that I was wrong, that it was just another car going by. Wishful thinking. His car would pull to the curb, and if he misjudged it, which he did from time to time, the rubber from the wheels would screech against the granite.

Sometimes he wouldn't get out of the car right away but would sit there listening to Sam Cooke or Marvin Gaye. During the summers, I could hear Sam singing about the chain gang or Marvin asking what was goin' on. Their voices soothed me, and for a moment I forgot how afraid I was. *Keep singing*, I would think. But eventually Sam or Marvin would stop singing, and Willie would exit. The car door would slam, and I would hear the *tink, tink, tink* of the car's engine settling.

Thirty seconds usually passed between the car door slamming and the screen door opening. I know it was thirty seconds because I counted every single one of them. And then I hung on the sound of the slow closing of the white screen door, the rusty hinges screaming in protest. My fate for that day hung on the time it took for the swinging door to rejoin its metal frame. If Willie called for me after the screen door closed, all was well. If he called before the screen door closed, a beating was coming.

Willie's inability to read and write bothered him a great deal. On several occasions he demanded that I teach him how to read. I was all too eager to do so because I believed that if I taught him how to read, he would feel greater empathy for me. But I was not a teacher nor was I able to explain how to do something that had come rather easily to me. He would grow frustrated, cursing and yelling that I wasn't teaching him properly and then, without warning, one of his bear-sized hands would thunder across my face, knocking me from the chair.

Not that I was the only object of Willie's wrath. The man was quick to pull a knife or gun on anyone he believed had offended him. Although I was only a child, I judged him as the type of person who lived for confrontation, constantly looking for a fight to show just how much of a man he was. More often than not, I would see his belligerence on display when I went with him on errands. A slow driver or someone who failed to move when the traffic light turned green or, worse yet, a driver who cut him off in traffic would incur his wrath. Never was this more evident than one summer day when I was eleven years old.

We were out on an errand and found ourselves on a one-way street in New Bedford's West End. Ahead of us was a taxi, and the cabdriver was helping an elderly woman out of the vehicle. The driver returned to the taxi several times to get the woman's groceries while she waited on the front porch. Willie was becoming impatient, but he also could see that the cabdriver was genuinely helping the woman. There was nowhere for us to go. Willie put the car in park and we waited. Finally, the cabdriver returned to his vehicle, and that's when the fireworks began.

Rather than pulling away, the cabdriver lingered even longer. Ten minutes or more passed, and Willie's patience had worn thin. He beeped the horn, but the cabdriver ignored him. So Willie rolled down his window and asked the man to move his car out of the way. The man stuck his head out the window, peered over his left shoulder, and yelled back, "Can't you see I just helped an old lady into the house? You'll sit there and wait you big . . . black . . . monkey!" He said those last three words slowly to make absolutely certain his audience did not miss their meaning. He then rolled up his window but not before hurling the most profane of racial epithets for closing measure.

Uh-oh.

Willie put two hands on the steering wheel and pulled himself closer to the front window, almost as if he were doing a pull-up. He stared out the window at the cabdriver and then back at me, as if to ask if he had really heard what he thought he'd heard.

"Did you . . . did he . . . aww . . . *no!*" Those last words came out more like a guttural roar, and for a brief moment it seemed as if he were asking my opinion. In a single, swift motion, he reached under his seat, pulled out a twelve-inch-long machete, and was out the car door.

The cabdriver, a thickly bearded mountain of a man, stepped from his vehicle just as quickly, intending to meet Willie halfway. For a moment, I had a vision of two adult rams gathering themselves for a head-butting collision. The cabdriver was a bigger man, but Willie was not impressed. The driver seemed to sense this, too, because as soon as Willie advanced toward him, he paused midstride and then took a step back. And if the driver needed any further convincing, the machete— no longer concealed behind Willie's back and glistening in the midday summer heat—certainly did it. The moment the cabbie saw the machete, all the bravado drained from his face.

Willie had undergone knee surgery a few months before, and he still walked with a pronounced limp. Yet this did not deter him. He chased the driver around his cab, waving and brandishing the machete, spewing profanity, and threatening to cut the man to pieces. The cabdriver believed him. Circling the taxi just quickly enough to stay out of Willie's reach, he tried to apologize, but Willie was hearing none of his pleas.

A few times, Willie reversed direction to try to cut the driver off. Seeing the move coming, the cabbie went back the other way. For what seemed like an eternity, they played this high-stakes game of cat and mouse until Willie, overcome by exhaustion and his throbbing knee, leaned against the taxi, both elbows across the hood, to catch his breath. Realizing that he was not going to catch the man, at least not today, Willie limped back to the car, but not before telling the cabbie, machete pointed at him for emphasis, that he would find him again soon. The cabdriver stood outside his vehicle—chest heaving, hand on the driver's door handle, waiting to make sure that Willie was fully inside his car. Then the driver jumped into his taxi and shot up the street, leaving the sound of screeching tires and the smell of burning rubber in his wake.

I had stayed in the car, not daring to get out, my mouth formed in the shape of an O. I knew what Willie was capable of, and I knew there was nothing I could do to stop him. Once the dust had settled and Willie was back in the car, I burst out laughing so hard that it hurt. I'm not sure why I did, but I couldn't stop laughing no matter how much I tried. As we drove back home, Willie yelled about how badly he was going to beat the cabdriver when he saw him again. That only made me laugh harder because I knew there was no way Willie was going to catch that man.

This was one of the few times at the Robinsons that I expressed genuine emotion without fear of retribution. As we pulled next to the curb of the house, I was still howling with laughter, tears rolling down my cheeks. Willie finally began to laugh along with me, and we sat in the car for several minutes, so overcome with laughter we could barely move. It was the only time I can remember really bonding with the man.

CHAPTER 9

All the world will be your enemy, Prince of a Thousand Enemies, and whenever they catch you, they will kill you. But first they must catch you, digger, listener, runner, prince with the swift warning. Be cunning and full of tricks...

—RICHARD ADAMS, *WATERSHIP DOWN*

I settled into a routine at the house on Arnold Street, to the degree one can ever become comfortable with monsters who disguise themselves as human beings. This is what they were to me: real-life boogeymen whose origins and intentions I could never fathom. Children rarely ask where monsters come from or how they came to be; children simply accept them as a fact of life, something to be dealt with, the way you deal with any other childhood fear.

One way I dealt with these monsters was to become a thief, and a very good one at that. My devious plots were elaborate, complete with escape routes and explanations if I were ever to get caught. I obsessed over the things I stole, and no matter how much I managed to get, I always tried to steal more. Once I stole something, I would stare at it, wondering how best I could hide it or preserve it. But I didn't steal just anything. I was fixated on one thing: food. At seven years old, I weighed just forty pounds, a fact the Robinsons explained away by saying I had tapeworms.

To avoid going hungry, I had to be creative—to outwit them. Nearly every morning of my days with the Robinsons, I would awake

26

and immediately try to determine how I was going to get food to hide in the basement. It took me a while to learn what to steal. My first foray into the art of thievery was a huge block of government-rationed cheese that Willie had hustled. I hid it in the basement and sneaked away one afternoon ready to feast, only to find the mice that roamed the cellar had already beaten me to it. After that, I placed my thieving eye on the unlabeled silver cans of peanut butter Willie brought home; I was confident that the enterprising mice couldn't chew through the metal.

I wasn't usually that picky; I would eat whatever scraps I could get my hands on. If it wasn't moving, then it was fair game. Whenever they went grocery shopping, I had to unload the bags. I would scan the bags quickly to see what was in them and hide the one with the most goodies underneath the car. When the coast was clear, I would take the bag and dash to the cellar, where I would squirrel it away. From time to time, they would realize that they had come up a bag or two short and would fume at the person who had bagged their groceries. They never figured out it was me. The joy of outsmarting the Robinsons became almost as sweet as the food I stole. Almost.

Another very important way of coping was to immerse myself in books. When, precisely, I began reading, I cannot say. There was no signature moment, at least early on, but I imagine I discovered books as part of going to school. Books for me were what the ocean is to the fearless explorer—deep and mysterious, boundless and soothing. I loved the smell of books, the feel of their weight in my hands, the rustle of the pages as I turned them, the magnificent illustrations on the covers that promised hidden treasures within.

Like food, books were hard for me to come by. The Robinsons never bought me any (Robinson Rule #10) and thwarted every attempt I made to get more. When I did bring home a book from the school library, I had to ask if I could read (Robinson Rule #11). If I were caught reading without permission, a merciless beating would follow (Robinson Rule #12). When permission was granted, it was granted begrudgingly and only under the condition that I read in the cellar. I was never allowed to keep books upstairs (Robinson Rule #13), nor could I read in their presence (Robinson Rule #14).

The cellar was cold, musty, and dank. Its walls tossed off long shadows in the dim light offered by a single swaying bulb. I frequently heard the mice clawing and scratching in the walls. The cellar was storage space for many of the home's utilities—washing machine, dryer, hot water and oil furnaces—but also for many of the things the Robinsons had no further use for, like broken furniture that didn't stand, ancient preserves no longer fit to be eaten, old clothes that had gone out of style. These abandoned items had served their purpose, but the Robinsons held on to them, believing that someday someone foolish enough to value them would come along and take them off their hands. To the Robinsons, the cellar was precisely where I belonged.

Amid all the clutter, I fashioned a makeshift reading space composed of mildewy clothes, torn pillows, and old box springs. I positioned this space directly under the stairs because, that way, I would be able to hear anyone coming down. And my hearing was finely tuned. I knew the stride pattern of each member of the family: Betty shuffled, Reggie had longer steps, and Willie's plodding was the easiest to detect, for he often walked with his oak cane. When they approached the cellar door, I would scramble to hide my book and stash of food. I kept a jug of water to wash away the peanut butter smell on my breath, a lesson I learned when Willie nearly caught me. If I had ever been caught reading down there with my moldy stash of hoarded food, I would have paid a dear price.

I loved the cellar, finding it a welcome refuge from the Robinson Rules. Yet it was not my favorite place to read—at least not during the warmer months. Across from the Robinsons' house, right next to Fuller's paint store, was Mrs. Blake's house. Alongside her yard was a small retaining wall. A large oak tree hung over the area, so large that it kept half the block in shade. The wall itself was no more than a few feet high and craggy, as if hewn from the side of a mountain, except for a single, smooth, square piece of rock at the wall's northern end. Once my chores were done and I had received permission, I would take my favorite book, go to that shaded haven, and lose myself in my latest mystery, none of which seemed as great as the mystery of where I had come from.

Nearly every summer day, you would find me sitting on that wall, accompanied by squirrels playing in the trees, as well as the occasional ant that tried to make my sneaker its home. I was never more at peace during my childhood than when I sat there. I loved the sound of the wind rustling through the leaves of the large oak, the smell of freshly cut grass brought on by neighborhood lawn mowers, the cacophony of birds that twittered as they flew by, the bumblebees that hovered by my head before moving on to more interesting things. This was my sanctuary, the place where I felt the most alive—and the safest.

One summer afternoon when I was about eight years old, I looked up from my perch atop my reading wall to see a woman strolling down Chancery Street toward me. It was a neighbor, Mrs. Levin. I had seen her on many occasions walking to Sunnybrook Farms, the neighborhood grocery store. She was a small woman with dark hair pulled away from her face, although now, looking at her up close for the first time, I noticed the first signs of gray. Mrs. Levin was plainly dressed as always and moved at a casual pace, thoroughly enjoying her walk.

She often waved and smiled at the Robinsons but nothing more than that. From time to time, her husband joined her. He was slightly taller, a balding man who wore red suspenders over a white T-shirt. They were Jewish, and the only reason I knew that was because as soon as they were out of earshot, Betty or Willie would fling anti-Semitic remarks at their backs. For quite some time I thought they said "jewels" instead of "Jews." For the life of me, I couldn't figure out why the Robinsons thought something as precious as jewels would be such bad people.

Now I looked down, careful not to make any eye contact that would initiate a conversation (Robinson Rule #15). The walkway alongside the Blake home was not paved, and I could hear the crunching of Mrs. Levin's footsteps on the gravel as she neared. As I so often did with strangers, I hoped that she would walk on by and pay me no attention. But that's not what happened. Her white tennis shoes, scuffed ever so lightly around the toe, stopped right in front of me. And though I was not afraid, I still swallowed hard. "What are you reading there?" she asked.

I looked up from the pages and showed her the cover of my Encyclopedia Brown mystery. Leroy Brown, "Encyclopedia" to his friends, was a boy detective who often sat at the dinner table helping his dad, the chief of police in the fictional town of Idaville, solve cases that had baffled the department.

"You like mysteries?" she asked.

"Oh, yes, ma'am," I said, making the conversation far longer than the Robinson Rules dictated. "I really like how you get a chance to figure out the clues for yourself."

"Now, if I remember, weren't you reading this book last week?"

It puzzled me how she could have known that. "Yes, ma'am. But when I finish a book, I go back to the beginning and start all over again."

"I see." She said nothing more and ambled on toward the store, but I still remember the long look she sent in the direction of my house on Arnold Street.

Later that evening, there was a knock at the door. I was in the pantry washing dishes when Betty answered. A voice I immediately recognized asked, "Is Steve here? I have something I would like to give him." It was Mrs. Levin.

I grabbed for the dishrag, began drying my hands, and heard Betty say, "I can give them to him." But Mrs. Levin was insistent: "If it's okay, I would like to give him these myself."

There was a pause. "Stevie!" Betty said, the sweet, melodic voice, and use of a nickname, telling me that she was "onstage." I came around the corner much faster than I should have, but my eavesdropping was either missed or ignored.

"You remember me?" Mrs. Levin asked. I nodded my head yes.

"Well, I thought you might like these." In her arms was a brown, open-ended box, but I could not see what was in it. She lowered it, and

I could barely believe my eyes. Inside the box were stacks of books, of different thicknesses and colors, their covers bright and promising.

"Whoa," I said.

"These," she said, "are for the boy who likes to read."

"Thank you, ma'am," I said, barely able to take my eyes off the box.

"You're welcome," she said, smiling; and with that, she left.

She was barely out of earshot before Betty's voice boomed, "Take those books downstairs! I better never see them up here."

"Yes, ma'am, right now, ma'am," I stammered. I feared that she would make me throw them away.

Nothing I write can accurately capture the power and timeliness of the gift Mrs. Levin gave me that day. Though I did not know it at the time, several years earlier, when I was one and a half years old, a babysitter had written: "Dropped Steve off at the latest family his mother is boarding him out to . . . he cried his heart out . . . this little boy doesn't have a chance in the world." Others believed this as well, especially those to whose care I was entrusted. I sensed it in their side-long glances and empathetic shakes of the head, their eyes saying what their tongue would not. *You are beyond repair.*

I had beaten my fists against this fate as long as I could. Now, frequently starved and beaten almost daily, failed and abandoned by the institutions tasked with my care, and waiting for a family that was never going to come for me, I was beginning to lose my desperate battle with the Robinsons. Caseworkers at the time described me as tense, nervous, and anxious. What was really unfolding was something far more damaging, something they never looked hard enough to see: I had begun to resign myself to this fate, to accept I was to be the Robinsons' prisoner and that their world would be the only one I would ever know.

But the characters that unfolded in those books and the worlds they lived in showed me a different life, a future far beyond the pain of the house on Arnold Street. I learned that not everyone lived the way I did, that most people came from intact homes that offered joy and laughter, freedom and exploration, promise and possibility. And because of what I read, I developed the ridiculously absurd notion that one day I, too, could have a life like the ones I read about.

At every opportunity I would steal down to the cellar to dive into my cardboard chest of hidden treasures, planting myself right in the middle of those adventures. I became a fearless explorer, a brilliant scientist, and a master riddle solver. I went to the depths of the ocean with Captain Nemo and *20,000 Leagues Under the Sea*, stood right by Howard Carter's side as he discovered the tomb of King Tutankhamen, and landed on the moon with the crew of *Apollo 11*. I unlocked more riddles with boy detective Encyclopedia Brown and joined forces with Alfred Hitchcock and the Three Investigators to solve even greater mysteries. My books became my shelter, protecting me as the Robinsons' slings and arrows rained overhead. And I returned my books' protection by guarding them the way most children guard their teddy bears. As a little boy, I was mystified when bookworms burrowed into their pages and crushed when a basement flood destroyed several of them.

Mrs. Levin's books gave me something else that I did not fully appreciate until many years later: a model for dealing with the Robinsons. It came from my favorite book, *Watership Down*, a novel I would read over and over again. Published in 1972 and written by the British author Richard Adams, this book tells the tale of a band of resilient rabbits searching for a new home. Led by the small but exceedingly clever Hazel, these rabbits encounter many obstacles in their search. One of their first challenges was one I knew all too well: they encounter a warren of contented rabbits—a home that seems to be exactly what the group is looking for—yet they learn that this new home is not at all what it appears to be and that it is, in fact, a cleverly crafted rabbit farm intended to ensnare them.

The rabbits escape the farm and often resort to trickery in their pursuit of a new home. Deception may seem unprincipled, but it is absolutely necessary if Hazel and his group of rabbits are to survive, especially when their very existence is threatened by another group of rabbits, the Efrafrans, and their evil leader, General Woundwort.

There comes a time when deception is not enough, and the group must take a stand against General Woundwort, although they know it will likely cost them their lives.

I found kinship in the rabbits of *Watership Down*. They became my childhood friends, the only ones I was allowed to have, and I could cite their names at the drop of a hat: Fiver, Bigwig, Pipkin, and Blackberry. My friends were smart, fast, elusive, and resourceful—their very survival was predicated on their ability to sense danger. Though confronted by bigger foes, they outwitted them. Perhaps most important, I saw the rabbits as fighters, their combativeness driven by a certainty that they could create a different and better life for themselves. For Hazel and his followers, it was never a question of *if* they would find a home; it was simply a matter of *when*.

Over the years, Mrs. Levin stopped by many times to deliver a new box of books. In my quiet moments of reflection, I often wonder what might have become of me had not this kind woman lit a pathway for me through the suffocating darkness of the house on Arnold Street. The Robinsons never refused her request, perhaps because they knew that would raise suspicions. But had they known those books would sow the seeds of my rebellion, they would have torched them the minute Mrs. Levin was out of their sight.

I do not know where Mrs. Levin is today, and neither she nor her family knows what has become of me. I don't even know if Levin was her real name, but that was the name penned inside the covers of many of the books she gave me. For the rest of my childhood, however, she would walk beside me. And as an adult I have found I cannot forget her. Sometimes Mrs. Levin walked from her home a block away; other times her husband drove her over to the house. On occasion I would look up from my reading to see her peacefully strolling to Sunnybrook Farms. The only way I knew to thank her was to hold up my book to show her that I was putting to good use what she had given me. She would smile and nod her head in approval. No words passed between us. None were necessary.

CHAPTER 10

We wear the mask that grins and lies,
It hides our cheeks and shades our eyes,—
This debt we pay to human guile;
With torn and bleeding hearts we smile,
And mouth with myriad subtleties.
Why should the world be overwise,
In counting all our tears and sighs?
Nay, let them only see us, while
We wear the mask.

—PAUL LAURENCE DUNBAR, "WE WEAR THE MASK"

There was no air-conditioning in the Robinson home. The only relief came from a broken-down electric fan whose whirring motion sounded like baseball cards stuck in the spokes of a bike. When the fan failed to ease the humidity, the Robinson family would have me run towels under cold water so they could apply them to their foreheads. On the morning of July 14, 1973, about a year into my tenure with the Robinsons, Betty asked me to fetch her a washcloth from the linen closet in the back bedroom. Her request set off a chain of events that would shape my sense of the world for many years to come.

Grabbing the washcloth, I caught wind of a strange smell but was too focused on completing my task to determine what it was. I walked back into the kitchen where Betty sat by an open window. She was brushing her hair with a heavy silver brush. "Go run that washcloth under cold water and bring it back to me," she said. "Hot today."

I returned and handed her the cold washcloth and stood waiting for her next command. She raised the washcloth to her forehead but wrinkled her nose. "What the . . . ?" she said. She unfolded the washcloth, and I could see the large yellow stain, bright against the white cloth. "Where did you get this from?" she demanded.

My ears pricked at the tone of her voice. "From the linen closet, ma'am."

Betty got up, the chair creaking against her weight. Still carrying the brush, she walked into the back bedroom much faster than she usually moved. Moments later she emerged in the doorway between the kitchen and the bedrooms and yelled, "You pissed in the linen closet!" I had done no such thing, but before I could protest my innocence, she swung the heavy brush, crashing it into my forehead. My legs came out from under me, and my arms pinwheeled backward. The kitchen began to tilt horizontally, and the fruit-decorated borders of wallpaper began to swim. She swung again, and I fell back to the ground, slamming my head against the linoleum floor. Bright flashes of light danced across my vision.

She stood over me, swinging the brush at my head again and again. I tried to use my arms for cover, but they were slow to respond. There was a sudden clattering, a foreign sound amid my wailing cries and her unintelligible screeching. I opened my eyes. Through a window of space between my elbows, I saw the large part of the brush skitter across the floor and come to a rest against the brown kitchen door. *Why was it in two pieces, and why had it changed color from just silver, to silver and red? Had somebody painted . . .*

An agonizing pain suddenly bloomed in my back. I screamed, pulling my arms away from my head to my lower back. That was when I first felt something running down my face. Betty must have noticed it, too, because she immediately stopped kicking me.

"Get over to the sink," she commanded.

The sink was only a few feet away, but given my dazed state, I couldn't locate it. I knew I had to stand up or more blows would fall on me. I managed to get to my feet, but the world started to tilt again. Like a gymnast trying to stick a landing, I put out my arms to regain my balance. My battle with equilibrium was interrupted by a sudden shove in the back. "Move!"

I lost my balance, and putting my hand down on the floor, I noticed a large pool of blood. *Was that mine?* Before I could answer my own question, I felt blood running down my forehead and into my eyes, blinding me. Now the blood seemed to be everywhere: on the floor, on my hands, on my shorts.

Another shove from behind and I stumbled forward, banging into the narrow pantry wall. I felt along the wall until I got to the sink. Betty forced my head down into the sink, turned on the cold water, and dipped my head under the faucet. She kept running her hands through my hair. The water running off my head pooled in the sink, and I watched it course in a crimson stream down the drain.

"Stop bleeding!" she said, fear and panic in her voice.

"I can't," I said.

How long Betty tried to stop the bleeding by running water over my head, I can't recall. I do remember her telling me to keep my head in the sink until she came back. She wasn't gone very long before I felt my head yanked out of the water. Wheeling me around to face her, she wrapped my head in a towel, which she fashioned into a turban. I noticed her heaving chest and the "Ooh La-La" stenciled in bright-pink cursive writing on her dark blue shirt. "Sit there in the chair and keep this towel on your head," she said.

I did, resting both of my hands on the turban. Though the towel muffled the sounds, I could hear her dialing the rotary phone. Her first two attempts failed. "Come on!" she screamed.

Her third effort succeeded, and when she began talking, her tone wavered between panic and eerie calm: "Hi, Edith . . . It's Betty . . . Yes, how are you? . . . Yes, it sure is hot . . . I know, I know . . . Look, Edith, little Stevie has fallen out of a shopping cart and bumped his head pretty bad . . . I need to take him to the hospital and there is nobody here ... Can you give us a ride? ... Great, thank you ... We'll be right outside."

Betty hung up the phone and turned her attention to me. "Everybody is gonna ask you what happened. You're going to tell 'em that you were playing in the backyard in the shopping cart when you stood up and fell backward. You kept playing and didn't know you were hurt until I told you to come in to take a bath." She grabbed me by the shoulder. "If you tell 'em anything else, they are going to send you right back to that bad home we saved you from. You got it?"

Through muffled sniffles, I nodded my head yes. Though I did not remember all the details of the Andrades', I remembered being left on the back porch, and that was enough for me to never want to return there.

"Now, whatcha gonna say?" she asked.

"Gonna say that I was playing in the shopping cart and fell backward."

A car horn sounded. She stood me up and, cradling her arms around my head, walked me through the front door and into the hallway. Before we left the house, she issued one last warning, a familiar refrain I would hear—and believe—with all my heart: "If you tell 'em anything else, we're gonna know. We know people everywhere."

We stepped out into the summer sunshine, ready to play our respective parts. We walked down the stairs, and then I felt Betty's suddenly gentle hands guiding me into the backseat of the car. She closed the car door and got in on the other side, again wrapping her arms around my head cradling me against her bosom.

"I didn't know it was that bad, Betty," Edith said, before putting the car in drive. She lived right across the street—a kind woman who always made it a point to speak to me.

"He took quite a fall," Betty said. "I didn't even notice until I gave him a bath."

We sped over to St. Luke's Hospital. The ride, which took a few minutes, was marked by a silence between the two women—strange given how well they knew each other. I've always wondered whether Edith, a part-time nurse, believed Betty's story.

To get to the emergency room at St. Luke's Hospital, you mount a slight hill that takes you to a circular driveway. As soon as Edith came to a stop, Betty got out of the backseat and came around to the other side, where I was sitting. She guided me out of the car and we walked, my head still wrapped in the towel and bent forward as if in prayer. Blood was spattered on my legs and sneakers, one drop formed exactly like a tear. The concrete sidewalk was gray and scattered with small pebbles. After several steps the ground suddenly changed to linoleum, the air from simmering heat to refreshing cool.

The environment wasn't the only thing that changed; Betty's demeanor did too. She became hysterical, demanding that someone attend to "her son," a term she had never used before nor would afterward. I felt a flurry of activity around me, and someone said, "We've got him now."

Betty let me go, but not before giving my arm a quick pinch. I knew exactly what that meant.

The next several hours were a blur of white coats, beeping machines, and painful needles. My head was shaved, and I received dozens of stitches, purplish, jagged tracks of yarn that would join the collection of mysterious scars I already had. At every turn I was asked what happened. I repeated the same story, despite the heavy silence that followed each time.

Things would likely have ended there, and I would have returned to the Robinson home without incident, if it was not for a woman I came to call Nurse Nancy. I don't know if that was her real name. As I think about it now, she must have been coming on to her shift after I'd been there for a while and as they were sewing me up. If she had been there when I first arrived, I would have noticed her. That's how it is for children who have been discarded and forgotten. When you first encounter people who are not willing to throw you away, you notice them immediately. You notice what they look like, what they say to you, and the way they look at you. You notice it all because you have to, because you need to. Some part of you knows that these images will be the only thing that will sustain you in the future, through the darkness you know is coming.

Nurse Nancy walked into the room from the right side and leaned against the wall, standing directly across from me. She said nothing that first time—just stood there, shifting her weight from time to time. She was a small woman, and her glasses dangled from a string around her neck. Her brown hair was cut short but curly, and her white shoes jumped out against her pink uniform. Her eyes were a deep brown and never seemed to leave mine. Each time I looked up, they bore into me, and I looked away, nervous and afraid that she would see the truth in them. Finally, I stopped looking altogether and kept my eyes pointed down at the floor. I could still see those pristine white shoes, though, and they jumped out even more against my blood-spattered sneakers.

Since we entered the hospital, Betty had not left my side, continuing her performance as the deeply concerned mother. She was patting my arm and holding my hand. I was confused. *Is this how it is? Do people hurt you and then are nice to you?* At one point Betty reached her hand up to touch my face, and I recoiled at the motion, believing that she was going to strike me again. Out of the corner of my eye, I saw Nurse Nancy shake her head and then walk out of the room.

She returned a short time later with two men. They wore long coats and had stethoscopes around their necks. They introduced themselves to Betty and began examining me. *Why does it take two of them?* I wondered. Their movements were more deliberate and purposeful than those of the other white coats. Though I was numb, I could sense movement around my head. One of the men lifted the back of my hospital gown and probed the area where Betty had kicked me. I winced at his touch, and the examination came to an abrupt end.

Nurse Nancy and the two men left the room together. Betty's gaze, hawkish and suspicious, followed them out the door. A few minutes later, they returned. "Mrs. Robinson, will you step outside, please?" one of the doctors asked. Betty, who had been seated, stood up and walked out of the room. Nurse Nancy remained in the room, along with the person who had stitched me up. "Quite a fall you took there, young man," Nurse Nancy said.

Though her tone was soft and gentle, her words made me nervous, and I kept my eyes fixed on the floor before I answered. "Yes, ma'am."

Voices sounded outside the room. Although I strained to hear, I couldn't understand what they were saying.

"You're going to be okay," she said. "We're going to keep you over-night, just to make sure that your head isn't broken."

I said nothing but was relieved that I wouldn't have to go back to the house on Arnold Street.

"Where is Mrs. Robinson?" I asked.

"She is outside talking with the doctors," Nurse Nancy replied. "Is that okay?"

"Yes, ma'am."

Nurse Nancy pointed at a strange-looking chair in the corner. "So here is what we are going to do. We have a nice room for you upstairs, and we are going to take you there in this nice little wheelchair."

I hopped down from the table and sat in the wheelchair. *What kind of chair is this?* I wondered as I used my feet to move it forward and backward, forgetting for a few precious moments everything that had recently happened to me.

Nurse Nancy was now behind me, and the chair began to glide across the floor, its wheels making no noise. I became conscious of how clean and quiet everything was. As we made our way through the hospital hallways, we saw all different types of people. They smiled and nodded at me. I had never felt such kindness.

We arrived at my room. Everything was white, clean, and orderly. There was a window to the outside, and through it I could see what looked like another part of the hospital. I hopped up on my bed, swing-ing my feet in the air, and began peppering Nurse Nancy with questions: "What is this place?"

"This is where hurt children come to get better."

So that's what I am, I thought. "How long am I going to stay here?"

"We don't know."

"Is Mrs. Robinson coming back?"

"She just went home to get some things you will need for your stay, then she will be back. Okay?"

"Okay," I said, but my heart sank at the knowledge that Betty was indeed coming back.

Nurse Nancy sat on the edge of my bed and folded her hands. "Steve, I want to ask you something. This story you are telling, about falling out of the cart and hurting your head—that's not what happened, is it?"

I looked out the window and into the myriad colors of an early evening sky. I so desperately wanted to tell her that what I had said wasn't true, that Betty was the one who had done this to me. Yet I knew what would happen to me if I told the truth, so I remained silent. My bottom lip quivered, and my eyes began to water.

"That's okay," Nurse Nancy said, patting my hand. "We can talk about it later."

Many years later, after reviewing my case history and medical records, I learned that a lot more was unfolding at St. Luke's Hospital those summer days in July 1973. From the moment I walked into the emergency room, the doctors and nurses who attended to me were suspicious about the story Betty had concocted. Nurse Nancy had summoned the two emergency room doctors to examine me, and they confirmed what she already knew: I had been badly beaten. When they asked Betty to step outside the hospital room where I was treated, it was to grill her about my injuries and how I could have sustained so many in a single fall. They were particularly concerned about the bruises on my back and believed they were inconsistent with the story Betty was telling.

Betty put on her best performance and repeated that I had fallen out of the cart. She could explain my other injuries no more than she could explain why I was seriously underweight. She had raised her own children and several other foster children and nothing like this had ever happened. "Call the Department of Social Services, and they will tell you what a great mother I am," she said. "I've taken in thirty-nine foster children, and I've won awards for what I've done." She told them that she'd taken in children nobody else wanted, including me, who had come to her abandoned by his own mother and horribly abused by several other foster homes. I had a lot of problems, including hurting myself, but she was doing her best.

Nurse Nancy and the two emergency room doctors were not convinced, so they admitted me to the hospital—to buy more time to determine what to do and to protect me from the Robinsons. What they decided to do next was call Dr. William Downey, the Robinsons' family pediatrician. They would share their concerns and presumably get his counsel.

They didn't know that Betty, feral in instinct and as shrewd as a con artist, had already called Dr. Downey, blasting my three protectors for accusing her of child abuse and asking that he vouch for her and what she had done to care for children. Downey, a graduate of Harvard Medical School, admitted that my injuries looked suspicious, but he "knew Betty to be a loving and caring mother who would not let something like this happen." He, and he alone, decided that I should return.

At the time, I was unaware that any of this was unfolding. What I did know was that almost no one believed Betty's story; the whispers in the hallway and empathetic attention I received told me as much. And because of this, I made a critical mistake: I continued telling the same story because I believed that the kind people at the hospital would figure it all out.

For a moment they had. Nurse Nancy and the two doctors had not only seen through Betty's charade but did something no one else had done up to that point: they took a stand on my behalf. Their strong opinions, though, were vetoed by the one person who, if he couldn't follow his own instincts, could have at least listened to my three protectors. His judgment was all that stood between me and freedom from the Robinsons. As it turned out, it was the closest I would come to freedom. Dr. Downey, who died in 2004, went on to enjoy a wonderful career in pediatrics. He was, I am certain, a good and honorable man. Yet his training and experience seemed to have abandoned him when it came to me.

I learned that I was going back to the house on Arnold Street from a nurse who had wheeled dinner into my room. "You're going home tomorrow," she said, in an effort to make conversation. "Aren't you excited?" Her words hung in the air long after she left the room.

My food was lined up neat and orderly. Normally I would have scarfed it down the second I thought no one was watching. Now I simply stared at it. *I was going back. They had not figured it out after all.* Tears came with this realization, and this time I did not try to hold them back or wipe them away. The tears, salty and bitter, ran down my cheeks and plopped onto my dinner tray, making small dark circles on the white paper place mat.

The following morning, Willie, Betty, Reggie, and Lisa all came to the hospital to pick me up. They carried balloons and stuffed animals, giving every appearance of the doting, affectionate family. When Nurse Nancy came into the room, they laughed and joked, and I found myself the center of attention, the apple of their eye. "Well, Steve, it's time to go," Nurse Nancy announced, pointing at the wheelchair.

"I know," I said. I didn't want to go. This hospital was the nicest place I had been, and the people were the kindest I had ever known. I got into the wheelchair, and we spun around to face the doorway. As we wheeled down the hallway, a number of people in bright-pink uniforms told me to take care and enjoy the best of luck. *Maybe they don't want me to leave*, I thought.

The going-home caravan arrived at the emergency room entrance, where I'd been dropped off two days earlier. As we exited, the cool of the hospital gave way to a heavy mugginess. Waiting for me was the Robinsons' yellow and brown station wagon, a sure sign that I was returning to the house of horrors. I stared at it for a long time, too afraid to move.

Nurse Nancy must have sensed this, because she kneeled down so that she was eye level with me. For the very first time, I caught a scent of her perfume, an airy fragrance that I wanted to grab and keep with me. Traffic glided by on Page Street, and a gentle breeze floated through the air. She patted my arm. "You are going to be just fine. You are a fighter, I can tell." She kept her hand on my arm for a moment longer. Wiping away tears, she stood up and announced in a firm voice, "We don't want to see you back here again. You stay away from shopping carts." There was seriousness to her tone that I hadn't heard during the previous two days.

I slid into the middle seat in the back of the station wagon. Reggie piled in after me and elbowed me hard in the ribs for not giving him enough room. "Get off me," he said, hissing. We pulled away from the curb, but I kept my eyes fixed on Nurse Nancy, craning my neck to watch her as we moved around the bend. The humidity in the car was suffocating. She did not wave but stood there watching the car.

"She can't help you now," Betty said. She turned her head to the left to look directly at me. "One of the first things you're going to do is clean up all that blood you got all over the kitchen floor."

"Yes, ma'am," I said, lowering my eyes.

Reggie leaned out the window, turned in the direction of Nurse Nancy, and launched a vulgar expletive in her direction.

Nurse Nancy, whose hands were holding the wheelchair, raised one of them to her mouth, shook her head, and walked swiftly into the hospital, leaving the wheelchair at the curb.

A month later, Patti Southworth, aware of my trip to the hospital and the intense discussion among the doctors as to whether I had been beaten, wrote the following summary in my case file:

> Steve is an odd six year old . . . he is extremely nervous and quiet. He is eager to please and will become very anxious and upset if he is reprimanded. Steve has expressed concerns about his future, and, wonders if he'll ever get "real" parents and why no one wants

him. I think much of his insecurity stems from his poor treatment at the Andrade home and that he had to be moved from there. Mrs. Robinson and her family seem to give Steve much love and attention and will give Steve good preparation for an adoptive home.

CHAPTER 11

One summer the Robinsons decided to reshingle their house. Scaffolding arose around the three-tenement home, almost magically to my nine-year-old eyes, reaching to the top of the third floor. Climbing the metal and wooden structure, workers undertook the arduous task of removing the old shingles and dropping them into large Dumpsters on the sidewalk.

We were told we had to stay indoors lest a falling shingle hit us. Staying in the house was not a problem for Betty, who never worked and watched TV most of the day; but for me, a curious little boy, it was cruel and unusual punishment. To pass the time, I grabbed a book and sat on the back stairs where it was a bit cooler. I tried to lose myself in my latest mystery, but I kept getting distracted by the white shingles that floated through the air before crashing into the Dumpster. I walked over to the screen door and pressed my nose against it, trying to look up. As I stood there, I noticed some of the shingles had missed the Dumpster and that a heavyset worker was picking them up.

"I can help," I said.

"Whatta you say?" he asked, in a loud voice that rose above the sound of banging hammers. He wore a yellow hard hat and dark shades. A T-shirt with the arms cut off at the sleeves showed his bulging muscles.

"I said I can help."

He eyed me warily. "How ya gonna do that?"

"Well, I can pick up the shingles that miss the bucket so you won't have to come down and get 'em."

I could tell he was thinking about it, because he didn't respond right away. He took a look up at the scaffolding, almost weighing the effort it would take to keep coming up and down the structure. "Where's ya mother?"

"Inside." As soon as I said it, my heart sank. She wasn't going to let me out of the house.

"Why don't you go get her for me?" he asked.

I found Betty sitting on the couch watching a soap opera. "One of the workers wants to see you, ma'am," I said.

"What do they want now?" she asked, irritated that she had to get up. I did not dare let on that I was the reason he wanted to see her.

With some effort she rose from the corner of the couch and walked to the back porch. By the time she got to the screen door, her demeanor had transformed. "Yes," she said, using her stage voice.

"Smart little boy ya got there," the man said. It wasn't a question, and though my expression never changed, inside I was beaming. Betty looked at me quizzically but did not acknowledge his remark. I did not return her gaze. "I'd like to put him to work, if ya don't mind," the man said. "Some of these shingles are on the ground, and he can toss 'em in the garbage for us. We'll give him a hard hat, kinda make him one of the crew."

She hesitated. The worker, believing that she was concerned for me, interjected, "Don't worry, we'll take care of him." With a sigh she relented, telling me that I was to listen to the crew at all times.

"Yes, ma'am," I said, barely able to contain my excitement.

For the rest of that day, I sat on the back porch, waiting for the loud clacking sound of a missed shingle striking the sidewalk. When I heard it, I bolted from the back porch, much like kids who shag errant serves in tennis tournaments. I picked up the shingle and heaved it into the Dumpster, enjoying the loud crashing as my toss found its mark. Then I returned to my spot and waited for the next one to drop.

After a few days of shingle shagging and other small assignments, I really did become part of the crew. My responsibilities included everything from picking up loose nails to getting tools they needed. I learned how to hammer a nail, how to use a level, and what a Phillips-head screwdriver looked like. The men allowed me to keep the hard hat, and soon they expanded my ensemble to include a tool belt and lunch pail. Each morning I raced through my chores to be ready in time for my new friends to arrive.

They taught me a great deal, perhaps without trying to. I saw how much pride they took in the small details, in doing a job well. I saw, too, the bond they shared with one another, reflected in their light-hearted banter during the lunch hour. They often took their breaks across the street from the house, where Fuller's paint store ran the length of the block and offered welcome shade from the summer heat. They sat with their backs against the cool brick wall, lunch boxes and thermoses at their sides. I joined them, and they asked about subjects I liked in school, who my friends were, and whether I liked any of the girls in my class.

One day the questions became more serious. George, the construction worker I had initially approached, put his arm around me. "Now, these people," he said, pointing his bologna sandwich at the house across the street, "they aren't ya real parents, are they?"

"No, sir," I said.

George was quiet for a moment. "Do ya know where ya real parents are?"

"No, sir."

He was quiet for a bit longer, and then he turned to me so abruptly that it caught me off guard; I actually backed up a couple of inches. "Don't ya worry about those people," he said, gesturing again at the house on Arnold Street. "God takes care of people like that." It didn't occur to me that George had sensed what was happening inside the house. Perhaps if I had thought about it a bit longer, I would have realized that the workers were in and around the house and would have heard many of our conversations and interactions.

"Yes, sir."

"Now, you like to read, I see. Always got books with ya. Don't ever stop readin'. Education is the most important thing you can get. Ya understand?"

"Yes, sir."

It never dawned on me that one day their work on the house would be finished. The last morning, the doorbell rang, and Betty answered. It was George, and although I was in the other room, I could overhear snippets of their conversation. She was signing some papers while thanking him for a job well done. As he got ready to leave, he asked Betty if I could walk him outside. A few minutes later, the two of us stood together on the sidewalk in silence. I adjusted my tool belt nervously. "We gotta move on to another job, Steve," George finally said.

It hit me that I wasn't going to see him and the crew any longer. Looking around at the crew, who were congregated a few feet away near their truck, I began to plead: "Can't I go with you guys? I won't get in the way, I promise."

George shook his head solemnly. "Sorry, Steve, ya can't. We'd love to have ya. Isn't that right, fellas?"

They nodded in unison. "Best little worker I've ever seen," one of them said.

"Works harder than you," said another to his friend, joking.

By then I couldn't hold back the tears. George got down on one knee to address me at eye level: "You remember what we talked about?"

"Yes, sir," I said, crying harder.

"Good. Don't you forget it now, ya hear."

They climbed into the truck and drove off. I stood on the street corner, watching the truck wind its way up Arnold Street. When I couldn't see it any longer, I ran down into the cellar and cried until there were no tears left.

CHAPTER 12

Maybe there's a chance for me to go back there
Now that I have some direction
It sure would be nice to be back home
Where there's love and affection
And just maybe I can convince time to slow up
Giving me enough time in my life to grow up
Time be my friend, let me start again . . .

—CHARLIE SMALLS, "HOME," *THE WIZ*

For most of us, home is the place where our life story begins. It is where we are understood, embraced, and accepted. It is a sanctuary of safety and security, of deep and abiding connections, and perhaps most of all, a place to which we can always return. Down in the dank basement, amid my moldy, hoarded food and worm-eaten books, sat another precious possession: the idea that my real home, the place where my story had begun, was out there somewhere and one day I was going to find it.

I cradled this notion as intensely as I did my beloved books. I was absolutely convinced that my real family was coming to rescue me from these real-life monsters. I concentrated this emotion nearly entirely on the idea of my father, a man I imagined to be strong and heroic, the only one brave enough to ascend the concrete stairs of the house on Arnold Street, bang loudly on the front door (no polite ringing of the doorbell for him), and say, "I have come for my son; give him to me." We'd walk off together, me nestled safely in the crook of his arm, headed for the place fathers and sons go to recapture time.

I grew impatient waiting for him, though. And so one summer day when I was eleven years old, I went looking for him. The occasion was an outburst from Betty. We were sitting in the living room, and she was furious at me about something I've long forgotten. "You're gonna be no good," she said, "just like your father!" The comment about my father stunned me, for no one had ever acknowledged that they knew who he was. The only thing I'd been told about him was what Betty said on many occasions—he didn't want me. I had learned to keep my features unreadable, but I broke that unwritten rule at the mention of my father's identity. My head snapped up, giving away my shocked expression.

"That's right, you heard me," she said, a nasty grin spreading across her face. She had my attention now. "Lemme tell you, boy. After they killed your father, they broke into the funeral home and set his body on fire." She shifted her weight on the couch, getting more comfortable as she warmed to her story. "Yep, they sure did. They hated him so much they hadda roll a rock over his grave so nobody would dig up his body. He was no good, and I can tell you something right now—the apple don't fall far from the tree. Not far from the tree at all."

Although I was not allowed to make eye contact (Robinson Rule #15), I couldn't help it this time. I stared at her long and hard, and this one time she let me violate the rule. *Was what she said true? Or was this yet another one of her poison-tipped verbal daggers?*

I looked away and resumed my habitual mask of indifference. But inside, my mind was churning. *How could I find out if she was telling the truth?* I turned my attention to the only person I could ask without being concerned about repercussions. "Hey, Ed," I asked some hours later, when he and I were alone in the bedroom.

"Was my father killed, and did they have to roll a rock over his grave or something?" My tone was deliberately casual, but my heart was thumping and pounding.

"What?!" he replied. "Is that what Ma said, that Kenny Pemberton was your father?"

"I dunno," I replied, repeating the name Pemberton silently to make sure I remembered it. "She didn't say a name. She just said what happened to him."

Ed looked up from tying his shoes. "Only one person died that way, and that's Kenny Pemberton. Was one of the best boxers this city has ever seen. But he got mixed up in some bad stuff, and he got killed in some kind of fight. I don't think he was your father, though."

This didn't satisfy my burgeoning curiosity. "But you're not sure, are you? How about you ask your mother for me?" Here I reverted to my own, more distanced, way of referring to Betty, which drew a sharp glance from Ed.

"All right, but don't get your hopes up. Kenny's still got a lot of family around, so if you were his son, I think somebody on his side woulda told us."

Weeks went by without Ed mentioning the boxer, and I was afraid to bring up the subject again. Then in April or May of 1978, my fifth-grade class went on a field trip to the New Bedford Public Library. Among other things, we learned how to look up old articles in the newspaper. You went to the reference desk and asked for the year during which the articles ran. They handed you a boxed spool of microfiche film, which you put in a projector. Then you scrolled through the papers for what you wanted. The task of searching interested me so much that I returned to the reference room that day during our free time. I grabbed a microfiche of old newspapers and ran them through the projector, captivated by the snapshots of the past.

I don't know exactly when I got the idea, but soon after that visit, it sailed into my mind like a ship into port: if Kenny Pemberton was as great a fighter as Ed said he was, he would have been a big deal in the local community. The *New Bedford Standard-Times*, our daily paper, would have had lots of stories and even pictures about him—and definitely something about his murder. If I could just look at a picture of him, I figured, I could tell if he was my father.

The problem was I had no idea when this man had lived or died. Here again, Mrs. Levin came to my aid, albeit indirectly. From the detective stories she brought me, I knew that when someone dies, an official record is created, a death certificate. If I could get that record for Kenny Pemberton, I'd know when he died. Then I could go to the library and ask for the right spool of microfiche. But where on earth would I get a death certificate?

"A what?" Ed asked, when I talked to him later that week. "What do you need a death certificate for?"

I had anticipated this response, and I was ready, even though it had taken me most of the week to figure out what I would say. "Oh, I'm doing a summer book report on local boxers, and I thought maybe I'd put in something about that boxer you mentioned a few weeks ago. What was his name?" I didn't want to let on that it was engraved in my mind.

"Kenny Pemberton. But Steve, I'm telling you, I don't think he was your father."

"Oh, I know, I know, that's not why," I said, trying to maintain my poker face. "It's just a book report. Everybody has to do one over the summer."

"Well, okay, it's not that hard," Ed said. "You go to City Hall, go to like the Vital Records Bureau or something like that, and ask for the person's death certificate. They'll give it to you. They have to. It's pretty easy."

My plan took shape. I would somehow get to City Hall, get the death certificate, dash across the street to the library, look up the story, and find out what I wanted to know. I just needed a good excuse to be away from the house long enough to do it. Some days later, I got my chance when the Robinsons asked me to pay the electric bill the next day. To save the cost of a stamp, they paid that bill in cash at a discount department store in downtown New Bedford that took utility payments. If I ran fast and got there early, I could get to City Hall and then the library and be home in an hour.

The following morning I went through my chores as quickly and quietly as possible, careful not to wake anyone in the house. When I was finished I grabbed the envelope, tiptoeing around the creaks in the kitchen floor that I knew would signal my departure. I had my hand on the gold doorknob of the kitchen door when I was suddenly startled by the sound of Betty's inquisitional voice, coming from her bedroom right off the kitchen: "Where are you going?"

"You told me I had to go downtown and pay the electric bill this morning." I held my breath during the long pause that followed. If she said I could not go, I'd have to wait a month until the bill had to be paid again.

"Okay, but you better be back in an hour."

"Yes, ma'am. But what if there's a line?"

"There shouldn't be no line this early in the morning. You be back here in an hour, or you know what you gonna get."

"Yes, ma'am."

I twisted the knob and walked out. My mouth was too dry to whistle, but I tried to amble out the door as slowly as possible, half expecting her to call me back at any moment and cancel my mission. At the stop sign on the corner near our house, I turned right onto the sidewalk along Arnold Street. Walking past the paint store, I knew I was no longer in direct line of sight from the living room. Now I just had the clock to worry about. One hour to pay the bill and find the father whom I'd waited for all these years. I shot off like a rocket, as close to a four-minute mile as an eleven-year-old in blue jeans can muster.

I ran up Arnold Street, passing the McAfees', the Vandivers', and other familiar houses, my feet striking the pavement in a rhythmic cadence. I was headed toward Star Store, an old jumble of a city department store well over a mile away. After several minutes I got winded and slowed down, but I didn't dare walk.

Making it to the store ten minutes before its nine o'clock opening, I waited right in front of the dirty glass doors. Others began a line behind me. When the doors parted, I sped down the "infants" aisle, past the carriages, hampers, and baby wipes, all the way to the back left wall, where a customer service counter took municipal utility payments. Without looking at me, a young clerk with too much eye shadow on her thick, tired eyelids took the envelope. She pulled out the bill and, licking her thumb, counted the money. She counted so slowly that I began to fear that Betty had made a mistake with the payment and my plan would be ruined.

Finally, the clerk nodded, and I was free to go. I tore back through the store and out onto the street. City Hall was about three blocks away, at the corner of Main and Pleasant. Running over there, I rehearsed my story once again: I needed the death certificate for a school report I was doing.

I felt hopeful—and nervous—as I crossed the street in front of City Hall and stood before the steps. Under my feet was a large emblem with strange writing I couldn't decipher, although I did recognize the words *New Bedford*. The heavy doors were an unexpected test of my physical strength. Whether a device forced them shut, perhaps to keep in the air-conditioning, or whether they were just unusually heavy, I struggled mightily to open the doors. The enormity of my task chipped away at my confidence. *What if they wouldn't give me the document?*

I managed to wrench those doors open, finding myself in a small foyer. All around me there appeared to be plaques of one kind or another. An enormous painting of a whaling scene dominated the right wall. Called *The Capture*, it depicted several men in a whaleboat harpooning a dying sperm whale overturned on its back. In the vestibule, I found the room number for the vital records section. I headed down a long hall that I noticed was very clean. People moved around this hall, their conversations echoing from the ceiling and walls. Still, they barely noticed me. I arrived at a large, high-ceilinged office with gray metal desks, yellowy light, and the languid buzz of clerks talking, file drawers opening, typewriters clacking, and phones being answered on the fifth or sixth ring. The business world had shifted to mainframes or minicomputers by 1978, but the shoe-box era would survive in this city hall for another decade. I took a deep breath and approached the long counter, standing on my tippy-toes so that I might appear as tall as possible.

A beefy, older black man with Popeye-thick forearms and a curly Afro was already standing there waiting for a document he'd ordered. He wore an orange-pocketed T-shirt and tinted shades. I recognized him immediately as a man who often walked through the neighborhood, a man the Robinsons used to call Charlie. His daughter was my classmate at Hathaway Elementary School.

"Can I help you?" a clerk asked me in that bland, all-purpose tone of officialdom.

"Yes, ma'am," I said. "I need the death certificate for a man who used to live in New Bedford." I swallowed hard, fighting my fear. "Um, his name was Kenny Pemberton. But I don't know when he died."

Conversations trailed off, file drawers stopped going in and out, and even the old Royals and electric typewriters seemed to stop clacking. *Uh-oh*, I thought. Two clerks looked at each other, exchanging that did-I-just-hear-what-I-think-I-just-heard expression. Charlie stared at me long and hard, but all I saw was his tinted shades. Just mentioning Kenny Pemberton's name had propelled me into the world of big people.

The head clerk came over. "What's a boy like you need a death certificate for?" Her tone was challenging, but it didn't really matter: I couldn't turn back now. I wouldn't turn back. I had come too far.

"Well," I said, struggling for composure, "each summer, we have to do a book report on some history of New Bedford, and I'm doing mine on local boxers."

Now it was her turn to pause. "What school you go to young man, and what grade are you in?"

"Hathaway Elementary, ma'am, and I'm going into sixth grade." I wondered what that had to do with anything.

"So if I called and talked to your teacher, would she tell me that you have to do this report you're talkin' about?"

I was amazed that she could ask such a silly question; it was summer, so of course my teacher wouldn't be around for her to talk to. "My teacher's Mr. Sladewski," I said. "And school's out, so I don't think he's there, but maybe he is, so you could call. Anyway, we have to do a summer report about New Bedford history."

This was half-true. At the end of fifth grade, everyone got a summer book list, with extra credit for doing a report on any books read. But the local history part was, I admit, an embellishment.

The head clerk seemed to know that there was more to my request than I was telling, but there was no easy way for her to find out what it was. "Hold on," she said, in a less edgy tone. "I'll be right back." When I again heard the droning of clerical business, I sensed that my explanation had worked.

I took a longer look at the room around me. Announcements of one kind or another were posted on the walls. On the wall behind me appeared a large map of New Bedford. To my left were rows of dark, singular shelves, and on each shelf sat a large yellow book, bigger than any I had seen. The head clerk walked over to these shelves and traced her hand along the yellow binders. Her hand came to rest on one of them, and with what seemed like Herculean effort, she heaved it down from its resting place and placed it on the desk. Her back was to me, but I could see her flipping the huge pages with enormous sweeps of her hand. My sense of wonder was interrupted a few minutes later by a very deep, gravelly voice. "Make sure ya get the story right, ya hear?" It was the man in the tinted shades.

I nodded my head vigorously in agreement.

"Look, you're gonna hear a lot of lies about Kenny," he said, "but don't pay no mind. No matter what ya hear, he was a good man. He just made some bad moves. Kenny wasn't afraid of nuthin'." Then in a much lower voice, he muttered, as if in an aside to viewers offstage: "That was Kenny's problem, I guess. He shoudda been afraid sometimes."

The head clerk had come back, carrying a single sheet of paper. "Charlie Carmo, leave that boy alone," she admonished. "He's just doing a report for school."

"I know, I know, Brenda," he said. "I just wanna make sure he gets it right." He turned back to me. "You're gonna get it right, aren't ya, boy?" Again, my head shook up and down. Affirmative. Yes! Charlie stared at me for another second before walking out the door. "Don't worry about him," the head clerk said as she slid the paper across the table. "It's just folks around here still have a lot of feelings about Kenny."

Years later I would find out exactly why it was so important to Charlie that I get it right.

"Yes, ma'am," I said. "Yes, ma'am."

Opening the City Hall doors to exit the building was somehow a bit easier than it had been pulling them apart to enter. Outside, I dared to look at the paper in my hand. My eyes scanned the sheet until I found it. *Yes, I had it! The date of Kenny Pemberton's death was August 2, 1972.*

The hour was dwindling away; I'd need to hurry. I bolted across the street to the tall, old public library on Pleasant Street, barely noticing the large statue at the front entrance. Founded in 1852, the New Bedford Public Library is famous for its collection of ship logs and memorabilia about the history of whaling. An imposing granite structure, it was built in 1910 in the style of a Greek temple. Although both the library and City Hall are municipal buildings, the dignified library, with its columned portico, was as serene as the redbrick City Hall was workaday and functional.

I hurried through the library's front door, my heart pounding. My success in getting the death certificate took my mind off Charlie's cryptic comment. I climbed the library's interior marble staircase to the reference section on the second floor. Walking into the room, I was as impressed as I had been on my field trip about two months earlier. Beneath the vaulted ceiling in the center was a wide, dark-mahogany desk flanked by white columns. On the walls were oil paintings of whalers in various stages of battle with the huge sea creatures. The shiny, marble-tiled floor reflected light streaming off elegant chandeliers. It was as far from the house on Arnold Street as I could get in 1978.

I got the microfiche for the *New Bedford Standard-Times* for July and August 1972 and set it up in the projector. The roll emitted a clicking sound as headlines flew by at warp speed, and my chest seemed to thump rhythmically with the images. As the date neared, I slowed the microfiche down. July 15 . . . July 19 . . . July 27. I was getting closer. Finally, there it was: August 2, 1972.

I scoured the headlines on the front page and local section for a mention of Pemberton, then inside those sections, then the other sections, then back to the front. Nothing. *This can't be right. There must be a mistake.* I checked the death certificate to be sure I was right. It still said August 2, 1972. I went back over every page of the issue. Still nothing. I was crushed.

I glanced at the clock; I had only a few minutes left before I'd need to hurry home. I saw the librarian and thought about asking for help. I decided not to, mindful of my close call in City Hall. For the first time since I had hatched my plan to find my father, I was faced with the possibility that I wasn't going to succeed. I put my head down on the table and began to cry.

"You okay?" asked a gentle voice. It was the librarian whom I hadn't wanted to ask for help. Her long hair was pulled back in some kind of bun, she wore a long skirt, and her eyeglasses dangled at the end of her nose. But the main thing I noticed was her kind face. Something about the way she looked at me told me I could trust her.

"I'm doing a report on New Bedford boxers, an' I'm trying to find an article about one of them who was—" I paused, swallowing hard, "was killed, actually. His name was Kenny Pemberton. I know the day he died, but I can't find any story about him in the paper for that day."

If she didn't recognize the local name, she intuited from my body language that whatever I wanted was very important to me. And she was compassionate enough not to ask why. "That's okay," she said, "I can help you."

"Really?"

"Sure. In fact, you're closer than you think. Remember, in a daily newspaper the stories are about things that happened the day before. So if he died August 2, you wouldn't see anything about it until the next day. Right?"

I nodded.

"I bet if you go to August 3, you'll find what you want." She stepped away, indicating that she wasn't going to do this for me.

"Thank you, ma'am. I really appreciate it."

I was sure she was right even before I scrolled to August 3, 1972. My mind was racing with so many thoughts that I skipped over the headline at first, but a half-second later I went back, and there it was, smack-dab on the front page: "Boxer Kenny Pemberton Is Slain in Fall River." Next to the columns of type was a small grainy photograph. I didn't really want to study the picture until I read the story, so I half-closed one eye to blur it.

My brain tried to make sense of the cryptic phrases: "Result of an argument in the bar . . . a third man passed the pair, turned and shot . . . three or four times in the chest . . . Pemberton was dead on arrival . . . no trace . . . fleeing through backyards . . . victim had been involved in a shooting incident in New Bedford at which time a Fall River companion was shot in the right arm." The jigsaw puzzle of police details was too hard, and so I stopped trying. But I did linger over some other words, ones easier for me to grasp: "Golden Gloves . . . middleweight boxing crown . . . Olympics trials . . . diamond class . . . one of three area boxers."

Now my eyes returned to examine the microfiche image of "Kenneth P. Pemberton." It showed a young man in a leather coat, his head tilted forward. He had a strong forehead and thick brow over deep-set eyes and a prominent jaw. His eyes were keenly focused on something. His mouth was half-open in an expression that held a hint of defiance—but that could also be a half smile. I stared and stared, but the shadowy image was unrevealing. Although its subject appeared African American, the photo gave no sense of skin or eye color. What struck me most about the man was his hair. It was straight and combed, in sharp contrast to my small Afro.

I leaned back and came to a decision: this man was not my father. I could see no resemblances between us, nothing concrete. Still, there was something compelling about him. I scrolled forward and found more. For most people, an obituary is the last thing a newspaper writes about them. But Kenny's story continued.

The next day brought another story speculating how and why he had been killed. And a few days after that, another story appeared, this time when someone broke into the funeral home, doused his body with lighter fluid, and set it on fire—a horrific and barbaric act that defied reason. What could he have done that was so terrible that killing him was not vengeance enough? Whoever he was and whatever he had done, he had paid a terrible and brutal price.

I became defiantly certain that my real father was alive. *I just don't know who he is yet.* And not knowing gave me what I needed most: the possibility that he would come back for me. I let out a deep sigh of relief and turned off the machine.

"Did you find what you were looking for?" the librarian asked, causing me to jump.

"Yes, ma'am," I said. "Thank you."

She said I was welcome and wished me luck. I smiled at her, marveling again at her kindness.

Whatever hope I had about the possibility of my father's return evaporated minutes later when I spied a familiar yellow and brown station wagon driving slowly up Pleasant Street. It was Willie and Reggie. They were looking for me, and even in that distance of a hundred or so yards, I could see the anger on their faces. Despite my best efforts, I had let time get away from me; I was at least an hour late.

I scanned the plaza, sidewalks, and trees around the library for a place to hide. Nothing! Then, in front of the library, I saw the large statue of a man carrying a harpoon. In desperation I dashed under its shadow. I watched Willie and Reggie drive by. Seconds later, I stepped out of my little shadowed recess, glanced at the statue, and ran home.

New Bedford had long maintained its ties to its history as the whaling capital of the world. The city's well-kept cobblestone streets, Seaman's Chapel where Herman Melville sat while researching *Moby Dick*, and widow lookouts—so-named for wives who waited for their husbands to return from the sea—were all reminders of a time long since passed.

The *Whalemen's Memorial* is another remembrance, a tribute to the brave men who sailed the seas in search of whales. It is a large bronze statue of a bare-chested whaler poised in the bow of a whaleboat, a long, sharp harpoon in his raised, muscular arms. A granite plaque is inscribed: "A Dead Whale or a Stove Boat." On sunny days, the protruding bow and its sculpted wake cast a small shadow on the sidewalk, and it was in that sea of dark that I hid that day.

I knew none of this history then, of course. Nevertheless, I briefly felt a kindred connection to the man in the bow, whose piercing eyes were so keenly focused on something off in the distance. He was searching—and so was I.

CHAPTER 13

The games of cat and mouse continued with the Robinsons for the next several years. The boy in me who believed that one day his parents were going to come for him gave way to the man who sensed that, in fact, he was on his own. And so I turned my attention to the future and how I could get out of the Robinsons' clutches.

As I saw it, my best hope for the future lay in attending college. I had my sights set on Boston College, largely because of a promotional brochure my seventh-grade guidance counselor had given me. I had no real sense as to how I would get there, but I knew that I needed to excel in middle school if I were to stand any real chance. Buoyed by my never-ending passion for reading and a quiet but fierce determination, I became a standout student, although the Robinsons never acknowledged any of my accomplishments.

Entering high school was the next step to getting away from the Robinsons. I had been looking forward to my first day of high school as much as I had looked forward to anything in my childhood. Little did I know that my first day as a freshman would be one of the most harrowing of my life.

New Bedford High School was about two miles from my house on Arnold, and I arranged to walk to school with my friend Duane Nelson. Along the way, I quizzed him on all the new things I would encounter, not the least of which was getting lost inside the building. He explained that even though New Bedford High School was one of the largest high schools in the state, it was really made up of four "houses"—green, gold, tan (my house), and blue. As long as you remembered what house you were in, you couldn't get lost. As we got closer to the school, I was struck again by its sheer size, which dwarfed my junior high school. Duane and I agreed to meet at the end of the day and walk home together. I reminded him that I needed to be home by 2:15 or I was going to be in trouble.

All members of the freshman class had to attend a mandatory assembly in the main auditorium. We were told to go to our house where we would select our classes. When I walked into the guidance counselor's office to choose my classes, I saw a small group of students huddled together with a guidance counselor, excitedly discussing what classes they were going to take.

I found a quiet corner and stared at the thick brochure, at a complete loss as to how I should choose my class schedule. My uncertainty was interrupted by Mr. Tabachinik, a cheerful gnome of a man. He wore a brown blazer and a tie that fell way short of his belt line. He had a bowlegged walk and a thick Yiddish accent. I liked him immediately. "Vell, young man, vhat classes are you going to take?" he asked.

"I really don't know, sir."

"No," he said quizzically, leaning forward. His eyebrows were dark and bushy, a complete mismatch for the snow-white tufts of hair that adorned both sides of his balding head. I shook my head again, embarrassed that I did not know the answer to this simple question.

"Vell," he said, rubbing his chin, "do you vant to go to college?" He had just said the magic words.

"Oh, yes," I said, "I am going to go to college."

"Gud," he said, the caterpillar eyebrows rising in approval. He pointed to the list of college-preparatory classes. "Then deez are zee classes you choose."

The rest of the day was a wonderful blur of bells, new classes and faces, and jostling bodies. For a time I forgot all that awaited me back at the house on Arnold Street. Like the explorer who senses land through the fog, I was still not certain of the pathway, but I was more convinced than ever that I was going to survive. All I had to do was outlast and outthink the Robinsons—something I had been doing for the past several years.

At the end of the day, I went to where I thought Duane and I were supposed to meet. Not seeing him, I started walking, thinking that I could catch him. The problem was that I had walked out the northern entrance of the high school, away from the direction of Arnold Street. For the next two hours, I was lost, wandering the southern end of New Bedford, trying to find my way back home. I recognized some places from the many errands I had gone on with Willie, but I couldn't connect the dots. And unfortunately I never stopped to ask anyone the way to the West End. Finally, I recognized the Little League field I had once played on with Eddie, and I ran home as fast as I could.

I wasn't all that worried about showing up late. The Robinsons knew I would never openly defy one of their orders, and so I figured that I would simply tell the truth—that I had gotten lost coming home from school. As soon as I hit the door, Betty and Willie were on me, peppering me with questions about where I had been. I told them what happened, but they wouldn't believe me. Willie pulled the strap off the wall, yelling, "You're gonna tell me where you've been!"

I cannot fully explain where the emotion came from, but I told myself that I wasn't going to let them win this time. I refused to cry, and the more I refused, the harder and longer Willie beat me. At some point he understood my resistance and yanked me over to the stove in the corner of the kitchen. He turned on the burner and placed the back of my hands over the flames.

The skin on the back of my hands rippled and bubbled, but I still refused to lie. I screamed in pain, but he held my hands in place. Betty yelled at him, telling him that burning the back of my hands was going to leave marks. (And she was right, because I still have the scars.) Only then did he stop.

Willie turned off the flames, and I fell to one knee, my head bowed, holding my hands, trying to will away the searing pain.

He stood over me for what seemed like an eternity, catching his breath, exhausted from trying to keep me still. Then he devised a new plan. He told me to grab my coat and get in the car; he would be right out. I did as he said, and he came out of the house a short time later with his hunting gear. I noticed that he had two of everything, including orange vests and rifles. This made no sense. He had taken me hunting before, but I was never allowed to carry a gun, let alone shoot it. And why was he now taking me hunting when he just spent the better part of an hour torturing me?

He opened the trunk of the station wagon, slid the rifles in, and slammed the trunk shut. Then he climbed into the driver's seat and told me to put on the orange vest. I put it on as delicately as I could to avoid scraping my burned hands. He sat there in silence, deliberately giving me time to try to figure out what he was going to do. After what seemed like forever, he turned to me and asked, "You remember what happened to that dog, a couple of weeks back?"

I did remember. He was referring to a hunting dog he had bought and then brought out to the woods and shot because it wouldn't hunt. And now I realized what he intended to do to me. "So, I'm going to ask you again, where did you go after school?"

I said nothing and simply looked out the window, defying him yet again, largely because I didn't think he was really going to shoot me.

"Still not going to tell me where you were, huh? I know whatcha thinking. You think I can't get away with it, huh?" Another long moment of silence. "I'll say it was an accident, tell 'em that it was your first time huntin', ya finger slipped off the gun." He chuckled to himself, a low sinister laugh. "Everybody knows huntin' accidents happen all the time."

He started the car and slid it into drive. "Now, I'm going to ask you one last time, where did you go after school?"

He wasn't bluffing. And now my defiance turned to fear. If I didn't tell him what he wanted to hear, he was going to shoot me, and I firmly believed that he would indeed get away with it. Except for

Nurse Nancy, no one had ever believed me, and in this case I wouldn't be around to tell my side of the story.

The problem was that I really had been lost. *How do you lie to get out of the truth? What was I supposed to say?* And then he gave me the answer. "You were over at a girl's house, weren't you?"

Slowly and reluctantly, I nodded my head yes.

He climbed out of the car, content that he had finally gotten the "truth" out of me.

A new realization came to me: *I am going to die here, at the hands of these people. And no one will know.* The tears that I held in for the last hour finally poured out of me. I sat in the passenger seat, my hands trembling and my back still stinging from the earlier beating. As I look back on my years with the Robinsons, this was the closest I had come to breaking. I had called on God many times before but never as fervently as I did that Monday afternoon in 1982.

"God, please," I said. "Please help me."

CHAPTER 14

He might not come when you call, but He's right on time.

—AUTHOR UNKNOWN

Early in my sophomore year, Ray Hernandez, a high school classmate told me about a college preparatory program. "It's the perfect thing for you, Steve," Ray said, barely containing his excitement. And it was. The Upward Bound Program's purpose was to provide under-resourced students with the support necessary to further their education. Weekly tutoring sessions that were focused largely on college planning gave me the tools I needed to chart my future—and my path away from the Robinsons.

But the program gave me something else too. The director of the program was Margery Dottin, better known as "Ruby," a member of the school board and a titan in the New Bedford community. She was a petite, African American woman with an incredibly sharp mind, a devout Christian faith, and a tireless passion for education and young people, and her name was synonymous with respect, honesty, and integrity. If you had a problem with Ruby Dottin, there was a really good chance the problem was you.

I had first met her several years prior, in elementary school, when she served as a judge for a citywide spelling bee. I had won the spelling bee that morning, and to this day I can remember the tremendous look of pride she gave me. No one had ever looked at me quite like that. She had continued with her passion for young people, now as director of the Upward Bound Program.

To her the program was far more than a college preparatory exercise; it was a family, and she treated all her students as she would her own children. Her passion for your future was so great that you never wanted to disappoint her. She understood that hope was not enough—that you needed someone who believed in you. Ruby Dottin thought the Spirit had put her here to do exactly that.

The Robinsons initially denied my request to join the program— that is, until Ruby Dottin telephoned the house and questioned Betty as to why I had not yet completed the application. With bated breath, I listened in the background as Betty tried every conceivable trick she knew, from not having transportation to her belief that I was not college material. As she hemmed and hawed, I detected in her tone something I'd never sensed in Betty before: fear. She well knew Ruby Dottin's reputation. Mrs. Dottin shot down every one of her objections. By the time Betty hung up the phone, I was a member of the Upward Bound Program at Southeastern Massachusetts University.

Had Betty known how much the program would further embolden me, she would have fought even harder to keep me out of it. The program's mission was to prepare students for entrance to college, which was perfect for someone who had set his sights on Boston College, the Jesuit Catholic university in the suburbs of Boston. Yet I had no idea what the steps were to apply to college and was even less certain as to how in the world I would pay for it. I would express these concerns to the Upward Bound staff, and each time they provided a plan.

What the program had no plan for were the Robinsons. One afternoon in my sophomore year, I came home with the PSAT registration form. I presented it to Betty, who promptly threw the paper in my face.

"No way I'm telling people my business," she barked, settling comfortably into her corner seat on the couch. The paper fluttered to the floor, landing right next to an open coffee can that had become Willie's spittoon.

"But if I don't take these tests, I can't go to college," I responded, in a rare moment of open challenge to her authority. "Who said you were going to college?" she said. "You might as well put that thought right outta your head. Now go get me a can of Tab."

I gave Betty my usual poker face, but inside I was in great distress. College had always been the next step in my escape plan, so much so that I kept the number of days in my geometry notebook. *They would never be able to touch me there*, I had reasoned. But now Betty had made it abundantly clear that she was going to stand in my way.

Looking back, this was a galvanizing moment. The Robinsons had taken away any semblance of my childhood, something I could never get back. But now this new edict, vile and ignorant, threatened my future. At some point in our lives, we all have to make a decision to take a stand, knowing full well the potential harmful consequences. For me that decision came in the fall of 1982, at the age of fifteen.

High school now took on even greater significance. As I progressed in high school, I became more determined to fight back against the Robinsons by working the system that had so far failed me. In January 1983, when I was a high school sophomore, I met with the social worker who had taken over my case, Jose Botelho. He had had my case for four years, and this was the first time we were meeting. The only reason he came to see me was because I telephoned him, a call I placed secretly from my guidance counselor's office. My complaint was very specific: I wanted to leave the Robinsons because they forced me to quit any school activity as soon as I started to have any success. What I was really doing was testing him. If he was willing to listen to that part, then he might be willing to hear more.

But he was not. Jose Botelho did not share my urgency; he was more interested in discussing how I could be more accommodating in the Robinson home. He tried to further dissuade me by suggesting that even if I found another family, which he doubted given my age, I would always have "little" difficulties. As soon as I sensed that he was not going to help me, I redirected the conversation and said that perhaps this was really my fault, that what I needed to do was work on being more cooperative. And I told him I would try and see if things got better.

But, of course, I knew they wouldn't. The Robinsons feared no god, and they had no mercy to which I could appeal. I thought that if I let a little time pass, I could convince Botelho. A month later, I met with him again and told him that the Robinsons' refusal to let me participate in extracurricular activities was jeopardizing my college chances. I told him that the Robinsons had made me quit the track team even though I had shown signs of promise. They had also forced me to quit the varsity debate team because I was required to bring money along to purchase a meal at the end of each day. He said he would look into this for me, but he still tried to convince me that staying in the Robinson home was the best option.

In their conversations, Betty Robinson continued to manipulate Botelho and his perceptions of me. She had a laundry list of offenses that I was allegedly committing: behaving disrespectfully, not doing chores around the house, stealing food. Of these, only the last one was true.

To his credit, Botelho called New Bedford High School, which gave him a good report about me, telling him that I had consistently earned a place on the honor roll. When he informed Betty of this report, she inquired why he had been asking the high school about me. She was becoming increasingly suspicious. Despite the conflicting accounts between the high school and Betty Robinson, Botelho continued to insist that the Robinsons were my best option.

In March of my sophomore year, I met with Botelho again and once more told him that I wanted to leave the Robinson home. Yet again, he tried to convince me that I should stay, but this time he added a twist: if I was so determined to leave, then it was my responsibility to inform the Robinsons that I wanted to leave. This I could not do. It would reveal without any ambiguity that I had violated Robinson Rule #1, which was to tell no one what went on at the house on Arnold. I said I would tell the Robinsons but only under the guise that I wanted to attend private school. He insisted that I tell them and be clear about my reason. For more than an hour, we negotiated how to approach the Robinsons. Finally, we came to a compromise: the Robinsons would learn the real reason, and Botelho would be the one to tell them. I went to bed that night and tossed and turned until the morning.

The next day Botelho came to the Robinson home. Their conversation took place in the living room, and Betty sent me outside. In a prerehearsed routine, I was to come back inside a few minutes after Botelho arrived and ask if I could play football with my friends. In an effort to appear to be the loving and caring mother, permission would be granted. The truth was, there was neither a football game nor friends with whom I could go play the game.

When Botelho told Betty why I wanted to leave, she went into a tirade and blamed him, accusing him of "putting thoughts in [my] head." Botelho feebly protested his innocence, going so far as to say that he was encouraging me to stay. But it was too late. He was barely in his car before Betty called the Department of Social Services and asked to speak to his supervisor. She ran off a list of complaints against Botelho, including that he had not seen me in four years, and demanded to be given a black social worker. When Willie got home, Betty replayed her conversation with Mr. Botelho. He immediately grabbed the strap and told me to strip and wait for him in the cellar. I did as I was told, shivering in the cold, waiting.

Fifteen minutes later, he came down into the cellar carrying the strap and a rope. When I saw the rope, I knew this was not going to be an ordinary beating. He intended to use the rope to tie my hands to the beams where I would dangle like a piece of flesh in a meat locker. I swallowed hard. For some time I had been able to steel myself against their punishments, but I questioned whether I would be able to withstand this one.

"You've been talking to the social worker, haven't ya, boy?" he said, tying the rope around my left wrist. I had spent hours thinking this through and playing all the different angles. And my response was ready.

"No, sir; *no, sir,*" I said. "He and I talked about going to private school because it would help me get to college. That way nobody would have to know your business. I didn't tell him I wanted to leave." It was a lie, of course, but I knew Betty would not be able to call Jose Botelho to verify my account. And even if she did, I was going to lie again. It would be my word against his. Still, it was a long shot. Willie eyed me warily, the strap hanging from his right hand, its strips dangling there like an octopus waiting to strike. But he actually stopped tying the rope.

"Betteh!" he yelled, his thick Southern accent bouncing off the cellar walls. The floor creaked above our heads as she shuffled toward the cellar door. "This boy here says the social worker didn't understand him right, says he only talked about goin' to some other kinda school."

"I knew it," Betty said. "Dem social workers always tryin' to start somethin'. That's awright. By the time I got done talkin' to his supervisor, I'd made sure he won't be comin' 'round here anymore."

Willie eyed me warily, the light bouncing off his glasses. "Boy, put your clothes back on and get back upstairs."

The verdict was in. Miraculously, the Robinson rule breaker had earned a reprieve. As for my unwitting accomplice, Jose Botelho, three weeks later he was removed from my case.

CHAPTER 15

My efforts to leave the Robinsons had not borne fruit, but the new caseworker's arrival brought another possibility. In early April of my sophomore year, Heather Pope was assigned to my case. She called Betty to set up an appointment to talk. "I can't this week," Betty told her. "My husband's in the hospital and just had a back operation." An appointment was set up for two weeks later. In the meantime, Pope contacted New Bedford High School and learned that I was on the honor roll and had made the varsity debate team as a freshman. What Pope didn't know was that the Robinsons had made me quit that too.

Betty and I met with Pope as scheduled, and under pressure from Betty, I told my new caseworker that I was very happy with my family situation. "We're so proud that he's thinking about going into law," Betty said, gushing. Of course, that was a bald-faced lie too.

Pope glanced down at her file. "Would Steve still be interested in attending boarding school?"

"Oh, no," Betty said. "He wants to stay in his school." She smiled at me. "Isn't that right, Steve?"

"That's right," I said evenly. "I'm not interested in that anymore. My parents and I discussed it at length, and we all agree that staying is the right decision." Saying these things almost made me sick.

In May, Pope arranged to spend time with me alone, away from the Robinsons' house. After I told her, in an evasive tone, that I really wasn't happy with the Robinsons, she asked if I'd like to reconsider attending a private boarding school. I said no, uncertain that a boarding school would give me complete separation from the Robinsons. Pope asked if

I'd like her to bring up with Betty whatever concerns I had. "No, please don't," I said. "If things become much worse, you can talk to Betty then, but not now." Still, I didn't want my fear of repercussions to hide the truth completely.

"Don't let Betty fool you," I told Pope. "She goes on about how she knows people at the Department of Social Services and could get you in trouble if you don't do what she wants." Pope asked again if she should talk to Betty on my behalf, but I begged her not to, the thought of Willie and his hunting rifles imprinted on my mind.

In early September of my junior year, it was time for my case's annual review. Pope called to schedule a meeting on the fifteenth of the month, but Betty made up an excuse, saying that she and Willie couldn't make it, as they had to be at a doctor's appointment in Boston. Pope suggested an alternative date, but Betty said she couldn't make that one either. "Steve doesn't want to meet with you anyway," she said. "He doesn't want to miss school. Isn't that right, Steve?" She nodded for me to take the phone. "Here," she said, "he'll tell you himself."

She handed me the phone. "Is this true, Steve," Pope asked, "that you don't want to attend our meeting?"

Betty was staring at me. "Um, yes, ma'am. I have some big tests coming up, and I can't miss them."

The next day, I called Pope from the Upward Bound office and told her that I did want to attend the review but that Betty had told me to lie and say that I did not. I also told her that Betty was lying about the doctor's appointment. My case review went forward as scheduled on September 15, without the Robinsons or me in attendance. At that meeting, Heather and her supervisor, Tom Amisson, set a strategy for how to proceed. They would have a case review with the Robinsons, me, and the staff at the department. At that meeting I would have an opportunity to talk about what had been unfolding at the house on Arnold Street.

Four days later, Heather brought me to the department to meet Mr. Amisson. On the ride there, Heather told me that if I wanted to leave the Robinsons, I would have to tell Mr. Amisson everything.

For years I had been trying to have it both ways: on the one hand I was desperate to leave the Robinsons, but on the other, I would never fully reveal the circumstances under which I lived, as I was too afraid that no one would believe me and was even more fearful about what would happen to me after. Deep down I knew Heather was right: if I was going to leave the Robinson home, I was going to have to make a stand, much like my friends in *Watership Down*.

For more than an hour, Heather and Tom Amisson listened as I told them the Robinson Rules, their deliberate attempts to thwart my academic progress, my constant hunger, and their merciless beatings. Several times during my story, Heather broke into tears, while Tom shook his head in disbelief. I finished by telling them what had been the final straw: the Robinsons were not going to complete the forms I needed to apply to college.

Though they believed me, the agency could not simply remove me from the Robinsons. Several years earlier, the Robinsons had been appointed my legal guardians, and given the rules then in effect, this seemingly meant they had to have some say in the matter. The challenge before the agency was to force the Robinsons to come to a review, something they had skillfully managed to avoid for the last several years.

The agency ultimately decided to hit the Robinsons where it would hurt the most: in the wallet. They would lure the Robinsons to the review, telling them they wanted to discuss the compensation the Robinsons received for my care. Once the Robinsons were in the room, they would announce that the compensation would be cut off. This line of approach emboldened me. I expected that once the Robinsons were no longer being compensated, they would let me go without a fight, and I would not have to endure any repercussions for revealing the truth.

The review meeting was scheduled for 3:30 p.m. on the afternoon of October 12. Right before I left for school, though, Betty told me that I was not supposed to attend the meeting. I was absolutely certain this was not true. In between classes, I ran several times to the tutoring offices of the Upward Bound Program, trying to call Heather to verify whether I should come. I kept missing her, and as the school day neared its end, I became increasingly nervous.

I finally reached her at 3:00 p.m. "Yes," she said, "you are supposed to attend the meeting. Do you need a ride?"

"No, I'll get there by myself. But please don't tell the Robinsons that I called you, okay?"

"Don't you worry about that at all," Heather said. She was now clearly on my side.

I was the last to arrive at the meeting. When I walked into the small conference room, Betty and Willie stared icy daggers through me. I knew I would be in real trouble as soon as we got out of there. Heather saw my fear and told the Robinsons that she had called me at school and asked me to attend the review. Willie kicked off the meeting by lying about a doctor's appointment he supposedly had at 4:15. Tom jumped right in, saying that the department was no longer going to pay the Robinsons for my care. Immediately the energy in the room changed. Betty became very agitated, conveying her disapproval of my previous social workers, who, she suggested, had broken several promises to me. Willie was even more blunt, demanding to know what the department was going to do for me, now that his family would no longer receive financial assistance.

The staff at the agency expressed their interest in helping me continue my pursuit of higher education and, if I so chose, providing me with a voluntary social worker for as long as I stayed at the Robinson home. I quickly agreed to this, knowing full well that if the agency wasn't involved, I would be at the Robinsons' mercy. Any possibilities of my release would be gone forever. I didn't need to look at Betty and Willie to know that I had committed the greatest of offenses by requesting a social worker. The Robinsons had so far succeeded in avoiding virtually any institutional oversight of my case, something that I had upset with my brazenness. And in addition, they were no longer going to be paid for having me in their home.

I was now afraid of what might happen to me back at home—really afraid. I said very little for the rest of the meeting. After the conference, Heather asked me to stay behind so we could talk about my college plans. "They are really going to hurt me now, Ms. Pope," I said, as soon as everyone had left.

"No, Steve, they aren't," Heather said, putting her hand gently on my forearm. "They know we are watching."

This was no consolation.

"You don't know them, Ms. Pope," I said. "You don't know what they are capable of."

Heather offered to give me a ride home, but I declined. Walking would take longer and delay the inevitable.

When I opened the door of the house on Arnold Street, I saw the leather strap, the rope, and a box of salt on the dining room table, right next to the floral centerpiece. *What is the salt for?* I had barely asked myself the question when Willie's voice boomed from the living room: "Get down in the cellar, and lemme tell you, boy, you better be naked as a jaybird when I get down there."

This time, there would be no miracle.

CHAPTER 16

Two days later, I met with Heather Pope and told her what had happened when I got back to the house on Arnold Street. "Can you show me?" she asked. I gently lifted the back of my shirt, wincing as I did. I looked over my shoulder to see her eyes go wide and her hand fly to her mouth.

"There really is only one thing we can do now," Heather said nervously, sitting across from me in a conference room at the department's offices. "You will have to file a 51A against the Robinson family."

"What is a 51A?" I asked.

"Well, it's a form you have to complete if you want to file a complaint against the Robinsons. You'll have to describe what has been happening to you in the home."

I nodded. "Okay. What happens after I fill out the form?"

"An investigation is conducted by the agency to see what the facts are."

"And then will I be able to leave?"

"Yes, Steve, you will be able to leave," Heather said. She smiled, but the smile didn't reach her eyes. There was something else. "There's a little problem, Steve. I think it's a problem we can fix."

I said nothing and waited.

"It's just that when you fill out the form, you have to be very specific about what's happening, and Steve," she paused, taking a deep breath, "Steve, they're going to know it's you who filed the form."

"I don't understand, Ms. Pope. I file the form . . ." My voice trailed off as I finally unpacked what she was really saying. "You mean I have to go back there, after I've completed the 51A, after they know it was me?" My voice escalated in anger.

Heather just looked at me, her eyes brimming with tears, her silence all the answer I needed. I bolted upright from the small conference table, knocking my chair over in the process. "No!" I said. I backed up against the wall, put my back to it, put my face in my hands, and slid down to the floor. I could not wrap my mind around what she was telling me. *Didn't they know what the Robinsons were going to do to me? Hadn't I told them enough? What more did they need from me?*

Heather came over and kneeled beside me. "They're not going to hurt you anymore, Steve. Once you file this form, they will know that if something happens to you, we're going to come after them."

It took her a long time to convince me, but finally I relented, and then only under the condition that Heather tell the Robinsons the department would be watching them. As I walked back to Arnold Street, Heather's words kept ringing in my ears: "We're going to come after them." *What*, I thought, *would she do if the Robinsons decided to come after her?*

I was going to find out soon enough. The Robinsons did learn that I filed the 51A, and just as Heather predicted, the beatings stopped. But the Robinsons now directed their anger at Heather. She received threatening phone calls, and Willie, who found out where she lived, also stalked her. Some weeks thereafter, Heather requested that my case be assigned to someone else. For the second time in a year, the Robinsons had successfully removed a social worker from my case.

In November of my junior year, Mike Silvia became my new social worker. One afternoon he came to the Robinsons' house to talk with us. With Betty and Willie present in the room, I told Mike that I didn't need a social worker. Later, when we left the house to speak privately, I told him that I did, in fact, want a social worker, and that I had been pressured to tell him that I didn't. "Please," I said. "Get me out of there. I'm desperate. I want to leave and never come back. I'll go anywhere."

By this time the Robinsons had changed their strategy from physical abuse to mental warfare. Still, I would not yield; their cruelty only furthered my defiance. They refused to feed me; I would save half my school lunches, hiding the food in my book bag. They called the Upward Bound Program and tried to convince them that I needed to be removed; I explained to my Upward Bound counselors what was happening and why I needed the program now more than ever.

I came home from school to find several of the books Mrs. Levin had given me shredded and torn, their pages left in a heap on the basement floor; I had already hidden my favorites, including *Watership Down*. They wouldn't let me bathe or shower in the house; so I ran as fast as I could to school and showered before classes began. They forced me to sleep outside in the doghouse with Rustina, the red Doberman pinscher; so I stole a blanket from a neighbor's clothesline and kept both of us warm. Worst of all, Betty would tell me she knew where my mother and father were—that she had always known, that she could call them if she wanted to. *You aren't going to be the one to introduce me to them*, I thought.

Amid all this, Mike Silvia was working furiously on my behalf. He continued to coordinate with the department staff and their attorneys to secure my release. I was growing impatient and called Mike frequently, asking when I would be moved. "It takes time," he told me. "There are processes we have to go through."

"What processes?"

"You have to undergo a psychological evaluation."

"A what? For what? What did I do? These people are starving me, making me sleep with the dog, for crying out loud, and I have to go through a psychological evaluation, like there's something wrong with *me*? And only then I can be moved? What kind of system is this?"

Despite my trepidation, I went through the psychological evaluation on December 15. Although the final summary would not be available for several weeks, the conclusion was that enough immediate evidence existed to justify moving ahead with my release. Freedom date: December 30, 1983. The agency, now fully concerned for my safety, withheld this information from the Robinsons.

Now all I had to do was hang on. I was terrified that something would happen to affect my release. Maybe Betty would find some new angle to use, or the department would lose its nerve. I was most concerned that one of Betty's alleged moles would tell her of the agency's plan. If that happened, there would be nothing to protect me. The possibility that I was going to die seemed very real. I feared Willie would take me hunting and only one of us would return or that some calamity would befall me in the night. I took a broken table leg and carried it to bed with me, prepared to use it against any threat. Sleep was hard to come by. When I did drift off, I jerked awake. Convinced that somebody was attacking me, I jumped up, swinging the table leg. It would be many years before I slept peacefully through the night. Each morning, I awoke exhausted but grateful to be alive, one step closer to freedom.

December 30 couldn't come fast enough. The Robinsons continued to find new ways to inflict mental anguish. On Christmas Day, they told me to sit down on the couch in the living room and watch while Willie, Betty, Reggie, and Lisa all opened huge piles of gifts. They went to great lengths to shower each other with holiday spirit— a spirit that pointedly didn't include me.

I steeled myself by counting the minutes, hours, and days. I imagined what it would be like to wake up on December 30, knowing that it would be my last day at the house on Arnold Street.

As it turned out, my face-off with the Robinsons would come sooner than that. Around nine o'clock on the morning of the twenty-eighth, with Willie away on a hunting trip and the rest of the house still fast asleep, I threw caution to the wind and called the Department of Social Services. In hushed tones, I asked Mike if I was still going to see him on the thirtieth. "Yes," he said.

"Will I be leaving?"

"Yes."

"Is there any chance that this won't happen?"

"No, we are absolutely coming to get you."

"I'm not sure how much more I can take, Mr. Silvia."

"I know, Steve, hang in there, just two more days. Hold on, someone wants to talk to you."

It was Heather Pope, who wanted to wish me a Merry Christmas and tell me that I had to hang in there.

"Thank you, Ms. Pope," I said. "I have to go now. If they find out I'm talking to you, I'm in serious trouble."

Just as I was about to hang up the phone, I heard the phone line on the other end click off suddenly. *Oh, no!* At some point in my conversation, Betty had picked up the other phone and had been listening in. A high-pitched, bloodcurdling wail came from her bedroom. Reggie burst out of his bedroom and lifted me off the floor by my neck, cutting off my air supply. His eyes were bulging with rage, white spittle flying out of his mouth. He used his weight and size to choke me.

For a moment I thought, *They are going to kill me just as I said they would.* But then my thoughts turned to survival. I scratched and clawed at him and then searched around me for anything I could use to hit him. I was losing consciousness. I could hear Betty yelling in the background, but I could not make out her words. Just as I was about to black out, he let go, and I slipped to the floor, collapsing onto my hands and knees. I stayed there, trying to catch my breath.

"Don't put any marks on him," Betty said. It dawned on me that she was giving him permission to continue his assault. He stood over me, trying to figure out how he could hurt me more while leaving no evidence. I sensed his weight shift suddenly, and before I could react, he placed a vicious kick squarely into my ribs, knocking me flat onto my back and taking whatever wind I had managed to gather. He unleashed a flurry of kicks and punches to my face and midsection as I did my level best to cover up. Finally, I heard Betty say, "That's enough."

I staggered to my feet, determined not to give Betty and her attack dog any satisfaction by lying on the ground. "Betcha won't use the phone anymore to call no social worker," she said. "Now get in the bathroom and clean yourself up."

I limped into the bathroom and looked in the mirror. I could hear the sound of my breath, tortured and raggedy. When I raised my head to look in the mirror, I barely recognized myself. I had large welts on my forehead and a long scratch down the side of my face. My lip was gashed, my mouth full of blood. One eye was completely closed. Every breath I drew in hurt where Reggie had punched and kicked me. Through the years I had always managed to fight back by not yelling out in pain, by excelling in school, or by plotting my escape. These small victories, cloaked in silent defiance, were monuments of dignity that I built to protect me from the Robinsons' brutality. But this beating had stripped me of that. It left me cowering and covering up like an animal.

There was something else as well: by filing the 51A and pulling off the veneer of the "kind and caring" family, I had revealed their true nature. They would never again be allowed to care for foster children and would lose a source of income. Once Willie got home and heard that I had called the department, we were almost certainly going on a hunting trip, a sojourn only one of us would return from.

A white-hot, blinding anger arose in me, the first signs of a temper I would struggle to control in future years. I had tried it the Department of Social Services' way, had filled out their forms. My reward was getting pummeled to within an inch of my life. I spat a crimson stream into the sink and looked in the mirror again. "I will not take this anymore. I am going to do this my way," I said, to no one in particular. I was going to get away from this house and these monsters—today. But how? There had to be a way.

Reggie banged on the door, interrupting my conversation. "Hurry up and get out of that bathroom."

I opened the door, and he brushed past me, burying an elbow into my ribs, bumping me off stride. He slammed the door behind him.

By now it was late morning. I had to get outside. That was the first thing. If I did, I would have running room, and they wouldn't be able to catch me. I'd worry about the "where are you going to go" part later. I glanced over at the garbage can and saw that it was only three-quarters full. I grabbed a pile of newspapers and several bottles off the kitchen counter and stuffed them into the garbage can, tying it so it wouldn't be apparent that there was more room inside the bag. I went into the bedroom, grabbed my winter coat, put it on, and was about to walk back into the kitchen when I realized that Betty was seated at her perch in the living room watching morning television. If she saw me, she would put an end to my mission right then and there. Yet in walking from the bedroom, through the kitchen, to the front door, I had to walk past her line of sight, roughly twenty feet away. My only hope was that she would be so engrossed in her program that she wouldn't notice me.

I stood in the bedroom, ready to bolt, when I heard the sound from the television. It wasn't a television program but a commercial. *Can't go when commercials are playing because she will definitely see me.* I heard the theme music from *The Price Is Right* and knew that high drama awaited—the moment when Bob Barker announced the newest contestant by saying, "Come on down." That was my chance. I waited in the bedroom for Barker's signature call, every muscle in my body tense. *There it is . . . wait, wait . . . not too quick or she will see you . . . "Come on down!" . . . okay, go now!*

I emerged from the bedroom, grabbed the bag, took three steps to the front door, put my hand on the golden doorknob, turned it, and—

"Where you think you're going?"

Betty's words cut through the air. A bolt of raw fear, sudden and arresting, shot through me. My hand froze on the doorknob. I let it turn back to its normal position. *So close!*

"The garbage can is full, ma'am," I said, trying to keep my tone as flat and even as possible. "I was just going to take it outside." My words hung in the air, and I stared at my hand, praying that I could just turn that doorknob, just one small turn to the right. Then I would be free.

The couch squeaked, and Betty emitted grunts of protest. She was getting up! Another surge of fear, greater than the first, washed over me. I removed my hand from the doorknob quickly and slumped my shoulders, trying to give every appearance of being defeated. I gave her a view of the top of my head because if she saw my eyes she would see the purpose they held. I prayed that my emotionless mask would work just this one final time. She shuffled into the kitchen and eyed me. "Take that coat off," she barked. "Knowing you, you'll try and run away."

You're right about that, I thought. And then another, more defiant thought occurred to me. *You're in for quite a surprise if you think not having a coat is going to stop me.*

I removed my coat and took it back into the bedroom. Reggie was still in the bathroom, belting out lyrics to Diana Ross's "Ain't No Mountain High Enough." Betty must have sensed something, because when I came back she was still standing there, those malevolent eyes trying to stare into my soul. I looked at the floor, again giving her a view of the top of my head. "I'm going to stand right here in the front doorway and watch you, just to make sure you don't run," she said.

My mind kicked into another gear as I grabbed the bag, Betty now trailing me. *How was I going to get away if she was standing there watching?* I opened the front door, and a cold, bone-rattling gust of wind hit me in the face. I glanced over at Rustina, the red Doberman pinscher, who was frolicking around, thinking that I had come outside to feed her. *Have to buy time. Think. Think! Got it.*

A couple of weeks earlier, Rustina had gotten loose and torn open a bag of garbage, strewing the contents all over the yard. I'd had to clean it up, but now it gave me an idea. As soon as I turned the corner out of Betty's sight, I dumped the bag on the ground, using my hand to spread it around while exclaiming loudly, "Oh, no!"

"What's your problem?"

I popped my head back around the corner, making a show of rubbing my bare arms in the bitter cold. I gestured at the mess that lay around me. "Rustina tore open a bag of garbage again, and it's all over the yard." I bent down and began picking up coffee grounds and eggshells.

Saying nothing, she stepped out of the doorway, wrapping the frayed red housecoat around her large frame. Surveying the mess, she said, "All right, but you'd better hurry up. And I'm gonna be watching you right through that window." She pointed to the window that overlooked the yard, providing a clear view of the front gate and up Arnold Street. She didn't mean she would be watching me pick up the garbage. She meant that if I tried to flee she would be able to see me.

The storm door slammed behind her, leaving me wondering just how I was going to get away without her seeing. I resumed picking up garbage off the ground. Looking up briefly, I saw the curtains shift. She was indeed watching me. I glanced at Rustina, chained to the doghouse, who seemed to be pondering my dilemma with me. I glanced around the yard, my eyes finally coming to rest on the garage. *Of course.*

The white-bricked garage, which ran right alongside the house on Arnold Street, had been a holdover lot for the auto shop down the street. I had thrown thousands of balls against this structure, nursing dreams of playing center field for the Boston Red Sox. Other times I had sat in its shade immersed in my latest mystery. I had scaled its walls and watched fireworks from its roof. The world always seemed so much bigger from its height, filled with a promise that eluded me. The garage had provided me refuge many times, but that cold, bitter morning it provided me something else: an escape.

Betty's eyes bore into me, watching my every move. I could not just up and bolt because she would call the police, charm them as she had almost everyone else, and I would find myself right back here. It occurred to me that if the police did come, my injuries would make my case for me. Then I remembered going to the hospital following the beating with her hairbrush. No, I had to slip away without her

87

knowing. My best option was to head to the Department of Social Services where someone would be willing to help me.

I continued my task of picking up garbage, but each time I returned to the pile, I moved a bit farther out of her line of sight. She probably thought I was moving farther into the yard, but in fact I was moving closer and closer to my escape. Satisfied that she thought I would keep returning to the pile, I bolted to the northern end of the garage, away from the front door of the house on Arnold Street. Ordinarily I could climb this building with ease, but now a combination of nerves and cold fingers hindered my escape. Several times I lost my grip. *Concentrate!* Finally, I managed to grab hold and moved around the green drainage pipe. Reaching the top, I lay down on my belly and crawled commando-style across the cinder roof, its rough surface tearing holes in my T-shirt and scraping my skin raw. As soon as I was certain no one from the house could see me, I stood up and moved to the other end. At any minute Betty was going to discover that I was no longer in the front yard. My heart pounded in my chest.

Climbing down the garage's other side, I leaped to the ground and paused there, pricking my ears for the sounds of pursuit. I listened for Betty's voice, expecting her to tear the door open and yell my name. No sound came. I began to run up the street and then stopped dead in my tracks. A car was coming. Was that Willie's station wagon? I ducked behind a parked car until the vehicle passed.

The passing car was not Willie's, but it did alert me to something I had forgotten: when Willie came home, he was almost certainly going to come looking for me, and he would be shrewd enough to head toward the Department of Social Services, located in downtown New Bedford. Rather than going my traditional route, I took a longer way, all the while looking over my shoulder. I received several curious looks from strangers, but no one stopped me.

About a half hour later, I walked into the lobby of the Department of Social Services, dressed only in a T-shirt and jeans, shivering from a mile-long trek in the cold, battered and bloodied. The young receptionist, troubled by my appearance, recoiled when she first saw me and then hesitated when I asked to see Mike.

"Please," I said, as evenly as possible, masking my fury at having to beg. "I really need to see him."

"Your name?" she asked.

"Steve . . . Steve Klakowicz."

She picked up the phone, dialed another number, and spoke in hushed tones. I sat down on a chair in the outer office, keeping an eye on the front door. At any moment Willie might come bursting in, shotgun in hand.

Moments later, Mike opened the door to the outer reception area. His shoulders slumped as soon as he saw my condition. I didn't make eye contact with him.

"Geez. Are you okay?" he asked.

"Not really, Mike."

"Are you hurt? Do you need to go to the hospital?"

To go to the hospital would be to admit that they hurt me. I looked him square in the eye. "No."

"Well, at least let me get you some ice."

"No," I said, standing to make my point completely clear.

Mike eyed me for a long while. Finally, he nodded his head in understanding. "Come with me."

His desk was in the middle of an open floor space. All eyes were on me as we walked. I sat down, and he put his coat around my shoulders. "Would you like something to eat?" Mike asked.

"I can't eat right now," I said, "but if you don't mind, I would really like something to drink."

"Sure, no problem." He put a hand on my shoulder. "You're going to be okay, Steve."

How many times had I heard that? "I'm only going to be okay if I get away from them, Mike."

"I gotcha," he said. He handed me a cup of water. I lifted it to my lips shakily. "We're going to get you out of there, today. I promise."

He picked up the phone and dialed the Robinson home. I could hear the phone ringing on the other end. "Hi, Mrs. Robinson. This is Mike Silvia, Steve's—"

Betty's voice came across the telephone line abruptly: "Steve ran away."

"No, he didn't, Mrs. Robinson. He's right here. And he's badly beaten up."

"Well, he busted up everything we got him for Christmas," she said. I grabbed a pen and piece of paper from Mike's desk and scribbled a note: "Didn't get anything for Christmas."

"Steve says he didn't get anything for Christmas. Is that true? Because the department gave you extra money to provide—"

Betty cut him off again. "He's lying! I've taken in thirty-nine foster children—"

Now it was Mike who interrupted, saying evenly, "So if I came by there in the next ten minutes, you'd be able to show me everything you've gotten him?"

The phone was quiet on the other end.

"Steve has a right to press charges against you and Reggie. But he doesn't want to do that. He says he just wants to leave your home as soon as possible."

"That's fine with me," Betty said. "We never wanted him in the first place."

Mike turned red and any sense of professional decorum he had tried to maintain vanished. "It's the other way around," Mike said, his voice rising. "You don't deserve him." His voice got lower then and took on a new intensity. "Now, you have a choice," he said through clenched teeth. "I can come by with Steve and get his things, or I can bring the police and have you and your son arrested. What'll it be?"

Again—that beautiful silence on the other end. After years of manipulating teachers, psychiatrists, police officers, and social workers, Betty had finally met someone she could not bend. "Fine," she said.

"Glad we understand each other. We'll be by in thirty minutes. Have his things ready." He hung up the phone.

Thirty minutes later, we were sitting in his truck outside the house on Arnold Street. "You ready?" Mike asked.

I took a deep breath. "I'm ready." And I was. I wanted to face them, wanted them to know that I wasn't afraid of them anymore, wanted them to understand that I had finally beaten them.

When I stepped out of the car, the neighborhood was eerily quiet. No dogs barking, no cars moving up and down the street, no children playing. It was as if the neighborhood, silent for so many years, would be quiet one last time, ringside patrons for the final showdown. Parked at the curb was Willie's yellow and brown station wagon. The *tink, tink, tink* of the car's engine settling told me he had recently returned home and was inside waiting.

We went single file up the porch stairs, Mike first. Blue-gray pigeons, their wings beating and voices cooing, settled on the garage roof where I'd clambered a few hours earlier. Rustina came out of her doghouse and cocked her head at me quizzically. Garbage was still strewn about the front yard. *I won't be cleaning that up. My days of cleaning up their messes are over.* A small dose of satisfaction ran through me as I pondered how long Betty had watched from the window, waiting for me to reappear. Reaching the top step of the small cement porch, I stepped out from behind Mike so that we stood shoulder to shoulder. He glanced at me and rapped loudly on the screen door. Lisa opened the door and went back into her room. It was the last time I saw her.

We stepped into the kitchen. Willie leaned against the counter, still dressed in his brown hunting gear, a lazy suspender dangling from his shoulder. His orange cap lay on the counter next to his car keys. Behind him was the brown jar I had stolen countless cookies from. His arms were crossed against his chest, and he was furious. He didn't acknowledge Mike, but he kept his hawkish gaze fixed on me.

Mike entered the living room where Betty was sitting. He was holding the papers that would release me from their custody. Reggie was nowhere to be found. Willie and I stood five feet apart, and he stared at me long and hard, trying to get me to look away, as I had done so many times in the past. If he was troubled by my appearance, he did not show it. I did not take my eyes off his. *You will look away before I do*, I thought. The silence was deafening. "Why didn't you wait until I got home?" he finally demanded.

"For what?" I asked, with every bit of contempt I could muster. "So they could lie to you again, and then you would beat me some more?"

"Nobody touches anybody in this house but me," Willie said.

"Look at my face," I said, addressing him in a tone he had never heard from me before. "He's always beat on me. And so did you. A lot of times for no reason. But no more. You'll never touch me again." I clenched my fists, my body shaking with anger. "You tell Reggie that I can fight back now and he'd better remember that, if he ever sees me."

"So you're a man now, huh?" Willie asked.

"I've been a man a long time now. You just never noticed."

I walked past him and into the living room. Mike was standing over Betty, telling her where to place her signature. She didn't read what she was signing but grew angrier as she signed each page. I watched as those pages turned, as my freedom crept closer and closer. "Do you have your things, Steve?" Mike asked.

Before I could answer, Willie, who had followed me into the living room, interjected: "He can't take nuthin' outta here until he pays fah all the things he has broken while he's been here. By my count, that's about a thousand dollars."

I was incredulous, as was Mike. He didn't acknowledge Willie's comment but turned to Betty. "We talked about this, Mrs. Robinson. I thought you said we weren't going to have any problems."

"Let them have it, Mike," I said. "They never got me anything worth keeping anyway. But I am taking my books."

"No, you're not," Willie snapped. "Those books belong in this house." Years later the irony would sink in. This illiterate man, who had whipped and beat me in frustration as I tried to teach him to read, was demanding to keep my books. At that moment, though, I was too angry to see it.

"No, they don't!" I shot back. "You people took everything I loved away from me. Made me quit anything I was good at—you even tried to take college away. Mrs. Levin gave me those books. You're not keeping my books." I turned to Mike, trying to fight the tears of frustration that had suddenly overcome me. "Mike, I will do whatever I have to do. I want to be rid of them, but I will take them to court and tell the judge everything they have done to me over the years. And I pray to God he sends them to prison."

Willie and Betty Robinson looked at me in stunned disbelief. For the past eleven years, I'd been nothing more than a discarded child, one they'd believed possessed no voice or vision. They didn't recognize this transformed person standing there with clenched fists, seething with fury and defiance. And it certainly never occurred to them that I had been there all along.

There was a long silence, and in that quiet I could hear the ticking of the kitchen clock. The refrigerator suddenly hummed to life, its low grinding suddenly louder than it had been. No one moved. Then it dawned on me that I was doing what I had always done: waiting for their permission. "I am going down to the cellar to get my books," I announced.

I walked into the kitchen, opened up the red basement door, and walked down the stairs, past the grime-stained window that had occasionally provided some light. The familiar smell of must rose to greet me. As I neared the bottom of the stairs, I suddenly froze, startled by sounds of movement farther into the cellar. My breath slowed. The cellar was pitch-black, and my books were farther back, in a green garbage bag tucked away in one of the corners. The furnace came on. As a young boy, I had run from that beastly sound; more recently, I had always turned my head in its direction. But now I did not move. I stared into the darkness, trying to discern shapes and movement.

Another sound, closer to the stairs now. Was that shallow breathing?

I pivoted toward the sound, and in that moment I knew Reggie was down here in the cellar, waiting for me.

I again felt the paralyzing fear that I wouldn't be able to leave the house on Arnold Street with my life. In orchestrating my release, I had violated every Robinson Rule in the book; there was no way they would let me go that easily. This concern, though, was replaced by a torrent of pulsing rage.

"I hope you are down here," I shouted to the darkness. The sounds coming toward me stopped—arrested, it seemed, by the rage in my voice. I heard shallow breathing. There was no mistaking it now, and I sensed its owner pausing, weighing his options, trying to figure out what to do next—a decision I tried to help along.

"Come on, then!" I yelled, crouching into a boxer's stance. "Come on out and fight me."

But I knew he wouldn't accept my invitation. He'd always been a coward who would never confront anyone on even terms. The sounds of breathing, joined by shuffling feet retreating farther into the cellar, confirmed this for me.

"Coward," I barked into the darkness.

I grabbed the garbage bag and ascended the stairs backward, giving me a full view of anyone trying to attack me. I left the bag of books in the hallway leading to the front porch.

When I returned to the living room, Betty was still signing the papers, her trademark red blotch of fury emblazoned upon her forehead, matching the tattered red housecoat she wore. Willie sat in his usual chair, again staring daggers at me as I walked in. I kept an eye on his hands, concerned there might be a knife or gun in them.

I watched intently as Betty signed pages of my release. She got to the final page, poised her pen above the signature line, and then stopped, drawn to the typed date to the right of her name. It said December 30, 1983—two days later. Her forehead wrinkled in confusion and then clarity as she realized that my departure had been imminent. She snapped her head up.

"You were planning this all along," she said, her voice rising an octave. Mike and I said nothing to this, our silence the only answer she needed. Her ballpoint hovered for a moment and then attacked the paper as she signed her name with ferocious strokes of the pen.

"That's the last page, Mrs. Robinson," Mike said tersely. He extended his arm, and she brusquely shoved the papers into his hand.

"You ready, Steve?" Mike asked. I nodded my head yes. Freedom was now only ten feet away, but Betty, furious at being outwitted, wanted to make sure I paid a price.

"Get out of here!" she screamed. Mike jumped at the sound of her voice. She followed that comment with more salvos: "We never want to see you again . . . We never wanted you in the first place . . . You were never family . . . We could have adopted you a long time ago, but we didn't want you . . . Nobody wants you, not even your own parents . . . You're gonna be no good, you hear me? No good!"

She offered those last words with the conviction of a traveling preacher, pausing at each word, trying to brand my future the way she had my childhood. The last several hours had thrown Betty off stride, but now she returned to her usual venomous self. In the shrillness of her voice, I sensed a last, desperate plea to extract the unconditional surrender she now knew I would never give.

I stared at her long and hard. "You stopped being able to hurt me a long time ago." I turned toward the kitchen. Remembering my conversation years earlier with George the construction worker, I turned back toward her and said, "God is going to take care of you."

Mike put his hand on my chest, nudging me toward the front door. But I wouldn't move. Finally, he whispered, "It's time to go, Steve." I nodded. I took one last look at Betty, whose head was bowed. She was crying and whispering over and over, "Just get out . . . just get out." I looked at Willie as well, but he avoided my gaze, looking down and away. I walked through the kitchen and opened the front door, stopping in the hallway to pick up the garbage bag, the only material possession I had after eleven years.

The minute I opened the outer door and stepped onto the porch, I was struck by the vivid colors and the sudden crispness of everything around me. My breath hit the cold air. Small clouds formed around my head and then dissipated. The neighborhood, so quiet a few moments earlier, now pulsed with activity. The pigeons, still lined up on the roof, craned their necks toward me in curiosity before flying away. Rustina bounded toward me, her shortened tail wagging back and forth. Across the street at Sunnybrook Farms, a clerk was unloading a milk truck, the wheels bumping down the metal ramp.

Amid this reappearing world was one sound I did not hear, and I knew I would never hear again: the *tink, tink, tink* of the yellow and brown station wagon.

Several weeks later, the psychologist's evaluation upon which my release was to be based finally arrived at the Department of Social Services: "Subject referred is clearly high functioning but anxiety and fear are masking what is very likely a superior IQ . . . it seems remarkable that Steve has been able to cope with his home situation for these many years. Immediate removal from present living situation is strongly recommended."

PART 2

A Mysterious Past

PART 2

A Mysterious Past

CHAPTER 17

It was late afternoon when we returned to the Department of Social Services. Because the office was one large space uninterrupted by cubicles, as Mike and I walked to his desk, all eyes were on us. A few of his colleagues came up to clap him on the shoulder, congratulating him on a job well done. He accepted these platitudes humbly, like a fighter pilot returning from a dangerous rescue mission. It dawned on me that the tough cases probably fell to Mike to resolve, and he had solidified his reputation with my departure from the Robinsons.

"How are you feeling?" he asked, as we sat down.

"Better," I managed to say. The realization that I would never return to the house on Arnold Street after a decade in their clutches had not yet sunk in. I was still literally shaking my head in disbelief.

"I'm glad. Let me update my supervisor, and I'll be right back."

After Mike left, his colleagues eyed me as if I were a vaudeville curiosity. If I looked in their direction, they looked away, pretending to be immersed in paperwork. *Don't you dare*, I thought, *don't you dare pity me*.

For the last couple of hours, adrenaline had masked the aching in my ribs and the pulsing in my eye. Now the pain returned, and I felt exhausted. I wrapped my arms around myself and rested my head on the front of the desk. In the background I could hear phones ringing, file cabinets slamming shut, snippets of conversation. After a time, this all blended together and faded away.

Hearing footsteps approaching, I popped my head up, forgetting for a split second where I was. Mike slid into his office chair and pulled a list of names and numbers out of a black binder. Looking me square in the eyes, he folded his hands together on his desk, the way people do when they are about to deliver bad news. "Well, now we somehow have to find you a place to stay."

Though I had left the Robinsons' only two days earlier than scheduled, the Department of Social Services seemed to have no plan for me. *I just need somewhere to go until I get to college*, I thought, as Mike scanned through his list. For a brief moment I felt intensely lonely, rootless, and disconnected.

Mike looked up and gestured to his list. "I have a woman here who may have room for you. She usually helps out in situations like this. You wouldn't be there long, but it's a place to stay until the start of the New Year, when we'll figure out a more permanent placement."

"Am I going to be able to do what I need to do to get to college?"

Mike nodded. "She's great about letting boys live their lives." I took this to mean that the place wouldn't be a home in a traditional sense but more of a group home for boys who had nowhere else to go.

He picked up the phone and dialed the woman's number but got no answer. He went to the next name on the list and dialed another number, but the person on the other end said that she had no room. "Don't worry," he told me, offering a reassuring smile.

Mike called number after number, going farther and farther down the list. Each conversation began the same way: "Hi, my name is Mike Silvia with the Department of Social Services, and I have a client here . . ." Hearing myself described in such clinical terms bothered me, but I said nothing, for my options were dwindling. All around me, chairs were sliding under desks, coats were removed from racks, and "see you tomorrow" was resounding across the large room. It was the holiday season, and judging from their hurried departures, these social workers were anxious to return to their families and warm homes.

As the room emptied, I became more and more nervous. I had always wondered where I was going next, but I had never quite answered the question, always telling myself, *Anywhere but the house on Arnold*. A half hour later, after the last social worker had departed with a cheery "good luck, guys," Mike hung up the phone and let out an exasperated sigh. He had reached the bottom of the list. "Sorry about this, Steve. It's just that it's two days after Christmas and families . . ."

His voice trailed off, and we sat there in silence, trying to determine what to do. Though I didn't know it at the time, I was among the most difficult type of foster child to place: teenager, male, African American. And during the holiday season, placing anyone was doubly difficult. Mike leaned back in his chair, his hands laced behind his head, staring at the ceiling. I glanced around at the large, silent office awash in piles of papers, filing cabinets, and binders. Somewhere in the corner of the room, a phone rang for what seemed like forever. "Nobody wants you" had been among Betty's final biting remarks, and now I was powerless to prove her wrong. The joy of escaping the Robinsons was gone; I felt lonely and defeated. Sighing long and hard, I buried my face in my hands.

"Do you know *anyone* you could stay with for a few days?" Mike asked. "Friends—anyone?"

I had been asking myself this very question. I thought about Mrs. Dottin for a moment, but given the Robinsons' vengeful nature, I didn't want to put her in harm's way. Nearly all the other adults I had known over the years were somehow connected to the Robinsons or the Arnold Street neighborhood, and I needed as much distance from them as possible. *But what about Upward Bound? Was there anyone . . . Wait a minute.*

I sat up straight in my chair. "Mike, I have an idea. It's a long shot, but it's worth trying." I leaned forward and put my hand on the desk. "There's a teacher in the Upward Bound Program, a Mr. Sykes. When Betty Robinson tried to remove me from the program, Mr. Sykes and another counselor refused her request." I didn't mention it to Mike, but I remembered a specific comment Sykes had made to the other counselor as I walked away: "I don't have any children, but if I did I would want my son to be just like Steve."

Mike leaned forward. "Do you know where he works?"

"At the college.* But I really doubt he's there; it's school vacation."

"Can't hurt to try," Mike said, picking up the phone. He called information and asked for the Upward Bound Program. I could hear the phone dialing. "Hi, Mr. Sykes. My name is Mike Silvia, and I'm a caseworker at the Department of Social Services. I have a client here, Steve Klakowicz, who has spoken very highly of you. Steve was removed from his foster home today and needs a place to stay for a few days while we sort out his living situation. Is that possible?"

I rocked gently in my seat, tossing up a silent prayer. I needed this to work. This was it, my last option. Mike held the phone to his ear, and I studied him for any telltale sign that Mr. Sykes was saying yes. Suddenly he switched the phone to his left hand and began to scribble on a piece of paper. "I see, I see," Mike said. "Well, it would only be for a few days, and I don't think Steve would mind, not after what he's been through today." He talked for a moment longer, twirling his pencil in his hand. "Okay, okay." Then he put the pencil down and shot me a thumbs-up. I let out a huge sigh of relief. For a moment I forgot all about the day's events, the Robinsons, and my injuries. Though my ribs ached, I exhaled deeply. It was the season of giving, and I had received the greatest gift of all: freedom, and, finally, a place to go.

---

* Southeastern Massachusetts University.

CHAPTER 18

Southeastern Massachusetts University,* where we arrived twenty minutes later, is ordinarily a beautiful campus. But on this overcast afternoon, as Mike and I waited in a large parking lot for Mr. Sykes to appear, its 1960s-era gray, hulking buildings seemed to blend into the gloomy, sunless sky. That was the second thing I observed. The first was the complete absence of activity. The school, then largely a commuter college, was closed for the holidays. There was simply no one there, except Sykes, a conscientious counselor who had come in on his day off to catch up on paperwork. To this day he insists he was meant to be there.

Sykes sauntered down the walkway, backpack slung over his shoulder. He was in his late thirties and far and away the most popular teacher in the Upward Bound Program. Outrageously funny and rebellious, he was a perfect fit for teenagers in varying stages of their own defiance. That he was white, wore his hair long, loved Harley-Davidsons, and listened to country music never mattered much to the African Americans, Cape Verdeans, and Latinos who dominated the program. We admired his passion for teaching, his witty intellect, and his love of learning. There was no greater joy than when one of his students "got it," as he liked to say.

We exchanged handshakes. If Mr. Sykes was alarmed by my physical appearance, he gave no sign. Mike and Mr. Sykes, who now insisted that I call him John, spent a few minutes talking while I hoisted the green garbage bag out of Mike's pickup truck and into John's weathered

---

* The college is now called UMass-Dartmouth.

green Volvo. The wind picked up, blowing about the few remaining autumn leaves. As they talked, I warmed my hands with my breath and watched the hibernating campus. Though I had been here many times as a student in the Upward Bound Program, it looked different to me, though I didn't quite know why.

"Good news, Steve," Mike said, a smile on his face. "You can stay with John through the holidays. That will give me time to find a more permanent place for you. Don't worry, I'll cook something up."

Mike and I said good-bye, and I got into Mr. Sykes's car. It was completely dark outside. John started the car and revved the Volvo's engine. "So, Mr. Syk . . . er, John, where do you live?" I asked.

"Westport. Do you know where that is?"

"No, sir."

"It's about twenty minutes from here, going toward Horseneck Beach. It's not the city, that's for sure, but I think you'll like it. And do me a favor, will ya? Please don't call me sir. Makes me feel as if we're in the military. And I'm pretty sure they wouldn't want either one of us."

I laughed, the first time I laughed that day. I had never gone much beyond New Bedford or the university campus. As we turned left out of the campus and away from New Bedford, a fleeting thought entered my mind, one I had first learned from the pages of Mrs. Levin's books: *There are other ways that people live in this world.* And I would now get a chance to discover them for myself.

CHAPTER 19

John was right: Westport wasn't the city. The trip to this quaint New England farming village was all two-lane roads with no streetlights in between. Headlights from an occasional passing car penetrated the darkness. Through that dimness I could see the outlines of the roofs of houses but little else. Had the day not been so wrought with strain and tension, I would have been struck by how eerily similar this trip was to another I had taken on a cold day in December some thirteen years earlier. But I was too overwhelmed with relief to make the connection.

Several miles later, we pulled into a gravel driveway, our tires crunching the stones underneath. More crunching followed as I stepped out of the Volvo and placed my feet firmly on the ground. I could see the outline of a small ranch-style house, easy to spot because there weren't any other houses around. We went inside, got settled, and a half hour later sat down to a deliciously terrible meal of half-baked chicken croquettes and instant potatoes. As it was almost nine o'clock, we then discussed where I was going to sleep. The room that adjoined John's was out—too small. We decided on an old cot he had stored in his basement.

As we lugged the dusty green thing up to the living room, one of the legs almost came off. I couldn't resist the opportunity to tease John. "Hey, John," I said, blowing off the dust, "did you use this cot at the Battle of Gettysburg or the Battle of Little Big Horn?"

He grabbed some duct tape to fix the legs. "I used it in both battles, if you really want to know."

"I thought Custer and all his men died in that battle."

"All of 'em did, except me," he said, pointing an exaggerated thumb at his chest.

"How did you escape?"

"I got out early. I always knew Custer was an idiot."

We both laughed.

I looked around; John's living room was sparse, to say the least. Three curtainless windows looked out onto the two-lane country road. In one corner an old television set with rabbit ears rested on a large lobster crate. In another, a radio sitting on a shelf gave off the faint sounds of holiday music. A small coffee table occupied the center of the room, a cribbage table its centerpiece, and nearby sat the largest piece of furniture, an ugly green couch that had seen better days.

We moved the furniture around, making space for the cot. "I'm glad to be here, John," I said. "Really glad. Thanks a lot."

He nodded. "Me, too, Steve." He began to turn away and then stopped. He paused for a moment before he spoke. "You're going to be okay here. I promise."

I offered a faint smile in return, still not convinced of this.

He went into his bedroom, and the door clicked gently behind him. I turned off the standing lamp and lay back on the cot. A half-moon illuminated the world outside my window. I could make out the faint outlines of trees that seemed to stretch on for miles. I heaved a big sigh. For the first time all day, I was alone with my thoughts. There was very little sound except that of an occasional lonesome car swishing down the country road, headlights blending in with the moonlight. The first few times a car approached, I bolted to the shadows of the makeshift bedroom, thinking it possible that Willie or Reggie had somehow followed me here. But the car always eventually passed, and after a while—after a *long* while—I started to believe that they would not find me in this faraway place.

Chapter 20

Meditation and water are wedded forever.

—HERMAN MELVILLE, *MOBY DICK*

I did not sleep on my first night of freedom. Today, even after all these years, I have trouble expressing the overwhelming sense of liberation that coursed through my soul on that moonlit night. *Had I really managed to escape the Robinsons?* This did not seem possible. But sure enough, when I returned to school after the holiday break, I had a new home and a new outlook on life and its possibilities. After a few weeks together, John had invited me to stay with him permanently and finish high school; and the Department of Social Services had consented to the arrangement. My task now was to heal old wounds as best I could and try to focus on two important tasks: enjoying life as a teenager and getting myself into the college of my dreams, Boston College.

Given what I had been through, I adjusted remarkably well to my new classmates and to life as a teenager. While living with the Robinsons, I hadn't been allowed to go out during my free time or take part in extracurriculars; relationships with peers were relegated to what I could manage in the space of forty-five-minute lunch periods. Now, high school blossomed into something that better resembled traditional American adolescence. To be sure, I never talked with any of my new friends about what I'd been through; there were vast stretches of my experience that remained my own private business. Yet I could now accept invitations to basketball games, birthday parties, and the mall. For the first time ever, I could have fun.

I remember my first movie. One Friday night in February, John dropped me off at the North Dartmouth Mall so that I could meet up with two of my classmates, Ray Picard and Kevin Rousseau. All week we had been talking about seeing *Footloose*, about a group of students who defy a town that will not allow them to dance. I was transfixed by the sights and sounds of the big screen—especially the movie's final scene, in which the teenagers take to the dance floor as if they were freedom personified. Later that evening, Ray, who had recently gotten his driver's license, drove me back to John's house on Horseneck Road. One slight problem: I had forgotten John's address. We drove around for the better part of an hour, relying on my rather shaky sense of direction. Eventually we did find it, but not before taking an involuntary tour of Westport's seemingly endless country roads.

Making friends became even easier as I became involved in school activities. I joined the track team and immediately became one of the conference's best sprinters and jumpers. I ran anchor on the relay in large part because I loved to chase people down and would go to almost any lengths to do it. I also joined the yearbook staff and became one of its editors. I had a great time making friends and finding activities I could excel in. It was, I suspect, a leadership ability that I'd always had but that I was now free to express.

When I wasn't doing sports or attending club meetings, I was beginning to explore relationships with girls. During my senior year, I began a relationship with Alicia, a wonderful young woman from New Bedford's South End. She was cute and sincere and, perhaps most of all, always able to see the good in others. Soon I found myself lost in the comfort of a first love. As the months passed, the relationship became an anchor for me. I'd always been cautious in all relationships, and it often took me a long time to trust anyone. But Alicia's grace and care for me lowered those walls of defense, and I eventually became convinced that she would not let me down.

During this time, however, my main preoccupation was academics. I knew, as I had always known, that a lot rode on attending college. My desire to attend college had driven me more than anything else to risk all in escaping the Robinsons, and I was not going to let anything, or anyone, get in my way. I had strengths in the classroom, including the ability to think quickly, honed from years of daily battles for survival. I'd decided in middle school that I was going to Boston College, and the intervening years had not changed that.

At least now I didn't have to fight the Robinsons for time to study or suffer their disparagement when I read a book. On the contrary, I enjoyed the consistent support not only of John but also of his parents, Theresa and John Sykes II. When I first met them, Theresa wrapped me in a long embrace without saying a word. Behind me, I could hear her husband teasing her in his gentlemanly tone: "Give the boy some air, Tree." He was a twinkle-eyed older version of his son, standing as erect as when he had been a soldier. After his wife let me go, he took both my hands in his. "It's a pleasure to meet you, young man." Never before had I been welcomed and loved so immediately and unreservedly.

Some of my fondest memories from this period are of times when John and I swung by his parents' house in Dartmouth, one town over from New Bedford, to say hello and visit. The four of us sat for hours around the kitchen table, talking about the Red Sox and Celtics, my experiences in school, and my college plans. (John's parents knew how I had come to live with their son, but we rarely spoke of it, except in general terms.) Our meals together were lengthy affairs, for Grandma Sykes insisted on stuffing us with baked chicken and rice, garden salad with tomatoes picked right from her garden, homemade soup, and nearly every vegetable imaginable. "Have to keep my boys fed," she would say.

After we ate, we settled in the adjoining living room. John and I read, Grandma Sykes fidgeted around the two of us, and Grandpa John sat in his chair, staring out the window, eyes twinkling, rubbing his hands together in satisfaction. One day after a fine family meal, I noticed a picture the Sykeses had hung on their living room wall, right next to a picture of John. I did a double take to make sure my eyes had not betrayed me. That was indeed a picture of me. I wore a brown sweater and plaid shirt and was clearly in need of a fashion lesson. But the Sykes had hung me on their wall anyway.

The Robinsons had never taken pictures of me, let alone added them to their family album. I had never been woven into the fabric of a family, and it now felt odd. The moment of confusion barely registered before I was overcome by the Sykeses' kindness. I stared at it long and hard, still not completely sure that I had been so unequivocally accepted.

And yet, for all the warmth and positive growth I experienced, I was never truly free of the Robinsons. I awoke often in the middle of the night, tormented by a recurring dream: I have left the tail-wagging Doberman pinscher and garbage-filled front yard and am running toward downtown New Bedford, taking the strategic route I believed would keep me out of the sight of Willie's all-seeing eye. Anxiety and fear threaten to swallow me, but if I can just get to the Department of Social Services, I will be safe. This comforting thought vanishes amid the roar of Willie's yellow and brown station wagon. He is driving up hard behind me. I jump off the sidewalk and skirt through a backyard that will carry me over to the next block. As I emerge from the backyard, Willie is waiting for me. His window is rolled down, and his shotgun, the one he used to kill rabbits with deadly efficiency, is pointed right at me.

Nor was I freed from endless thoughts about the birth family I'd never known, especially on my frequent, solitary bike rides around the area. During the warm months, I got up at 6:00 a.m., hopped on the light-blue ten-speed bike I'd bought by saving up the weekly allowance John gave me, and rode down the several miles to Horseneck Beach. The sky was a beautiful light pink, tinged with orange. There was virtually no traffic, and save the humming of my wheels on the pavement, it was totally quiet on Horseneck Road. No matter how often I rode this route, I found myself transported back to an earlier era in rural America: stone walls, open fields, and quaint farmhouses dotted the landscape, and only the presence of towering telephone lines signaled that modernity had not completely escaped the countryside town of Westport.

A mile into my ride, a large, gray-shingled, abandoned farmhouse appeared in the middle of a grassy field. In the middle of its roof was a cavernous hole so large you could a drive a car through it. I always slowed to look; this structure, too, had its story. Then, driven by a voiceless urge and with a single, backward glance, I burst into furious sprints of speed, my legs churning, my lungs screaming in the cool morning air. A passerby might have taken me for an aspiring cyclist prepping for a triathlon rather than what I was—a young boy trying to pedal away years of pain and loss.

At the end of Horseneck Road, right where it turned into East Beach Road, the miles of bucolic farmland suddenly yielded to the powerful sea, a breathtaking picture only nature could create. Right at the intersection of the two roads was a small inlet. No sunbathers came here; the multitudes of rocks made it impossible. I leaned my bike against the large, yellow, weather-beaten "turn left" road sign and strolled down to where the rocks ended and the sea began. Off in the distance, endless water met God-brushed sky, the only interruption Elizabeth Island, the small island off of Cuttyhunk known as the final resting place of the *Wanderer*, the last whaling ship to leave New Bedford. Oftentimes the wind would howl off the water, creating ferocious gusts of turbulent air that threatened to knock me over. Yet if I faced it and dug my heels into the rocky soil, I found I could withstand that wind. And so I stood there, listening to the roaring waves thumping to shore in near perfect cadence, staring at an ocean that appeared as large and mysterious as the past I was trying to understand.

Morning after morning, my thoughts were the same. During my childhood, I had survived seemingly endless suffering on the unyielding belief that one day my mother and father would come rescue me. They never did. Now that I was free, I faced new questions: Where *had* I come from? What invisible forces had created my life, my unlikely last name—Klakowicz—and this mystery that was my past? The roiling ocean seemed to answer me. *This is your fate. You are never to know. And what did you need them for anyway? You survived without their help. Now you have yourself, and that has to be enough.* Morning after morning, with these thoughts still fluttering around in my head, I heaved a deep sigh, got back on my bike, and began the long trek back up Horseneck Road to John's house.

CHAPTER 21

Many rivers to cross
And it's only my will that keeps me alive . . .

—JIMMY CLIFF, *"MANY RIVERS TO CROSS"*

In April 1985, a beautifully glossed cream envelope arrived in the mail with my name on it and "Boston College" printed on the front. With trembling hands I tore it open, scanning past the address until I saw one word: "Congratulations!" Without reading any further, I tossed the letter up into the air, burst out the back door, and ran through the field behind John's house, the tall grass whipping at my legs, yelling from the top of my lungs. When I finally calmed down enough to read the entire letter, I was in for even better news: I had been awarded a full scholarship as well.

On the first day of college, in late August 1985, I tossed a small, beat-up, yellow suitcase, courtesy of another "hunting" expedition, into the trunk of John's new two-seater MG. As we drove the hour up to Boston, Dire Straits' "Money for Nothing" blaring out of the car's speakers, it felt as if there was nothing I couldn't do. I had beaten the Robinsons and, despite Betty's predictions, had finally made it to college. Yet within the first few weeks, it became clear that the next four years would not be smooth sailing. I had trouble clicking with my classmates, not least because the students on my dorm floor seemed intent on getting drunk nearly every night. Social relationships with both men and women often seemed to flow from alcohol; the only way to be accepted was to drink until you keeled over. I had never liked to drink, at least not to excess, and I was never willing to join in the binges.

It also wasn't long before my fellow students remarked on my last name, my appearance, and my race. The white students couldn't figure out if I was black or white or something in between. "What are you, exactly?" they asked. The question stung all the more because I didn't know either. On more than one occasion, the topic of affirmative action came up, and a white student grumbled that I had taken his high school friend's place in the freshman class.

My relationships in the African American community weren't much better. Skin complexion mattered in that community as much as alcohol in the white community, and my light skin, blue eyes, and strange last name made me a ready target for students who thought the African American experience could be reduced to a shade of color.

Things were even tougher in the classroom. I had been admitted to college on the basis of raw intellect and a curiosity developed during my years of furtive reading at the Robinsons'. Yet my academic foundation was, in a word, shaky. The language of college was entirely new to me; I didn't know what a GPA stood for, what a syllabus was, how to choose classes, how to take notes, or how to prepare for a college exam. My time-management skills were terrible, as was my self-discipline. I would spend hours reviewing homework assignments because I had no sense of what was important and what wasn't. John had advised that I not miss a class no matter the circumstance, and I listened to him. Still, I would sit as far in the back as possible in the hope of avoiding being called on, averting my glance if the professor deigned to look in my direction. Though I could follow the discussion, I was far less certain of my ability to contribute. Nevertheless, I was confident I had kept my secret well concealed.

Embarrassment was inevitable. Once, when I received a disappointing grade on a political science paper, I went to my professor's office seeking redress. We had been reading *The Peloponnesian War* by Thucydides, and the language was completely foreign to me, a far cry from the books Mrs. Levin had given me. But I was convinced that I had rightly captured the political view of one of Athens's politicians, who had made the case for war with Sparta. I couldn't understand how the instructor, Professor Landry, had thought otherwise.

Waiting outside Professor Landry's office, I overheard him speaking with another student; I couldn't even begin to follow what they were saying. *This won't be pretty,* I thought to myself. And indeed it wasn't.

Professor Landry was a graying, bespectacled man; his office was awash in all types of books. He leaned back in his chair, resting his chin on a makeshift podium created by his hands. "Professor Landry," I began, licking my lips a bit nervously, "I think you made a mistake."

His eyebrows arched above the rim of his glasses. "I see. How is that?" he said, taking my paper and scanning it over.

I held my book close to my chest as if it were a protective shield and launched into my opening testimony. As I spoke, I could see him scanning my paper more closely. Before I could finish, he held up a hand to stop me.

"Are you sure you read the text assigned to you in the syllabus?"

"I did." I now held my small green copy of *The Peloponnesian War* out before him like a sacrificial offering, showing how heavily I had highlighted it.

He took the book and flipped through it. "The problem, Steve, is that you have to read the *whole* section, not just part of it. If you had read the whole thing, you would have realized that the politician's position changed later on." He took the book and flipped through it. "I can tell you didn't read the whole section, because it's not highlighted." He cracked a smile. "Next time, don't you think it would be easier to dip the whole book in highlighter?"

My face fell; he was right. And I was devastated. I may not have had a home or parents or some of the advantages of my classmates, but I had thought that I was intelligent. I had often been told so, and I had latched on to that belief as one of the few things I could truly feel proud of. Suddenly I felt horribly exposed—a feeling that would last for months.

Beyond these newfound doubts, I was also struggling with loneliness—the sense of having no "home" to return to. When holiday break came and my classmates traveled to their warm homes and family gatherings, I was forced to apply for an extension to stay in the dorms. Some classmates asked if I wanted to spend the holidays with their families, but I politely refused, unable to shake the feeling that I would be intruding. That same feeling of imposing would overcome me when I thought of visiting the Sykes family. The holidays were times for family, I reasoned, not for wayward souls.

Most days during break, I got on the trolley, or the "T" as it is called, at the foot of the campus and rode into downtown Boston. The trolley car was slow and far too often would come to a screeching halt to pick up passengers. From my window seat I enjoyed all the beautiful sparkling lights, red ribbons, and wreaths of holly decorating the homes along Commonwealth Avenue. I got off at Boston Common, which was always beautifully lit, or at Downtown Crossing, where I delighted in the smell of roasted peanuts and the ringing of bells. At some moments as I strolled around the historic city, passing colonial-era churches and magnificent monuments, I felt connected to a larger community and to a greater spirit. Ultimately, though, I knew I would have to get back on the train to return to my dorm room, where empty hallways and cold Italian submarine sandwiches awaited.

As the start of second semester approached, the disappointments were adding up. I had naively thought that college would erase the past and allow me a fresh start. Instead, I found myself facing new setbacks. And, in the midst of those discontents, I still longed for my parents, despite my greatest efforts to pretend that they were no longer necessary. But I was determined to stick it out. I had come too far, and I was not going to quit now.

CHAPTER 22

A turning point came the summer after my freshman year when I took a job with the custodial staff. I needed the money, but I was more motivated by the free housing, which eliminated the persistent problem of where I was going to live. As it turned out, I was given something far more valuable: mentors.

The university's custodial crew was a collection of salt-of-the-earth men whose own dreams of attending college had fallen short. There was Sumner, diminutive and irascible, with a penchant for short-sleeved plaid shirts, whose sole purpose for working as a custodian appeared to be hunting for items that departing students had abandoned; Jimmy, an older African American man, considered the crew's unofficial leader; Tony Cherin, a thick-accented Italian immigrant who doubled as my supervisor, also a self-defined ladies' man who took special delight in blasting nagging pigeons with a water hose and sharing his amorous conquests; and Dave, the spitting image of a young, red-bearded Santa Claus, who spent his days driving around in a maroon van, trying to catch his crew lying down on the job (he rarely succeeded; I often started my 6:00 a.m. shift by taking a nap among the mops and brooms in the library supply closet).

I enjoyed the lighthearted banter of these men ("What'd you hustle today, Sumner?") and their obvious affection for one another. I also came to respect their work ethic embodied in their weathered and calloused hands. They were perfectionists who took tremendous pride in their jobs, no matter how menial others thought those jobs were. They saw themselves as protectors of the university's image and believed

117

that a squeaky clean campus said as much about the school as the number of volumes in the university library. In their perspicuity, Sumner, Jimmy, Tony, and Dave also reminded me of the construction crew I'd met as a boy. None had a college degree, but they had another kind of wisdom, much of which they aimed directly at me.

One blazingly hot day, while we were eating lunch in the shade next to the library, Dave asked about my first year in college. A campus tour of students and families walked by, and I watched as a college student walking backward recited the university's great history. I debated for a moment whether I should say anything at all to Dave, but I decided to speak because we had developed a great camaraderie by then. "Well, to be honest, this past year wasn't that great," I said, looking off into the distance.

They listened as I related some of the issues I had faced.

"What do ya folks say about that?" Dave asked.

"Uh, they're not really around."

"So, that's why you're here working with us," Jimmy said playfully, a mystery-solved expression dancing across his creased face. "And here I thought it was because of our charming personalities."

To my relief, more banter followed, mainly about Sumner's sunny disposition. Sumner said nothing to this but sat there glaring back at us, munching on his sandwich, muttering under his breath. A large piece of bologna fell from his sandwich onto the ground, and he grew furious, throwing the rest of the sandwich down on the ground in anger and storming off. This only spurred us on to new howls of laughter. When we finally calmed down, Dave returned to our conversation.

"But you're going to stick it out, right?" he asked.

"I'm still thinking about it," I said, half-jokingly. Had I been paying better attention, I would have realized that no one was laughing. "How about I just come work with you guys in the fall?"

Jimmy made a big show of crumpling his brown paper bag. "What ya wanna come work with us fah?" He was serious. I looked around at the other guys in the crew, and none of them were smiling either. Jimmy's voice softened, but only a bit. "Stevie, ya got it all. You're a young kid; ya got your whole life in front you. You're smart, handsome; ya go to one of the best schools in the country. I mean, just *look* at this place." He gestured with pride at the beautiful tree-lined campus and its Gothic buildings. "Any of us would change places with ya in a minute."

That comment barely registered before Jimmy continued: "Don't let me come here in Septembah and find ya workin' with us." He narrowed his eyes and pointed his half-eaten sandwich right at me. " 'Cause if we do, we're all gonna stand in line and give ya a good kick in the pants!"

Tony stood up, sunlight bouncing off his rimmed spectacles, and pantomimed a soccer kick. "Jep, kicka you right in de pants." The rest of the guys laughed. I rubbed my newly toughened hands together and smiled but didn't say a word. I didn't need to. I had gotten the message loud and clear.

CHAPTER 23

I did return the following fall, and things improved. In the classroom, I came to identify with the unofficial Jesuit philosophy of service, questioning all things and refusing to accept the world as it is. I now looked forward to going to class, where with some confidence I debated with my classmates the differing views of Hobbes, Locke, and Rousseau. Professor Robert Faulkner's class on modern political philosophy greatly affected me. Initially I struggled to understand Francis Bacon and his method of scientific inquiry, but my own persistence and Professor Faulkner's patient efforts helped me grasp the concepts. The value of looking at the world objectively, of gathering all information before jumping to conclusions, soon became evident. From then on I applied the principle constantly in my academic and social life.

At the same time I was wrestling with Francis Bacon, I was also uncovering the deep history and long struggle of the African American experience. My own struggles for identity had never been about race; I had always seen myself unequivocally and proudly as an African American. Still, I lacked any real understanding of my people's history. That changed when I saw *Eyes on the Prize*, the documentary of the African American civil rights movement. The enormous sacrifices required in the pursuit of freedom struck a chord, for I well understood the lengths one would go to for the right to choose his or her own destiny.

What I had not understood was how prominent New Bedford had been in the historical quest for access and opportunity. The city was an important stop on the Underground Railroad; it was the first place the great abolitionist Frederick Douglass had lived when he escaped to the North. Several members of the 54th and 55th Civil War regiments, two of the first official African American infantry units, hailed from this area. The most famous was William Carney, the first African American to receive a Congressional Medal of Honor. Several decades later, New Bedford had remained in the forefront of the struggle.

Like many of my peers, I felt a connection with esteemed historian and sociologist W. E. B. DuBois, the first African American to receive a doctorate from Harvard. DuBois's emphasis on education and leveraging that knowledge to exact social change echoed the sentiment of many African American men on campus. So deep was our admiration for DuBois that we founded an organization called the Talented Tenth, based on DuBois's concept that those of us who achieved a certain level of success had a further responsibility to become leaders.

Some of this history had been much closer to me than I had known. New Bedford had deep roots in abolitionism and the Civil War. At the turn of the twentieth century, its whaling reputation rapidly coming to a close with the advent of kerosene, New Bedford kept its ties to equality, rivaling Boston and New York in reputation as meeting grounds for those anxious to address the inequalities suffered by African Americans. In the western end of the city, at the home of prominent attorney E. B. Jourdain, the nation's most renowned African American leaders would gather to debate how to best address the blight of segregation.

W. E. B. DuBois was a frequent visitor to New Bedford; his grandfather, Alexander DuBois, had moved to the city in 1873. For years DuBois would write of meeting his grandfather in New Bedford, remembering him as a man "in passionate revolt against the world." Clearly transferred to his grandson, some of that passion for equal rights manifested itself in those heated discussions at Jourdain's home. From those meetings would come the position papers, transcendent speeches, and organizational plans that ultimately led to the creation of the NAACP. To my utter amazement I learned that the gathering place for their meetings was 279 Arnold, right down the street from where I had grown up.

Armed with a better understanding of my own cultural history, my relationships with my peers changed. Those who had questioned my authenticity because of my fair skin and blue eyes now encountered a person ready to acquaint them with the African diaspora that rightly included people who looked like me. My peers came around, to my great happiness and relief.

In the fall of my junior year, I pledged the historically black fraternity Kappa Alpha Psi. Our brothers came from all the city's top universities and carried themselves with confidence and purpose. The fraternity had a motto—"Achievement in Every Field of Human Endeavor"—and the older brothers made sure you lived up to it, not merely in the classroom but also in the community. There was no question about your responsibilities: you had to execute community service projects and prepare reports on what you did. Accountability was critical, and the judgment of the older brothers was harsh and unforgiving if you failed. Also, you had to conduct yourself in an upright way, mindful that you were little more than a link in a chain that dated back to the early 1900s and that you needed to behave as a God-fearing steward of that history. I tried hard to live up to that and was soon named president of the chapter. Shortly after that, I was recognized as the Undergraduate Brother of the Year in the province.

One brother with whom I became especially close was Tim Palmer, a student at Northeastern University. Whereas I was stubborn and strong-willed, Tim was easygoing and took life as it came. I would jump right into the thick of a situation; he would take time to look at an issue from all sides. His parents, Herbert and Cookie, and sisters, Angela and Mary, welcomed me into their home and showed me again the power and the beauty of a tightly knit family.

The Palmers were not my only close connection. My relationship with Alicia, my high school sweetheart, continued on into college. After freshman year, holidays found me seated at her family's table, watching in envy as they recounted prior holidays and childhood memories. And during my summers, I returned to the Upward Bound Program to work as a tutor and counselor. Part of what always drew me back was the sense of home and family I found in the program and the opportunity to make a real difference in the lives of young people who needed guidance and direction as much as I had. I was especially drawn to the larger-than-life figure of Mrs. Dottin, the closest thing to a mother I had known. The pamphlet the program produced to attract students contained a simple phrase: "This program has made a difference; let it make a difference for you." And as I entered my junior and senior years at Boston College, I realized that it was true.

These institutions and people were all important to me, giving me what I needed most: a sense of connection to something greater than myself. But what was their history, I could not make mine. More than anything else, that was what I wanted: my *own* story, my own history, my own home to return to—not that of the Jesuits, or of the fraternity, or of Tim's or Alicia's families.

Though I was free I was not yet home, and so my quest to find my past would return again and again in the years to come, like a lighthouse beacon that flashes bright and then fades only to return again. And ultimately, like that lighthouse beacon, it would have the power to guide and to save.

CHAPTER 24

O ne bitterly cold January night during my senior year, the telephone rang. I was putting some books in my backpack for a trip to the library, and I used my free hand to pick up the phone. The caller was a female adult, but I couldn't recognize her voice; it seemed weak and far away. "Hello, is Steve there?"

"Yes, this is Steve, but I'm sorry, I'm having a hard time hearing you."

The voice, slightly agitated, was stronger now. "Can't you hear me?" There was no mistaking who it was: Betty Robinson, of all people. She was calling to see how I was doing—or so she said. She had never called me before, never been interested in my well-being, not while I was with her nor after I left. I sensed another purpose and was immediately on guard. In the background, I could hear beeping and a faint voice coming over an intercom.

"Where are you?" I asked.

"In the hospital." There was an uncomfortable pause on the line. "In Boston." That meant it was serious.

I sat down on the edge of the bed and placed my backpack on the floor. "I'm sorry to hear that. What's going on?"

"I'm not doing that well." Another pause. "You didn't leave here the best way, you know."

I grew angry, but sensing the seriousness of her condition, I tried to measure my words. "It was the best way for me."

"You wanted to get out in dem streets, be free and live how you wanted to live."

I couldn't believe it. *Was this the reason she was calling? To tell me that?* I stood up, and now I had no intention of disguising my feelings. "You were always wrong about me. You always said I'd be no good, but you were wrong then, and you're wrong now."

"Is that right?"

"It sure is. And it always was."

I was going to say more—that I had made it to college after all, that I was succeeding here, that others had seen in me what she never could. But I stopped, knowing that I had nothing to prove to her.

She sighed, a deep heavy exhaling of air that told me she had been in considerable pain and was tired. Another series of electronic beeps came over the line. I recalled my last conversation with her when I told her that God was going to take care of her for what she and her family had taken from me. But the intervening years and my own deepening faith had given me a different perspective; her judgment, be it reprisal or forgiveness, was to be left in God's hands, not mine. He would decide.

There was another long silence, and for a brief moment I thought she had hung up. "Well, you take care then," she said. The line went dead, and I dropped the phone back in the cradle. I stared at it for a long while. Then I stood up, put on my coat, and slung my backpack over my shoulder. I opened the door of my room and stepped into the hallway. The door was heavy and swung closed behind me, the lock clicking in the latch. Whether Betty Robinson was calling to apologize, say goodbye, or reaffirm her position, I never knew. A week later, while presiding over a meeting at my fraternity, I received word that Betty Robinson had died of complications from diabetes. She was fifty-three years old.

CHAPTER 25

As a child growing up with the Robinsons, I had spent a lot of time looking in the mirror, trying to discern whatever secrets about myself I could. On the morning of May 22, 1989, my college graduation, I spent a good hour in my room, adjusting my cap and gown. The person looking back at me from the mirror was far different from the shy, inexperienced, and uncertain adolescent who had entered college four years before. There was a stride in my walk now, a quiet confidence that came from having traveled a most unconventional path to the glorious morning that waited right outside my front door.

The mirror still held secrets. The blond tints were still there, though less noticeable than before. My last name, Klakowicz, felt more foreign to me than ever. I still tilted my head when I listened to people. As I often had during the past few years, I shook my head to clear the fog. I didn't want to deal with all this now. I had put away these nagging questions, imposed my will on them, forcing them into a mental drawer labeled "For Further Review." On this day, though, they'd come back as never before because, while everybody else had family members who'd come to wish them well, I had nobody.

The campus was awash in the colors and sounds of commencement. Flowers of different shades and hues encircled trees that sat magnificently on perfectly manicured lawns. Maroon and gold balloons hung from light posts, twisting and turning in the light breeze. Off in the distance, I heard the strains of a commencement song, often interrupted by the ringing of bells from Gasson Tower. Beaming parents, radiant grandparents, and awestruck younger siblings all hovered around my classmates, marking this day in the annals of their families' histories. Several times, fellow classmates asked me to serve as an impromptu photographer. The families huddled together, and through the camera lens I saw those boundless, timeless human connections, the overflowing smiles, the pride. "Thank you," they said, and I handed back their cameras, wished them luck, and continued on my way. Within a few steps they had almost certainly forgotten about me, but images of their families remain in my mind to this day.

We walked into Alumni Stadium in our black caps and gowns, barely noticing the blistering heat. Classmates around me shielded their eyes from the sun and scanned the stands, trying to locate their families. When we were all in place, a hush fell over the stadium. Jonathan Kozol—award-winning activist, educator, author, and native Bostonian—rose to give the commencement address. In a solemn voice he reminded us that there remained tremendous suffering in our country, hardships that we sons and daughters of this great Jesuit institution were uniquely qualified to address. Noting the 500,000 homeless children in this country, he said, "These children have done nothing wrong. They committed no crime. Their only crime is to have been born poor in a rich nation." A thoughtful murmur arose in the stadium, and I nodded my head in complete understanding. *All children belong to somebody*, I thought. *Or at least they should.*

After the ceremony, I headed to the student athletic center to attend the individual diploma ceremonies for the College of Arts and Sciences. The heat in the building was oppressive, the air heavy and thick. Because of my last name and the way the ceremony was organized, I sat in the back and would be among the last to receive my diploma. For more than an hour, I watched scenes of family bliss that I could only dream about.

For each of my fellow students, a small herd of parents, grandparents, aunts, uncles, and siblings clapped and bellowed their appreciation. They called out to my classmates and snapped photos. I kept my eyes fixed straight ahead and read the commencement program over and over because I knew that if I looked back for even a second, the wave of emotions I was holding inside would certainly wash over me. I'd never allowed myself to feel self-pity, and today, graduation day, was not the time to start. As the names got closer to mine, however, so did the hard truth: there would be no roar of celebration for me. John Sykes was immersed in finals, and travel would have been too difficult for the elder Sykeses. Though I couldn't remember either of my parents, I missed them more on this day than on any other.

My classmate Debbie Henderson sat next to me, her family directly behind us. Suddenly I felt a tap on my shoulder. Debbie's mother tried to hold back tears as she wished me congratulations. Her awareness that I was alone moved me, and for a brief moment I forgot the overwhelming feeling of loss. Then my name was called, and I ascended the stage to receive my diploma from the dean. On the way back to my seat, I stared at the regal lettering and my last name so elegantly embossed on the sheepskin. Another, quite strange, thought arose then: *The reason I have never been comfortable with the Klakowicz surname is because this is not my real last name.*

After the graduation, as the final snapshots were taken and the graduates slipped off to dinner or parties with their families, I made my way back to my dormitory. I pulled open the heavy brown door and noticed a sign taped to it: "All students must depart by 4:00 p.m." I let out a long, slow breath of air.

My footsteps echoed in halls that hours earlier had bustled. I packed my remaining belongings, thinking about the day's events. *Where was I going?* In the short term I'd return to New Bedford to work for the Upward Bound Program, as I had the previous few summers. *But what about after that?*

As I zipped up my suitcases and piled them in a corner, the thought that had gnawed away at me suddenly took hold: in order to develop any real direction in my adult life, I'd need to learn where I had come from and to whom I belonged. *All children belong to someone,* I thought once again, *and that includes those who have been left to the whims of chance.*

Trying to find my family was going to be difficult. Yet I had always found safe harbor in the person I believed God had made me, in my strength, my resilience, my competitive nature, and my loyalty toward others. I may not have had a family, but I did have that. And that would be enough. Whatever was out there to learn would be easy to handle compared to the hardships I'd already endured or the persistent shadow of knowing nothing at all.

Or so I thought.

I put the last of my boxes into my rented U-Haul and turned around to look one last time up and down Commonwealth Avenue. I was going to miss Boston College. My dorm had been right at the foot of Heartbreak Hill, named for the punishing inclines that challenged marathoners each spring during the Boston Marathon. The humidity had finally eased. A long white string, likely from a balloon that had long since left its mooring, blew about a tree. I stood there for a moment strangely entranced, wondering which way the wind was going to blow the string next. Then I started the truck, shifted into drive, and began the long trip back to New Bedford.

CHAPTER 26

I didn't begin probing into my family background right away. The summer after graduation in 1989, I returned to the Upward Bound Program in Dartmouth, Massachusetts, and threw myself, as usual, into tutoring and counseling work. At summer's end, I returned to Boston looking for work. The job market was difficult, and I struggled largely because I didn't know what I wanted to do. I only knew I wanted to make a difference. I took the first job offered me, at an auto-rental company. I wore a shirt and tie on the job, but that was where the professionalism ended. The pay was terrible, and I barely had any money left each month for food. All day long I towed rental cars, fought traffic, washed cars, and ruined my clothes with dirt and oil. It was humbling work and a far cry from the meaningful career I had envisioned. In the summer of 1990, I left the auto-rental company to return yet again to Upward Bound's six-week summer residential program.

My dissatisfaction with work was nothing in comparison to the restlessness I was feeling in my personal life. The summer after college, my longtime girlfriend, Alicia, had stunned me by abruptly ending our relationship. I was too reliant on her and her family, she said, and she wanted "space." She was there one day, and then the next she was gone, disappearing from my life so quickly I wondered if she had been there at all. With her went her mother, with whom I was especially close. Though I had seen difficult times, her departure brought a new kind of pain. I suddenly lost my bearings, struggling to find the fighting determination that had long been my hallmark.

Holidays came and went that first year after Alicia's departure, and

I found myself in my small apartment, quietly asking the one question I had not dared ask before: *What had I done wrong?* I had survived the Robinsons and graduated from one of the country's best universities, and my reward seemed to be this disconnected life. When would I feel as if I belonged to something? To someone?

The coming months brought closure to the end of my relationship with Alicia and in time I would come to see it as a blessing. Though I was grateful to her for the time we had spent, the suddenness with which I became an outsider reminded me again of the importance of having your own family. And therein was my problem. For years I had been trying to replace my family. Everything had fallen short and would continue to, I suspected, until I found the place I had come from. Yet I had no idea where to begin.

I turned again to Mrs. Dottin, asking to speak with her one day after our daily morning staff meeting. I sat down in the chair next to her desk. Behind her, through a ceiling-to-floor glass window, you could see clear across campus. I fidgeted with my hands, not knowing where to begin.

"Why don't you just jump right in," she said, peering at me over the top of her glasses. Her calmness and quiet manner had always belied an amazingly perceptive mind.

I took a deep breath. "Mrs. Dottin, I've been wondering about my parents. I have no idea who they are or where they are. Most people in the situations I was in had someone, Mrs. D, but I had no one. And I want to know why."

"Did you ever think that there are some things you are not meant to know?"

I bobbed my head slowly. "I have, Mrs. D."

"And?" she said, raising an eyebrow.

"And I refuse to accept it."

She laughed and reached over to pat my hand. "Steve, that is why you have become the young man you are. That and, of course, a few blessings from on high."

I smiled, nodding my head in agreement. Ruby Dottin never failed to remind me how blessed I was.

"Do you know anything at all?"

"Not much, except what Betty Robinson told me when I was a boy." I recounted Betty's description of my father, my search at the library, and my subsequent conclusion that Kenny Pemberton was not my father.

She sat back in her chair. "You were quite the little investigator, weren't you?"

I laughed, recalling just how much of a detective I had fancied myself as a boy. "I sure was. I thought I could solve the mystery of my heritage the same way the Hardy Boys so often solved mysteries. But I never did."

Now my tone became more serious. "When you don't know, it's a weight on your soul. And I've carried this weight my entire life. I want to put it down."

She eyed me for a long moment. "I *do* know, Steve. I never knew my father, and it bothered me until I finally realized that I simply wasn't meant to know. But that answer isn't going to work for you, I can see that." She leaned forward, and I shifted my backpack on my shoulder, as if moving it would allow me to hear her better. "Here's what I can tell you. The person Betty described to you was Kenny Pemberton. There was nobody else who met an end like that. But I don't know if he was your father. I do know he came from a big family, lots of brothers and sisters, and if he is your father, I am sure one of them would know. Come to think of it, we have a speaker coming to talk to the kids tomorrow during the life skills class. I am almost certain he knew Kenny. I can ask him if you like."

I accepted her offer, but I still did not believe there was a connection. As Mrs. Dottin had rightly pointed out, Kenny had come from a large family, and certainly someone would have known about me. Besides, I had done my own sleuthing years before, and the answer seemed clear and definitive. The fighter who had died so tragically was not my father.

The next day, several of my students burst into my classroom, breathless. "Steve, you have to come over to building 1A. There's a man over there who says he knew your father."

I nodded; this must be the speaker Mrs. Dottin had referred to. "Okay, guys, I'll be right there." I took my time putting my books and papers in my backpack. I was in no particular rush to hear something I already knew wasn't true.

"No, you have to come *now*," they said, pulling me by the arm. "He saw a picture of you and everything!"

That piqued my curiosity. I turned the classroom over to my assistant, and the students and I walked across the campus to the life skills class. I found a well-dressed African American man of average height standing before a blackboard. He was dark complexioned and wore a neatly groomed mustache. Like a student late to class, I tried walking to the back of the room so as not to disturb his lecture. But all heads turned in my direction. Caught in the act, I reversed direction to greet him. In the few strides it took to get to where he was standing, I could see a look of familiarity cross his face, as if he knew who I was. The room was silent save the gentle rustling of the blinds.

He held out his hand to me, and I accepted it. "So you're Kenny Pemberton's son. I'm Russell Almeida. I use to spar with your father."

There was certainty in the way he said "your father," so I rushed to correct him. "Mr. Almeida, I'm sorry to disappoint you, but I've seen a picture of Kenny Pemberton, and he is not my father. We don't look anything alike." Out of the corner of my eye, I could see the students turning their heads from left to right as if watching a tennis match.

"And I'm sorry to disappoint *you*," he said, smiling, "but he *is* your father. I don't know what picture you've seen, but you do look just like him. You tilt your head when you're listening to somebody, just as he used to." He stepped back for a brief second to look at me again; behind me, the students whispered excitedly. "A good man, Kenny was. Fierce, loyal, and would do anything for a friend," he said.

I remained unconvinced, yet I sensed the great respect Russell still held for his friend.

"You don't believe me, do you?" he asked.

I held my hands up, conveying that I was guilty as charged. "No disrespect, Mr. Almeida, but no, I don't."

He nodded. "Tell you what. I am going to come by and see you Friday night."

I shook my head in protest. "Mr. Almeida, really, I don't want to put you to any trouble."

He held his hand up, in a gesture that said this would be no bother. "I will bring a picture of Kenny with me. Maybe then you'll believe me."

CHAPTER 27

I lived in the Fort Hill section of Roxbury, sharing a small two-bedroom apartment with a fraternity brother. At seven o'clock that Friday evening, the doorbell rang. I peeked through the blinds to see Russell standing there. With his left hand he lightly thumped a black leather briefcase against his leg.

I showed Russell into the living room, settling into a chair across from him. He accepted my offer of something to drink. Our reflections shimmered in the glass of my old television set. Russell pulled from his briefcase a black-framed eight-by-ten picture. He held it out to me, his hands open and extended like a ring bearer gravely protective of his possession. "Here he is, Steve. This is your father."

The picture I had seen as a young boy years earlier—the one accompanying the announcement of Kenny's death at age twenty-six—looked nothing like this one. In Russell's photograph, Kenny's hair was dark and had been straightened in the style that many African American men wore in the 1960s. Eagle-wing eyebrows framed deep-set, brown eyes. His nose was straight and lean, his lips gently curved, and there was just the shadow of a mustache and beard on a handsome face that bore no scars. Kenny was crouched in a boxing pose, leaning slightly to his right, his right hand positioned beneath his chin, his left a bit lower, poised to throw a jab. Veins bulged from his large forearms. He was bare-chested, and his lean, sculpted physique resembled a coiled spring. His face was as serene as a slow-moving river, giving no hint to the rage that seems to flow within boxers.

I looked away for a moment and thought back to my stolen dash to the New Bedford library as a young boy. For years, I had believed that childhood quest to find my father had failed. So my search had continued. For many days after my library search, I had stared in the mirror, trying to determine who I resembled. Now, nearly more than a decade after that boyhood quest, I realized I had actually solved the mystery of my father's identity that summer morning in 1978. There were physical differences—my skin and hair were lighter, and our eyes were a different color—yet I was, in essence, looking at a darker version of myself at the same age. The search was over: Kenny Pemberton was my father.

The failure to find Kenny had been a blessing because it kept alive the possibility that my father would return one day. But now the truth, lying before me in an eight-by-ten picture frame, brought a harsh reality: Kenny was not here and never would be. The full weight of his absence overcame me as I mentally ticked off the things I would never know: a father's pride and counsel, his strength and protection, and most of all, his love. I got up, walked over to the window, and sat on the small sill, looking out through the protective iron bars. The sun was setting, turning the sky a dazzling array of orange, purple, and yellow. I sighed deeply.

After a few moments I asked Russell to tell me what he knew of my father. He said that my father was a local legend, and that he always would be for the people who had known him. "You ever see Sugar Ray Robinson fight?" he asked, referring to the great middleweight, generally considered the best pound-for-pound fighter in boxing history. I nodded yes.

"Well, that was Kenny. See, I used to spar with your father. He patterned himself after Sugar Ray, stenciled his name on his gym bag, wore his hair like him, and fought just like him. Most fighters have one or two things going for them, but Kenny, he had them all—speed, power, toughness." He nodded his head in approval at the not-so-distant memory. "He could take you out with either hand and his left hook to the body." He stood up and threw a phantom left hook. "Well, it just took the wind out of you. He got that punch from watching Sugar Ray Robinson. Nobody wanted to fight him, and I think one of the reasons he liked me was because I would trade blows with him. Yeah, Kenny had it all. He was a man among men and a god among women. Yep, Kenny was going to be champ of the world, and everybody knew it."

I nodded. A short distance away, a car door slammed. "But he didn't, right?"

Russell sat down and shook his head solemnly. "No, he didn't."

A few moments of quiet passed, and during that time I sensed there was another story about Kenny, one that Russell wasn't telling me. I furrowed my brow and looked at him quizzically. "Why not? If he had all this talent and all these people who believed in him, why didn't he become a champion?"

Russell shifted on the imitation leather couch. "When all that stuff went down with Kenny, I wasn't really around. There are other people who know more about it than I do." He took a sip of water. "But I do know about his reputation in the streets. I actually saw it for myself."

I traced my finger around the black coaster that protected the table. "What do you mean?"

Russell looked at the ceiling, searching for the right words. "He would walk down the street, and people just crossed to the other side. You could see the fear on their faces. He was a good man, but you didn't want to cross him, because he would show you no mercy."

He fidgeted with his hands as he said this and looked away. He was struggling to protect me from something. But from what?

Russell must have sensed my thoughts because he leaned forward on the couch and addressed me in a low, intimate tone: "Steve, Kenny was a man's man. People *loved* your father, and not just because he was a great fighter. He was loyal and protective. If you were his friend and you needed something, he would give it to you, no questions asked. Most times you didn't even have to ask."

Then Russell told me about riots that broke out in New Bedford in the summer of 1970. Massive unemployment, abysmal living conditions, and reports of police brutality had ignited the city's southern and western neighborhoods in rebellion. "Your father was right in the middle of that—in a good way. There was all kinds of looting and burning, and he grabbed a bullhorn, jumped up on top of a car, and calmed everybody down. When that poor kid, God rest his soul, got shot, it was your father who came out of the crowd to pick him up and help get him to St. Luke's Hospital. Senator Brooke came to town and created a committee to negotiate with the mayor and the police. Your father was on that committee, appointed by the senator himself. There was a picture in the paper and everything."

I looked again at the photo now standing on the coffee table between us and pictured my father as the community leader Russell described. And I remembered the headline relaying the news of my father's tragic death: "Boxer Kenny Pemberton Is Slain in Fall River." *Only heroes are slain,* I thought. *Was he really a hero?* The front page of the newspaper that day and articles the following day had hinted at a life that was less than heroic. *Who was the real Kenny Pemberton?*

I asked Russell about the circumstances of my father's death. He leaned back, as if fending off a jab. "I had left New Bedford by then, so I don't know all the details."

I pressed him. Was it true what I had read in the newspaper and what Betty Robinson had told me—that my father's body had been burned in the funeral home? Who does that to a man already dead? Why wasn't his death enough?

Russell shook his head gravely and sighed. "That is true. It was different times. Harder times. But I know this. He would have been proud, real proud, to call you his son."

The phone rang, yanking me out of the 1970s and into the present. It was my friend Tim, asking when we were going to head out for a party. When I hung up, I pressed Russell about another topic that remained a great mystery to me. "Did you know anything about my mother? Who she was? Her name? Anything?"

He eyed me for a long while. "Well, looking at you, I'd guess your mother was white. And that makes sense, too, because white women were all that your father dated. But no, I don't know who your mother is. I do remember your father being with this gorgeous redhead; Evelyn Brown was her name. Could that be your mother?"

I shrugged. "I don't have any idea. I've never heard that name before."

"Here's what I'll do. I'll ask around New Bedford and see what I can find. There are still a lot of people around from back then, and they might know something." He grabbed his briefcase and stood up to go.

I stood up with him and faced him squarely. There was another question I needed to ask him, perhaps the most important one of all: "Did Kenny know about me?"

Again, Russell leaned away. "Well," he said, rubbing his chin nervously, "I remember hearing a rumor in New Bedford about Kenny having a child. But he always denied it. If you want my opinion, and I know this may be hard to hear, I think he did know." I folded my arms across my chest as if doing so would protect me from this crushing revelation.

Russell put a hand on my shoulder. "You know, you might blame your father for how he treated you. But you're like him, more than you know. I can see him in you. You're a fighter and a leader just like he was. I could see it in the kids in the program and the way they talk about you. Those kids will never forget you for as long as they live. That was like him too. Kids loved him. They knew he was the real deal. When he walked down the street in New Bedford, they swarmed him. And he loved them back. You remember that."

CHAPTER 28

For almost a year after meeting Russell, I did nothing more to learn about my parents.

I didn't want to dwell on the similarities I bore to my father, as Russell had urged. Part of me, maybe even the predominant part, didn't want to know anything more about him. Thanks to this man, Kenny Pemberton, I had been abandoned to the foster care system and forced to suffer more than a decade of servitude to the Robinsons. To say that Kenny had abandoned me would not even be accurate; he had conceived me, and that was all.

But Kenny had bestowed on me a lesson: an entire universe of difference existed between a father and a dad. He had lived for the first five years of my childhood, plenty of time to intervene, to do something, *anything*. But he had not. To hear how great a boxer he was, how much people worshipped him, and most of all how he loved children only made me angrier because, although I had been many things—foster child, college graduate, student-athlete, fighter—he had denied me the identity and role I had most wanted, that of a son.

Like untold numbers of African American children, I had been consciously discarded by a man who seemed to define manhood by everything except being present for his son. That decision and its repercussions had blown across time, like tumbleweed in an arid desert. Immeasurable voids and endless questions are often created when a father deliberately abandons his child. Far too often, those empty spaces are filled by opportunists who see that vulnerability as something to exploit. In my case, it had been a cold and calculating foster family.

Night after night, I sat on my bed with the picture of my father sitting on my chest, his face now frozen in time, recalling Russell's fervent admonition that Kenny would have been proud of me. *What right do you have to be proud of what I have become? Whatever I am, you had nothing to do with it. I can never call you Dad.* As I held the picture, I noticed the burn scars on the back of my hands, courtesy of the Robinsons. The intervening years had faded them, but they were still there. Another harsh judgment arose within me. *That was your fault. You sent me to them. No matter the circumstance, I was still your son. You were supposed to protect me.* Yet despite that simmering anger, I couldn't fully remove him from my heart.

The summer of 1990, around the time I spoke with Russell, I had applied for and received a position in undergraduate admissions at Southeastern Massachusetts University. Driving a gray, beat-up Volkswagen Scirocco, with a cracked dashboard, temperamental heater, and car radio that did not work, I canvassed the state, extolling the virtues of higher education and the university and helping to make college a reality for low-income students. I found my thoughts drifting to my father, albeit in a more distanced, philosophical way. The college admission process is a life event for child and parent; in my daily work, the elements comprising the timeless child-parent bond—love, hope, sacrifice, letting go, and holding on—were on constant display.

I'd come away from intense scenes of family pride and emotion between fathers and children and would conclude that a man could build whatever monuments he wanted in the worlds of politics, sports, entertainment, and business, but if they come at the expense of his children, then he has failed. Once the attention fades and the crowds stop cheering his name and his accomplishments are little more than fine print in a history book, the only thing that truly survives him is his child. That is his legacy. That is what defines him. All else is but a footnote.

Kenny's legacy was cemented in my mind, so I turned my attention to the person who could fulfill my last remaining hope to have a family: my mother. But I retained no more memory of her than I had of

Kenny, and I had not the slightest clue who she was. The only thing I knew with any certainty was that she was white.

In April 1991 I called Mike Silvia, my former caseworker. We'd kept in touch during my college years and it was always a pleasure to hear his voice. Mike told me that he wasn't supposed to give out any information, but that he would see what he could find and call me back in a week. The following evening, I arrived home from work to find a message on my machine: "Hey, Steve. It's Mike. Give me a call when you get a chance. I'll be in the office."

It was past five, and I worried that Mike might have left for the day. I picked up a glass of lemonade and walked back into the living room, holding the cordless phone in the other hand. To my happy surprise, he picked up on the second ring. "So, Steve, I have some information, but I'm not sure how helpful it's going to be. And remember, you didn't get it from me."

"I gotcha, Mike."

"Let's see here." I could hear pages flipping in the background. "Your mother's name is Marian Klakowicz. Maiden name, Murphy. There is no record of your father anywhere in your file. We lost track of your mother somewhere around 1975. The department never knew where she was after that."

"Wow," I said, taking notes furiously. Every detail I jotted down made my mother seem more real, closer to me. For the first time, I heard her name: Marian. I wrote it down and underlined it twice, whispering it softly to myself. "Is there information on anyone else?" I asked.

"There is." Mike's voice fell to a whisper. "Remember, you did not get it from me. I could get in big trouble—like lose-your-job trouble— if anyone ever found out."

I nodded my head. "Mike, I give you my word. It's the most precious thing I have."

"Okay. In that case, did you know you had siblings?"

I jumped up, nearly knocking over my glass. "Wow. Mike, I had no idea." Through all my imaginings of what was or could have been, it never occurred to me that I had brothers and sisters. I had always seen myself as a lone entity, this lost child, disconnected from everyone.

"Well, it says here that there were four boys, including you, and a girl."

Questions flooded my mind. *Where were they now? Were these Kenny's children? Do we look alike? How come I don't remember them? Did they live with my mother?*

"There's one other thing, Steve. The only information we have on your family is the town and state where your grandparents lived in 1972. The name here in the file is J. Murphy, but I don't know if that is your grandmother or grandfather. The last address we have is in Pucker, New Jersey."

I tapped my pencil on the table, so astounded I stopped taking notes. *That was such a long time ago.*

"Before I let you go," Mike said, "I have been going through your case file. It's huge, by the way, and . . . well . . . there are just some very tough things in here about your family. It was tough for me just reading it. I know you went through the fire with the Robinsons, but things were pretty tough long before you got in their clutches. That's all I can really say. So be careful. And be prepared."

CHAPTER 29

*The voice of parents is the voice of gods, for to their children they
are heaven's lieutenants.*

—LEWIS THEOBALD, *DOUBLE FALSEHOOD*

*S*iblings, I thought, after hanging up with Mike. I shook my head
again in astonishment. *How do I go about finding them?* I paced
around the apartment. I knew my siblings existed, but I didn't have
their names. *What else do you know? The town where your grandparents
lived. What was the name of the town again? Pucker. Strange name for a
town, but that is what he said. There is no way my grandparents could still
live there. How else could I find them? Take a trip to the town and start asking
around?*

As a first step, I called information to see if they had anything.
Not only were there no Murphys in Pucker, New Jersey, but no town
named Pucker even existed; nor was there any town with a similar
name. Hanging up the phone, I dropped heavily onto my couch. Mike
had told me the notation was from 1973. Maybe the name of the town
had been written down incorrectly. I picked up the phone again and
called information several more times, trying to find anyone with the
last name of Klakowicz in the New Bedford area. This strategy failed
too. There was no one by that name in the area.

I had no idea what to do next, so I wound up putting the project
on hold for several weeks. In June, after I celebrated my twenty-fourth
birthday without a single call or card, I sat down and called information

again, asking this time to be put through to the operator in New Jersey. Everything seemed to hinge on the town in New Jersey where my grandparents were last known to reside. If I could determine the name of that town, then I could find them. A pleasant female voice answered, and I gave the name of the town I was looking for. She confirmed Pucker did not exist.

"Let me explain why I'm looking," I said. I proceeded to give her the Cliffs Notes version of my search. "So, I know they were in a town in New Jersey," I wrapped up, "but I just don't know where."

She was quiet for a minute. "That is quite a story. Are you sure you have the name of the town right?"

"That's just it. The notes were written almost twenty years ago, so I can't be sure. Is there any town that has a similar name to Pucker?"

"Not really," she said, "but there is a Tuckerton, New Jersey, which seems to be the closest thing to what you are looking for."

I jotted down Tuckerton and underlined it twice. Even if it was the right town, and *if* there were Murphys living there, they likely wouldn't be the Murphys I was looking for.

"Now, what listing were you looking for again?" she asked.

"Murphy." I could hear the pounding of keystrokes in the background.

"Well, I'll be," she said. "There is a listing for a Murphy—J. Murphy to be exact. They are the only Murphys listed in Tuckerton, which is odd since it's such a common name. It would be a miracle if they are there after all these years, but here's the number." I wrote it down very carefully, starting with the area code, 609.

"Thank you, ma'am," I said, overwhelmed with gratitude. "You've been really helpful."

We hung up, and I paced my apartment, steeling myself against the inevitable disappointment. *There is no way, absolutely no way, this is your grandparents' number. You've had enough disappointments. Don't get your hopes up. You'll only be let down. You will find them someday; it just won't be on this day.* Still, it was important that I exhaust every avenue. A few minutes later, I rushed to the phone, anxious to get this setback out of the way. As the phone rang once, twice, then three times, I realized I hadn't given much thought to how I was going to begin the conversation.

"Hello," said an elderly voice on the other end.

She sounds just like a grandmother should. My heart began pounding in my chest.

It's not her, Steve. It can't be that easy.

"Hi. Mrs. Murphy?" I asked.

"Yes."

"I'm, uh, sorry to disturb you, and, uh, I don't know if I have the right number, but my name is Steve Klakowicz and—"

On the other end, I heard an exclamation of "Oh!" and the phone clattering to the floor. Then she drew it to her ear and uttered the words I'd longed to hear: "Steve, oh my goodness, we always wondered what happened to you."

"You know who I am?" I asked, incredulous.

"Oh, yes. The last time we saw you, you were a little baby."

Even in the midst of the overwhelming possibility that I had finally found my family, my ears still perked up with her use of the word *we*. *Was she referring to my mother?*

"So you're my grandmother?" I asked, trying to verify, to be absolutely certain this was not another false hope.

"I am," she replied, laughing lightly. "You were a beautiful little boy. When we took you out, people would stop and stare. You had these beautiful blue eyes and blond hair. Your mother used to call you the 'golden boy.'"

"My mother," I said, my voice breaking, "where is she?"

She paused for a moment, and in that brief swallow of time, I knew the answer. "I'm sorry, but your mother was very sick. Steve, she died many years ago."

I closed my eyes and leaned my head against the door frame. *She's gone too. Both of them. They're gone.*

In my sophomore year at Boston College, we had a debate in philosophy class triggered by the question, "Can you miss something you never had?" For nearly an hour, the debate raged while the professor watched in delight. My seat was in the back, and at some point he noticed that I had remained silent. "Steve," he asked, "care to weigh in?"

All heads swiveled in my direction. I shifted a bit uncomfortably in my seat, unaccustomed to having the focus on me. Still, my answer was ready. "You absolutely can. I miss my mother because I've never been able to stop imagining her."

Over the years, in the absence of any memory, I had created my own detailed picture of my mother—her hair, her laugh, her mannerisms. I had imagined at times her pushing me in a stroller, nestling me in her arm, pushing me in a swing while I squealed in delight and screamed, "Higher, Mommy, higher!" I'd pictured her telling stories of bringing me home from the hospital, the first words I said, my first steps. I'd imagined asking why she had decided to name me Steve. Perhaps most of all, I imagined our long-awaited reunion: me trying to pick her out in a crowd, she running to me with open arms, an embrace that could bend time, me trying to brush away her tears, telling her that her son has come back and everything would be fine. Yet all this was not to be.

"Steve, Steve, are you still there?" my grandmother asked. How much time had passed with my head against the wall, I don't recall.

"I'm here," I said, sitting down heavily on the couch. "I'm sorry, it's just that—"

"I understand."

"And my father? Did she ever mention him?"

"Your mother never said much about him. Only that he was a well-known fighter."

"So she said he was a fighter," I said. If there was still any doubt that Kenny Pemberton was my father, my grandmother had just put it to rest. "Did she say anything else about him, his first name, his last name, anything?"

"No, nothing at all. But I do know where your brothers are."

A Chance in the World

"My brothers? You know where they are?" Strange as it sounds, I hadn't thought of this possibility. A gentle breeze wafted in from several open windows, bringing the scent of fresh air and the rose bush next to the porch.

"Oh, yes, Ben and Marc live here in New Jersey, not too far from me. There were six of you. We don't know where Joni and Bernie are, and we didn't know where you were either, until this phone call." My siblings' names came at me in a rush, and I grabbed my pad to write them down. I had only written down Ben's name when I stopped suddenly; the phone beeped, signaling another call was coming in.

"You said there were six of us," I said, ignoring the sound. "Who is the sixth?"

There followed a brief moment of silence. I had my pencil in hand, ready to write down the name. "You mean, you don't know?" she asked.

"Know what?"

"Steve, you had a sister, a twin sister. Her name was Starla. She passed away a little while after the two of you were born. I'm so sorry. There's so much I need to tell you."

148

CHAPTER 30

My grandmother Loretta and I talked for a couple of hours that evening in June 1991. I learned that she was not my biological grandmother but my step-grandmother, having married my grandfather, Joseph Murphy, after the death of his first wife. During that conversation, she also filled me in on the basics of my mother's life.

Marian Klakowicz née Murphy was born in Philadelphia in 1937. She dropped out of school after ninth grade and held a series of odd jobs, including working as a telephone operator. She moved around a bit, living at one point in Biloxi, Mississippi. While visiting friends in Texas, she met a fisherman, Rudolph Klakowicz, and they were married in February 1958. Later that year, Rudolph and my mother came to New Bedford, and their child Ben was born. My mother was twenty years old.

Her marriage was in trouble from the beginning, hampered by her increasingly erratic behavior, including her drinking, as well as by Rudolph's constant unemployment. By 1960 he had left her, and the two were barely in touch after that. Marian struggled to survive. She left Ben with just about anyone and didn't return for days. After one such incident, Grandfather Murphy rescued Ben and took him back to his home in New Jersey for good, to be raised by himself and Grandmother Loretta.

One might have expected my mother, too, to return to New Jersey, but her relationship with her family was strained. The Murphys continued to support her, but they expected her to live by their rules, and Marian wouldn't comply. She remained in New Bedford and held another series of odd jobs. In 1961 she was suspended for public drunkenness and disorderly conduct, just one of several charges she would incur that year and for which she'd receive probation. By 1962 she was destitute, desperate, and pregnant with her second child. She managed to get by on welfare and gifts from charitable organizations. Later that year a son, Marc, was born, and two years after that, a daughter, Joni, each by a different father.

The next few years saw more poverty and trouble with the law. In December 1965 she was arrested for disorderly conduct and sentenced to the House of Corrections for six months. Marc and Joni, three years and one year old respectively, were placed in foster care. When my mother was paroled in March 1966, she spent nearly a year looking for work in order to get her children back. In early 1967 my grandfather tried to get social services to allow the children to live with my mother in an apartment he'd pay for. Yet my mother refused his support and continued, unsuccessfully, to try to find work.

Soon she was pregnant yet again—with me. She later told my grandparents that a well-known boxer was the father, although she seemed not to have revealed that to anyone in New Bedford. I was born June 15, 1967, as was my twin sister, who died five days later of a brain hemorrhage. I apparently stayed with my mother as an infant, while she continued efforts to get Marc and Joni back. By early 1968 she had a steady boyfriend in her life, and by May 1968 she had succeeded in reclaiming Marc and Joni. Later that fall, Marian announced that she and her boyfriend were expecting a baby, due right around the holidays. It appeared she was turning her life around.

Yet it didn't last. By the summer of 1970, right around the time Kenny was immersed in the riots, my mother's life had unraveled again, for reasons my grandmother didn't elaborate. The state stepped in; Joni and I went into foster care, and Marc went to New Jersey to live with our grandparents. Only Bernard, her youngest child, remained in her care. For the next several months, Marc lived in relatively good conditions, but at the end of September 1971, he returned to foster care. My grandparents could no longer afford to keep him. I can only imagine the effect this must have had on Marc and my grandparents. At the time, I was bound for the abandoning-on-the-porch Andrades and, later, the ruthless Robinsons. Bernard stayed with our mother for another three years before he, too, was placed in foster care.

Marian Klakowicz continued to battle the courts and the state to have her children returned. Meanwhile she sank further into despair and depression. Her family heard from her from time to time—usually when she needed money. In the late morning of a cold January day in 1978, in Union, New Jersey, a building superintendent followed a trail of smoke to a small apartment shared by a woman and two brothers. He broke down the door to find a woman collapsed in a chair, her arm still in the outstretched position it had been in when she dropped the cigarette that ignited the fire. Paramedics tried to resuscitate her but to no avail. Either because of smoke inhalation or damage done by alcoholism, Marian Klakowicz née Murphy was dead. She was forty years old.

CHAPTER 31

Though I mourned the passing of my mother and my sister Starla, I came away from the conversation with Grandmother Murphy beaming with excitement at the idea of having siblings. I couldn't wait to share the news with my work colleagues. The next day, I heard from current and former students who also congratulated me on finally finding my family. But in many ways, the story was just beginning.

Susan Pawlak-Seaman, a reporter from the *New Bedford Standard-Times*, called that afternoon in June 1991 to ask whether these stories she was hearing about my quest for my family were true. She interviewed me for the better part of an hour and a half, trying to unravel all the complexities of the story. The following morning, Mike Silvia called with information on my sister Joni's adoptive parents. A family in Taunton, Massachusetts, twenty minutes from New Bedford, had taken Joni in and raised her.

I called Joni's adoptive mother, Muriel Johnsen, who now lived in Reading, Pennsylvania, and told her who I was. Muriel was completely stunned to hear from one of Joni's siblings. "Joni has looked for all of you for years," she said. "She would often go to New Bedford trying to find anybody who had the last name Klakowicz. But she never knew where to look."

"Where is she now?" I asked.

"Biloxi, Mississippi. She just moved there."

I had been taking notes, and my pencil froze on the paper. "I'm sorry, can you repeat that?"

"Biloxi, Mississippi. Why? Is there something significant about Biloxi?"

"There sure is. Joni's and my mother lived there for a few years."

"Oh my gosh!"

"Is there any chance Joni would have heard about Biloxi from our mother?"

"I don't see how," Muriel said. "She was very young, just five years old or so when she came to us." She paused then—a long, mysterious silence. "Steve, I think it's important that you know that Joni has struggled a lot. When she came to us, she had been through a really traumatic experience with your mother. We've always tried to help her as much as we could, but Joni has never quite gotten past it. Maybe finding all of you will help."

I listened quietly, understanding well the possibility of closure that finding your family would bring and the questions it could answer. "Please let her know we are looking for her and would love to hear from her," I said.

"I will. She just moved there, and as soon as she gets a phone, I'll ask her to call you."

I said good-bye and placed the phone gently in the cradle. Leaning back in my chair, I shook my head in amazement at the recent events. But the week was still young, and more was yet to happen.

The next day, Wednesday, June 19, 1991, the *New Bedford Standard-Times* ran their front-page article about my search for my family. Under my picture was the following headline: "Quest pays off: After 21 years he has a family." The article went on to detail my path to adulthood and my long search to know my heritage. Toward the middle of the story, Kenny Pemberton was named as my father.

The paper ran in the late afternoon, before I left my office. By the time I arrived home fifteen minutes later, several strangers had called and left messages. These people all said the same thing: they were friends of Kenny's and wanted to talk to me as soon as possible. While I was writing down the messages, the phone continued to ring. And ring. The last message came from Susan Pawlak-Seaman, telling me that she needed to talk with me as soon as possible. I called her back immediately, pacing my usual path through the apartment. "Steve," she said, "I'm hearing from several Pembertons who are giving me a hard time because I wrote that Kenny was your father. They are pretty upset. They're saying Kenny didn't have any children, and if he did, they would have known. They're saying you should stop saying you're Kenny's son. But I told them you were absolutely certain."

"I am certain, Susan. The only thing my mother ever said about my father was that he was a well-known fighter."

"I understand, Steve. I just wanted to make sure you were aware."

I heard a similar message from Mrs. Dottin. Around noon the following day, we met for lunch at her request. No sooner had we sat down than she broached what she had come to say. "The Pembertons have been calling my office," Mrs. Dottin said cautiously. "They're telling me you're wrong, that Kenny didn't have any children."

It was now a familiar refrain, and I was frustrated. "Well, they're wrong, Mrs. D. Besides, I'm not asking for their permission or for them to believe me. You know better than anyone how long and hard this road has been. I've got no patience for someone who tells me that somehow I've gotten it wrong. Have they ever asked why someone would claim Kenny Pemberton as their father? It's not as if he left this great legacy."

A silence followed. She poked around at her salad and then gave me that familiar look over the top of her glasses.

"Steve, you have to realize what a shock this is to everyone, especially his family."

I put down my fork. "Maybe that's what I don't understand, Mrs. D. If I had lost a family member as they have and then learned years later that he had a child, I would welcome him with open arms."

She nodded in agreement and slid me a piece of paper across the table. "Give Kenny's sister a call. Her name is Geraldine, and this is her number."

Rather than taking the number, I leaned back. "If this is how it's going to be, Mrs. D, if I have to get into a debate with anyone about who I am . . ." I left the sentence unfinished.

She held her hand on the paper a moment longer and lowered her eyes as she so often did when she wanted to get a point across to one of her obstinate students. "You do need to talk to her, and you need to go see her. She is the oldest of all the Pembertons. I didn't know Kenny, but I do know Geraldine, and if I remember correctly, she and Kenny were very close."

I took the number and promised that I would call.

CHAPTER 32

Geraldine Gomes, or Gerri, as people called her, lived at the top of Mill Street in a modest single-family home in New Bedford's West End. I parked across from the house and got out of my car, taking in the neighborhood. This part of town was more than familiar to me. I had passed through here countless times on errands with Willie. His battle with the cabdriver had happened right on this street, less than a block away. Years after that, I had often walked through this neighborhood of closely knitted homes on my way to school.

It was late on Friday afternoon when I pulled up to the curbside. A gentle breeze blew, and off in the distance I heard traffic humming on Rockdale Avenue. A silver-haired gentleman in a short-sleeved plaid shirt, who appeared to be in his midfifties, was sitting on the porch, rocking gently in a double rocker. We made eye contact as I emerged from my car; he bolted inside the house, moving so quickly that the rocker banged against the porch wall. As I approached the steps, I heard him calling "Gerri! Gerri!" from somewhere inside. I reached out to steady the rocker, which was still swaying from his sudden departure. I rang the doorbell, waiting for what seemed like an eternity. Finally, the man who had dashed inside appeared at the front door.

"Hi," I said. "I'm Steve."

He waved me off. "I know who *you* are. I'm Manny, Gerri's husband." He gestured toward the living room. "Come on in. She's in here."

He opened the door, and I stepped into the home's small foyer. One of my favorite poems, "Footprints in the Sand," hung on the wall. I walked deeper into the living room. The windows were open, and white curtains fluttered gently in the breeze.

Sitting on the couch in a pink nurse's uniform was a middle-aged African American woman. Her hands were clasped tightly in her lap. When she saw me, she put her head down and began nodding to herself.

Before Manny left the room, he gestured toward the couch, indicating I should have a seat. "You're going to have to give her some time."

Gerri kept her head bowed a few moments longer, and in that time I sensed that a flood of memories were coming back to her. When she finally lifted her head, I could see that she had been crying. "I can't believe it," she said, smiling. "You are definitely one of us." A flood of questions followed. Where had I grown up? (About a mile from your house, and I used to walk past your house all the time on the way to school.) Who was my mother? (A woman by the name of Marian Klakowicz.) Who raised me? (The Robinsons.) Do I have a girlfriend? (I'm still working on that.)

As we talked, I noticed the color of her eyes. Both of my parents had brown eyes, as did all four of my grandparents. Though I had already learned much about my biological family, I still hadn't figured out where my blue eyes had come from. I had assumed they came from my mother's family and her European origins. Now I was surprised to see that my aunt's eyes were bluish green. Gerri told me that my grandmother Mary Cabral was actually Cape Verdean and that my eyes likely came from my father's Cape Verdean origins.

Cape Verdeans are a beautiful people; they hail from a small archipelago of islands off the western coast of Africa and are of European, Portuguese, and African descent. Centuries of this fusion of cultures had created a people of skin hues, hair textures, and eye colors as diverse as the lands from which they came. Some of this had clearly been passed along to me.

As we chatted, she smiled from time to time and pointed out that I shared a lot of my father's mannerisms—from the way I scratched my head to the way I looked skyward while I was thinking.

I had many questions for her, but I was reluctant to ask. Mrs.

Dottin's and Marc's cautionary advice had stuck with me, and I knew enough about Kenny's life and death to know that I needed to be careful.

"Can you tell me about him?" I asked. "What was he like?"

She snickered. "You mean, other than that he thought he could walk on water?" Her voice turned more serious. "I know he had this tough street reputation, but he was always my mischievous little brother."

She proceeded to give me details of Kenny's story that greatly furthered what I'd already learned from Russell Almeida. Kenny was born into a large family in nearby Tiverton, Rhode Island, anchored by his mother, who loved and doted upon him just a bit more than her thirteen other children. Unfortunately, the family experienced a series of tragedies. An older brother, Gordon, died at eight years old, after surgeons botched his hernia operation. A sister, Elaine, died in a car accident at age fifteen. And then in 1956, faulty wiring caused a fire that burned down the family's home. The family scattered, the children going to live with various relatives and friends while Kenny's parents tried to piece their lives back together. Kenny's youngest brother, Greg, and two sets of twin sisters—Cynthia and Sheila, Beverly and Colleen—were put into a Rhode Island orphanage and eventually were raised in foster homes.

The strain split up the marriage; Kenny's father, Joe, moved to an apartment in Fall River. His mother suffered a coronary occlusion and died at age thirty-nine. She was upstairs in her bedroom when she collapsed. An ambulance sped Mary to St. Luke's Hospital, but she was already gone. Kenny flew into a rage, storming into the garage and breaking all the windows with his bare fists. He was just fifteen.

At that point, it seems, Kenny threw himself into boxing with the fearlessness for which he became known. But the ring was not the only mistress pining for his attention. Kenny was also drawn to the allure of the streets, and by 1971 he had plunged into the chaotic darkness of New Bedford's drug subculture, moving beyond recreational marijuana use to the more dangerous, violent pastime of selling and using heroin. As he fell further and further into addiction, Kenny became more emboldened as a thug, caring little about the consequences. One of his tactics was to beat up local dealers and take their drugs, usually for his own personal use. He also became embroiled in a dispute over territories, ignited by his unwillingness to respect previously defined boundaries.

Still, Kenny had a compassionate side. Geraldine told me that she, Kenny, and some of the other Pemberton children had a passion for horseback riding. "Kenny loved to ride," she said. "Whether from selling drugs or some legitimate work, he came up with the money to buy a horse he called Hawkeye, and he would often leave New Bedford to go riding." He stabled Hawkeye in Rochester, a small rural town nineteen miles north of New Bedford, and became familiar with the area. Perhaps it was the perfect escape for a city kid whose life was buffeted by poverty and trouble.

At the same time, Kenny made several vain attempts to kick his heroin habit. He turned to Geraldine, who tried desperately to keep the family together after their mother died. Kenny often came to her home in the West Lawn apartments at three or four o'clock in the morning, ringing the doorbell, looking for a place to crash and someone to talk to. She'd sigh and let him in. She made him sandwiches while he shared his emotional struggle. "I'm hooked, Gerri," he told her. "I'm trying to get off, but it's hard."

Geraldine convinced Kenny to try a methadone clinic, and she drove him there daily for his shots. "I told him, 'Kenny, you have to be careful. They're gonna shoot you if you keep this up,'" Geraldine remembered.

"They'll have to come at me from behind because nobody would give me the chance to see them coming." Even the weight of addiction had done nothing to humble Kenny.

"He was a born fighter and he just had no fear," Geraldine said, summing up my father's life. "You couldn't talk to him. Once he decided he was going to do something, you couldn't stop him. He was just a force of nature. The same things that made him the boxer he was are what got him killed."

We sat in silence for a moment. A warm breeze pushed the curtains aside, and the sweet smell of summer entered the living room. I had never known where my stubborn resolve came from. Now hearing Gerri describe my father and his unyielding nature, I silently asked myself, *Has he given me something after all?* I barely registered the thought before I noticed my aunt on the verge of tears. "I'll never forget the night Kenny died," she said. "I got a call in the middle of the night. It was from the hospital in Fall River, asking if I knew a Kenny Pemberton . . . they called me because my number was the only one he had in his wallet. When I got to the hospital, he was already gone. They had a sheet over him, except for his face. I can still see the bandanna he had wrapped around his head . . . when I saw him, I just hit the floor . . ."

She shakily raised a tissue to her eyes, and I felt a pang of remorse for bringing her back down that road.

I leaned over to touch her hand. "If you would rather we not talk about this—" I began. But she cut me off, shaking her head.

"No, it's okay," she said. "You need to know this." She spent a moment collecting herself.

"The thing about it was he had been trying to find me all day. He had come by my work, looking for me, and I was out on my break. He asked people on my job when I would be back, said he had something really important to tell me. He waited around for a bit, but then he left." She paused for a minute and took a deep breath. "That will stay with me the rest of my life, that we kept missing each other that day. I never learned what it was he wanted to tell me. Maybe it was to tell me about you."

It was time to say good-bye; I could tell Geraldine was exhausted emotionally, and so was I. I gave her a long hug and promised I would stay in touch. Manny walked me out to the porch. I paused at the bottom of the steps and looked around the neighborhood, thinking again just how many times I had walked past this house on my way to school. So many answers had been right inside. I turned to face Manny. There was a question I needed to ask. "Mr. Gomes, when I first came here, you ran inside, and I could hear you calling for Gerri. Can I ask what you told her?"

He looked up Mill Street for a moment and then turned to me. "I told her that she needed to sit down because Kenny's son was walking across the street."

It felt good to hear that—to hear myself spoken of so unequivocally as Kenny's son.

I smiled and nodded my head in understanding.

CHAPTER 33

During our conversation, my aunt Geraldine had warned me that Kenny's brothers, Warren in particular, would have a more difficult time coming to grips with my sudden arrival. Kenny's memory was difficult for them even after so many years, and they hadn't considered the possibility that he might have had children. Geraldine was right, as I'd discover a few days later when I went to see Warren. He was the one who had called the newspaper asking why they had written this "lie" about Kenny.

Geraldine had given me Warren's number and suggested I call him. I called him the following day from my university office. The voice on the other end was gravelly and curt. "So you *think* you're Kenny's son, huh?"

I wouldn't let this slight pass. "No, I *know* I am."

"We'll see about that," he said.

We agreed to meet in downtown New Bedford shortly after work. The location had been my suggestion. I wanted a large public venue with plenty of people. I had received enough warnings to know that when it came to Kenny Pemberton, I needed to remain cautious.

I found Warren dressed in a blue workman's jumpsuit and sitting on a small brick ledge beside some potted plants. It was unbelievably hot, the type of heat that only a thunderstorm can relieve. A McDonald's loomed over his shoulder. He wore a blue baseball hat pulled low, and large, dark sunglasses completely masked his eyes. Even with that disguise and from twenty yards away, I could see the resemblance between us. I saw later that he, too, had deep-set eyes and a strong prominent forehead.

As I approached, he mouthed something to himself. Then he

turned his head and looked off in the distance, his eyes fixed on something far off. By the time he returned his gaze to my direction, I was standing right in front of him. He wouldn't look at me and kept pawing the redbrick sidewalk in front of him, like a bull trying to break loose from his confines. I waited patiently, finally taking a seat a few feet away from him on the small ledge.

He pulled a pack of Newports from his breast pocket. "Smoke?" he asked, extending the small green-and-white box in my direction.

I shook my head. "No, thanks. I don't smoke."

He nodded, as if expecting this answer. Snapping open a stainless steel Zippo lighter, he lit his cigarette, took a long, slow drag, and expelled it into the atmosphere. A steady stream of foot traffic flowed in and out of the McDonald's. A big yellow city bus lumbered up the street, spewing exhaust in its wake. "Gerri tells me you went to college in Boston."

"I did."

He nodded his approval. "She also tells me that the Robinsons raised you over there on Arnold Street."

I shrugged my shoulders. "*Raised* is not the word I would use to describe it, but yeah, that is where I grew up."

He took another pull from his cigarette. "Sorry you had to deal with that."

I looked at him quizzically. A quick breeze came through the plaza, but it did nothing to alleviate the humidity. "You knew about them, the kind of people they were?"

"Everybody knew about 'em, how they took kids in for money, treated 'em like animals." He looked off in the distance. "If Kenny had known his son was there, he would have taken you out of there himself, brought you to us. And then he would have gone back and would have taken out Willie and Betty, too, for treating you like they did."

This picture of my father as the avenger was, I believed, revisionist history. I'd been told a great deal about Kenny, but Kenny had told no one of my existence. *Is Warren suggesting that Kenny had not known about me?* I dismissed the thought almost as quickly as it came to me. *New Bedford was too small for him not to have known,* I thought. Such a conclusion seemed less than concrete, however, and the question nagged at me: *Had Kenny known that he had a son?* Whether he had known about me or not, one thing seemed abundantly clear: by the time he died, he had no idea where I was or what had happened to me. The only thing that connected the two of us was a small sliver of time, a bitter irony I now shared with Warren. "I went to live with the Robinsons right after he died, August 1972," I said.

He winced at the mention of Kenny's death. Flicking away the remains of his cigarette across the plaza, he rose to his feet. "Has anyone taken you to his grave?"

"Uh, no," I said. "I don't even know where he is buried."

He stood up. "Come on, then. I'll take you."

I felt uneasy about going, but I also sensed a begrudging acceptance from Warren that I was indeed Kenny's son. We got in my car, and with Warren as my guide, wound our way through downtown New Bedford toward St. John's Cemetery, Kenny's final resting place. We traveled up Union Street, passing through the general area where I had grown up. I pointed out several childhood landmarks I recognized: my elementary school, Leed's, Tailor's, the small library next to Buttonwood Park. Staring out the window, Warren mumbled a word or two but said little else.

Many neighborhoods in the proud city of New Bedford are huddled together; homes are tightly clustered and there are few front yards or garages to speak of. Cars park on the street, and there is often a tango of traffic on the two-way streets. Located on Allen Street, fewer than ten minutes from downtown, St. John's Cemetery was nestled snugly in between neighborhoods just like this. The cemetery is enormous, covering several city blocks.

We turned left into the graveyard and immediately bore right at a huge maple tree, headed toward the cemetery's southern end. Gravestones of various sizes and shapes were lined up in perfect order, interrupted only by the smooth paved road. The larger stones rose above the earth, timeless shrines that seemed to suggest the largeness of the lives they marked. It was a warm and sunny day, only a few clouds drifting overhead. Large green maples in the full flush of summer stood like guardians over this sanctified place.

We drove until the road ended and got out. Looking around, Warren led us down a neatly ordered row. A gentle breeze greeted us, bringing some relief from the humidity. I trailed behind, looking at the weather-beaten markers. The hundreds of stones in this area were all small and humble, running flat with the land; a few had even sunk below the unkempt grass, the names of the deceased now invisible. Inspecting the graves, I noticed that the dates of passing were mainly from 1970 and 1971. Flowers brightened some of the stones, but for the most part these lives had seen very little in the way of commemoration. Time and distance had taken their toll.

Warren stopped in the middle of the row and gazed down at the ground. Walking slowly toward him, I felt a surge of finality overcome me—the same feeling I had when Russell brought me my father's picture. A childish thought danced in my mind: *Maybe if I just turn around and go, there is still a chance he will come back.*

Warren bent down and began pulling up weeds. Peering over his shoulder, I read the words inscribed on the light-gray stone, "Kenneth P. Pemberton," and above that, his title, "Brother." Kenny was born in 1946 and died in 1972, making him just twenty-six years old, two years older than I was when visiting his grave for the first time.

This cold, gray, emotionless slab of granite was all that marked my father's memory—miniscule compared to the largeness of Kenny's life and the long shadow he had cast over mine. A film of dust and dirt covered the stone, and grass and weeds framed its edges. I went to my trunk and grabbed the bucket and rags I used to wash the car. Spotting a nearby spigot, I filled the bucket and brought it back to the grave. I washed the stone while Warren dug out its sides, using a stick he'd found. We worked in silence, listening to the chirping of the birds and the sound of cars revving on nearby streets. I sensed Warren's acceptance that I was indeed Kenny's son, yet I also felt a subtle tension between us, one that I couldn't articulate.

The muggy mid-July heat hung in the air, coating us in a light sweat. The back of Warren's light-blue shirt turned a darker hue. When we were finished, Warren stood up and looked around the cemetery. His voice was barely audible as he spoke: "We kept getting calls threatening to hurt other members of the family. They said they were going to dig him up, cut him up, and put him in different parts of New Bedford. The whole area was surrounded by police when we came to bury him." He pointed a short distance away. "They were all lined up over there." He closed his eyes, pained by the memory. "They rolled a large rock over his grave so nobody could get to him."

He removed his glasses, and for the first time I could see his eyes, filled with pain and sorrow. He stared off into the distance and then suddenly turned to me, moving so quickly I nearly put up my hand in self-defense. "What did you bring all this back for?" He threw his hands out to his side, holding them out as if he were Lady Justice herself, holding the scales of fairness and impartiality. "He was my brother." He choked out the last word, his voice filled with pain.

"And he was my father," I said, an edge in my voice.

Tears of anger and frustration welled in my eyes. For years I had envisioned my homecoming: walking into a festive home where my family would suddenly swarm around me. There would be generations of Pembertons waiting to greet me—grandparents, aunts and uncles, nieces and nephews. They'd welcome me back as if I'd never been gone. Those idyllic visions had sustained me during the dark years of the Robinsons and beyond. In none of them had I ever imagined that, once I found my family, anyone would ask what I was doing there. I thought everyone would accept me without condition or prequalification.

Warren didn't respond. He bowed his head and stuffed his hands into his pockets, kicking at the ground, his black boots standing out against the bright-green grass. I leveled my eyes at him and jabbed a finger in the air. "I wasn't trying to bring back anything. I was just trying to find my father. And it doesn't matter what any of you say; I had the right to find him. You had a chance to meet your father, to shake his hand, to look him in the eye, to call him your own. You even had the chance to say good-bye. I never even got the chance to say hello. And I never will. Kenny is gone from me now. And none of you can give him to me."

Tears continued to roll down Warren's cheeks, but now he nodded his head in understanding. We stood there in a heavy silence punctuated by Warren's sobs. Off in the distance, shimmers of heat rose from the ground, blurring our view of the gravestones and giving the impression that they were melting. A lone crow flew by, cawing and screeching. I watched my uncle wrestling with his grief twenty years after the fact and remembered my aunt Gerri telling me that Kenny and Warren were particularly close; they were closest to each other in age, and Warren had idolized his older brother.

A lot suddenly made sense: our edgy first phone call, the protests to the reporter, the clipped, cold greeting in downtown New Bedford. Kenny's death, the tragic fall of this "golden boy," had become part of the fabric of his family's life. They had moved on as best they could, telling themselves that time would heal their wounds. Yet part of them had died too. And now, two decades later, I had suddenly appeared with my Kenny-like features and mannerisms, intruding on the tortured peace they had gradually found. In the relentless pursuit of my roots, I had naively believed that my presence could erase their pain. I had been so insensitive to their pain, so heedless of the great chasm left by Kenny's death—all that could never be replaced.

"I'm sorry, Warren," I said, resting my hand on his shoulder. "For all of us. I am sorry he's not here."

Warren wiped his tears with his sleeve. He put his sunglasses back on and took a long, deep breath. I peered down at Kenny's gravestone, shining a bit brighter now. "Kenny was a man's man. And he would have been proud of you, Steve. I can tell you that. Wherever he is, he is looking at you right now and sayin', 'That is *my* son.'"

I was never his to claim, I thought. Despite the newfound sorrow I had for Kenny and his fractured family, I still could not bring myself to forgive him.

CHAPTER 34

Starting again is part of the plan
And I'll be so much stronger holding your hand...

—GLORIA ESTEFAN, *"COMING OUT OF THE DARK"*

So much had happened in so little time. After half a lifetime spent regretting and mourning a family I didn't know, and tagging halfheartedly along with the families of others, I was finally realizing my dream. My parents were gone, but now I had grandparents, aunts, uncles, and siblings to call my own. I could envision future Christmases spent together, phone calls on my birthday, and a slew of proud faces on my side of the aisle at my wedding, should I ever be lucky enough to find a bride. No longer would I feel alone and disconnected in the world.

Now, in August 1991, about a month after the cemetery visit with Warren, I would take the next step and meet my siblings in Freehold, New Jersey, where my brother Marc was living. For the first time as adults, all four of Marian's children—the four who had found each other—would be in the same room.

I got up before dawn that Saturday morning, brimming with excitement and anticipation. The drive to Freehold—a town that, incidentally, was the inspiration for Bruce Springsteen's "My Hometown"—was going to take several hours, but I would ride in style, having traded in my beat-up Volkswagen Scirocco for a new red Volkswagen Fox. On the passenger seat was a map of central New Jersey;

in my cassette case was all the music I needed to keep me company in the early morning hours.

A soft rain had begun to fall by the time I reached the Garden State Parkway. It was nine o'clock in the morning, and Freehold Mall, where Marc and I were to meet, was empty, as the summer shoppers had not yet arrived. I peered out over the parking lot as the Fox's windshield wipers beat a steady swish. I had no recollection of having siblings; I was simply too young to remember. Questions darted in and out of my mind. *What did Marc and Ben look like? What do they remember of our mother? Did we look alike? Would I recognize them if I saw them? Could I pick them out of a crowd? And what about Joni?*

A late-'80s burgundy Camaro approached, its engine roaring as if it were on a raceway. Heavy, thumping bass and the screeching of a rock guitar poured from its speakers as the car came to a hard stop. The door opened, and out spilled a tall, white, mustached man dressed in blue jeans and a blue T-shirt. His hair was brown and feathered down to his shirt collar. A cigarette dangled precariously from one side of his mouth; I remember first thinking, *It's going to fall.* My second thought: *My brother is white.*

He didn't close the driver's side door. Rather, he stepped around it to extend an open hand. "You're Steve," he said.

"And you're Marc," I said, smiling.

I took his hand, and then we embraced. A lifetime of searching, wondering, and imagining had brought me here to this near-empty parking lot in central New Jersey, to the embrace of a complete stranger who doubled as my brother. *Finally,* I thought. *I have finally found where I've come from.*

"It's good to finally meet you," I said.

"You too."

We stared at each other for an awkward moment. My grandmother had known nothing of Marc's father, and my mother had stubbornly refused to tell her. These last few months, I had trouble imagining what my siblings looked like. Now, try as I might, I couldn't discern any resemblance between my brother and me. *It's a good thing we met this way,* I thought, *because I could have passed you a thousand times on the street and never known we were brothers.* I shook my head in disbelief.

"Well," he said, leaning one hand on the driver's side door, "let's head over to my girlfriend's house. Joni is there, and she really wants to see you too."

"Sounds like a plan," I said.

We got into our respective vehicles, his door creaking as he slammed it shut. I rolled down my window. "Hey, Marc, slow down a bit. My car probably can't keep up with your mean machine." He shot me a thumbs-up and peeled off anyway, water spraying off the Camaro's tires. I burst out laughing and gave chase.

A short while later, we drove down a tree-lined street and pulled into the driveway of a modest home with brown shutters. Marc's small, blond girlfriend greeted us at the door: "Come on in. Joni is in the shower, but I'm sure she will be right out."

We stepped inside to a small kitchen. An older, stocky gentleman in a bright-yellow, sleeveless T-shirt sat at the table. His graying hair was combed straight back, and his hands were large and calloused. I judged him to be in his midfifties. He extended his hand. "Hi," he said, "I'm Mason." That was all he said. Nobody told me who he was or what he was doing there. After we shook hands, he walked down the hallway and rapped on the bathroom door. "Joni, ya bruddah, he here." His accent was thick and Southern but somehow different from the drawls I'd heard over the years.

Joni yelled something back. Suddenly the bathroom door burst open, and she emerged amid a torrent of steam. I was taken aback. A tan towel was wrapped around her hair like a turban. Another towel with green horizontal stripes covered her body. She was pale and very thin. Dark circles hung under brown eyes that were recessed and hollowed. Her cheekbones protruded. Rarely had I seen someone's life experiences so clearly written upon his or her body. In the short time it took her to reach me, I thought, *She looks like a prisoner of war.* Sorrow and a desire to protect her overcame me. I opened my arms, and she ran up, hugging me close and weeping on my chest. Wrenching sobs came from the depths of her soul; her body wracked and convulsed against mine. Several times she tried to speak but couldn't.

I understood her pain and kept whispering, "I know, I know."

When she finally pulled away, her eyes were red, her face flushed. She wiped her eyes quickly and furtively, as if embarrassed. "I have to go get dressed," she said softly. She disappeared into a back bedroom, the door clicking behind her.

I looked at Marc, searching for an explanation. He shrugged his shoulders in an I-have-no-idea gesture. "She's been crying since she got here yesterday. She's fine one minute and then the next . . ." He sighed heavily. Mason bobbed his head in agreement.

We all sat down at the small kitchen table, a basket of flowers its centerpiece. Marc's girlfriend offered something to drink, and I accepted a glass of Coke. I had so many questions for Marc, but I didn't want to plow right in. Marc spared me the need. "So," he asked. "How did you find all of us? I went back to New Bedford several times trying to find you guys, and I never could."

I told him the sequence of events, and we both marveled at this quirk of fate. "So you remember us?" I asked.

"Oh yeah. I remember all of you. We were always hungry, and I used to put sugar and water in your bottles and give them to you to try and keep you quiet."

"Was our mother there?"

"Sometimes. But sometimes she would leave us with people, and other times she would just leave us by ourselves."

I shook my head in disbelief. "How old were you?"

"About seven or eight." There was a distance to his voice as if he were talking about someone else. He snapped his fingers as if an idea had come to him. "If I remember correctly, you should have a huge scar on your left foot."

He was right. I had always carried a long scar that ran horizontally across my foot, but its origins had been a mystery.

He opened his can of Coke. A loud pop and hiss sounded across the small kitchen. "You got it when you were about two or three. Our mother had left us, and we went out looking for food in garbage cans around the neighborhood."

I shook my head in disbelief. "Marc, no."

"Oh, yeah," he said, lifting the can to his lips. He took a long swallow. "That's how it was. Me, you, and Joni went looking for food all the time. We'd leave Bernie in the apartment, figuring he couldn't get himself into too much trouble." His tone was still even, but I could detect a certain haunting in his eyes. "Anyways, we were in a neighbor's backyard rooting through their cans, and you fell into a pile of glass. You cried and hollered like nothing I'd ever heard. Me and Joni got you back to the house, and I just remember there was blood everywhere. I think the neighbors took you to the hospital, and when you came back, you had this huge bandage on your foot."

A year before, I had met Lois Gibbs, a wonderful woman. She had been a friend of my mother's, having lived in the same apartment building. One day my mother had asked Lois's father and her to drop me at a babysitter's. That event led Lois's father to write in his diary that I didn't have "a chance in the world." Lois also told me of my mother's neglect, and I knew that was the reason she lost her children. But absent any memory, it had not truly hit home for me. Marc's story made my mother's actions real, and for the first time I began to sense how perilous life with her must have been. Joni emerged from a bedroom in the rear of the house and sat down at the kitchen table. She wore acid-washed jeans and a man's T-shirt that said "Big Dog" on the left front. On the back it said, "If you can't run with the big dogs, stay on the porch."

She sat at the kitchen table rocking gently, her eyes skittering across the room, as if she were trapped. I stared at her, swallowing hard, trying to hold back tears. *What has life done to you, Joni?*

Marc continued to tell us about his upbringing; how, after we were taken from our mother, he came to live with Joe, Loretta, and Ben in Tuckerton, New Jersey; that for years he thought Ben was his cousin and not his brother; that after a year his grandparents could no longer afford to keep him and he was sent back into foster care; that he lived with foster parents who treated him as if he were an indentured servant.

"I remember a lot too," Joni suddenly whispered. She stared straight ahead at the floral basket with the plastic flowers as her audience. "I remember being hungry—always, always hungry." She repeated "always, always hungry" as if it were a tribal chant. "But that's not what I remember most. I remember these men touching me in places they shouldn't. I remember that *a lot*. I wasn't no more than six years old." We said nothing, listening in stunned silence. But Joni said no more. Off in the distance a car horn beeped, reminding me of the world that existed beyond our collective pain.

Marc asked about the circumstances in which I'd grown up, and I recounted my tale. He listened, interrupting when I told him about college. "You went to Boston College? You must be pretty smart."

I shook my head in denial. "Oh, I don't know about that. I worked pretty hard. I knew education was my only chance."

Marc waved me off. "Naw, you're pretty smart. You found us, and nobody else done that."

"Well, almost," I replied. "We still haven't found Bernard yet. This won't be complete until we find him."

Joni had been quiet the entire time, but now she looked directly at me and said, "You're not black. You can't be." She said this almost pleadingly, as if saying it would make it so. I was so stunned I nearly asked her to repeat herself. I let out a long sigh. I had experienced racism before, but I had never expected it would factor into my family reunion. I had known my mother was white, and as far as I knew, I was the only one of her children who was of mixed race. But I had believed that such considerations would have no place here, that the loss we collectively suffered would transcend any difference.

"But I am, Joni," I said gently. "I know our mother was white, but my father was African American, and I grew up in an African American community."

Like many children of mixed race, I had grown accustomed to questions about my identity. Most people wanted to know which side you identified with, and there were others who demanded you choose a side. I never had any patience with the latter and would admonish anyone who crossed that line. Yet with Joni I knew I needed to tread lightly, no matter how annoyed I might have been at the question.

"You're not black!" she said again, her voice this time panicky and shrill. She burst into tears and bolted from the kitchen table, slamming the bedroom door behind her.

An awkward silence took hold of the room. I looked around the table and met with downward glances. Marc spun the Coke can around in his hands. Mason had his hands folded but tapped his thumbs together. Somewhere in the back bedroom, I could hear Joni's muffled sobs. None of us knew what to say.

We were meeting our brother Ben for dinner that night, and we decided to pass some time by heading over to the Freehold Raceway Mall, where Marc and I had met a few hours earlier. The enormous mall had opened the previous year. Long, pristine corridors and wide hallways held hundreds of shops and thousands of shoppers. Beautifully architected high, glass ceilings gave the place a palatial feel. In its center court was a majestic water fountain, framed by three smaller fountains and large potted plants, while a beautifully sculpted, ten-foot sand castle stood at the foot of one of the escalators.

We walked around the stores looking at things none of us could afford. Joni and Mason stopped into several jewelry stores while Marc and I waited patiently outside. It was clear that Joni wanted to keep as much distance between me and her as possible. She and Mason, who by now I realized was Joni's boyfriend, stayed a few yards back from Marc and me.

After half an hour, we stopped in the food court on the lower level. Joni and Mason sat at one table, and Marc and I sat at another, eating our Wendy's and Chinese food. A children's carousel spun nearby, and its gilded music wafted over the food court, blending in with the birdlike chatter of a hundred conversations. Out of the corner of my eye, I could see Joni casting curious glances in my direction. Each time I tried to make eye contact, she looked away. After a while I stopped looking her way, thinking that eventually she would come around. This was a departure for me; I usually ignored those who held racist views, believing that racism was its own prison. But this simplistic philosophy seemed terribly insufficient in trying to come to terms with my own sister.

Marc and I talked a bit more about his job as a mechanic; I laughed as he told me some of his favorite stories about irate customers, and he did the same as I told him about some of my college pranks. Both of us had mischievous personalities, and it occurred to me just how much havoc we might have raised as children had we grown up together. We laughed at this prospect, but soon my thoughts returned to Joni. Though she was sitting less than five feet from me, she might as well have been a universe away.

I poked around at my food, trying to determine what to do about Joni. *What had I done when faced with seemingly insurmountable obstacles? I had pushed through them. Why would this be any different?* It was decided: I wasn't going to let something as trivial as race keep me from my sister. Time, distance, and circumstances had done enough damage, but we hadn't authored those conditions. Racial attitudes could be changed, but only if you are willing to fight through it. The only question was whether Joni would be willing.

"Hey, Marc," I said. "Would you mind taking Mason for a walk? I want to try and talk to Joni."

Raising a questioning eyebrow, he got up and walked over to Mason. Soon they were headed to the escalators. I let a moment pass and then walked over to where Joni sat. A new version of the carousel music began. "Do you mind if I sit down?" I asked.

She glanced at me briefly before returning her eyes to her plate. Again I was struck by the hollowness in her eyes. I pulled the chair out and winced as the metal legs screeched against the floor. "Look, Joni. I don't know why you feel the way you do about black people. But when I look at you, I don't see someone white. I see my sister, a sister I haven't had my whole life. You're the only sister I have and am ever going to have. We both have lost too much to let something like that keep us apart."

She began to cry, deep sobs that shook her rail-thin frame. She held a small, gray purse that she kept twirling in her hands. "The man who touched me when I was a little girl was black." She offered this as neither an explanation nor justification but simply as a statement of fact.

"Was this when we were with our mother?"

She nodded her head vigorously yes. I let out a long, slow breath of air. Joni's childhood innocence had been yet another casualty of our mother's wayward life.

I swallowed hard. "I won't pretend to understand what you went through, Joni. And I am so sorry you had to go through that. I really wish I could take away the pain that you have, that all of us have, but I can't. All I can tell you is this: whoever that monster was, he had nothing to do with me or anyone else who is black."

She raised her head up then and looked down the mall toward the crowded shops, putting a hand to her mouth to keep the sobs from escaping. "It still hurts," she whispered. Tears sprung from my eyes at this confession. Never before had I so wanted to assume another person's pain.

I stood up from my chair and came to kneel beside her. I put my hand on top of hers, and to my relief she did not pull away. I leaned close to her and whispered, "You have brothers now, Joni. No one will hurt you as long as we're here." It was the only thing I knew to say. Off in the distance, the music from the carousel had finally stopped.

Later that evening, the four of us were standing in front of La

Dolce Vita, an elegant Italian seafood restaurant twenty minutes away from Freehold. Joni's attitude toward me had thawed considerably; she even held my hand as we walked in. We milled about the lounge area for a few minutes, snapping pictures and looking at paintings, when the front door swung open.

As soon as Ben—neatly attired in a tan blazer, yellow shirt, and black jeans—walked in, I knew he was my brother. He was a shade over six feet, with an athletic build and a shock of perfectly coiffed blond hair. It wasn't these features that gave him away but the striking resemblance he bore to Joni. Both had deep-set, dark-brown eyes, pale complexions, and strong jawlines. Joni must have seen it, too, because as soon as he stepped into the small reception area she ran over to give him a huge hug, a scene similar to the one when she and I had met earlier that morning. And as she had with me, she was holding on to Ben for dear life.

When Joni finally let him go, Ben and I gave each other a warm embrace. "So you're the investigator," Ben said, once we separated.

"At your service," I said, laughing.

Marc and Ben shook hands, and I envied their familiarity. The hostess escorted us over to our table where a wonderful view of the ocean awaited. We sat down, Marc and I side by side; Mason, Joni, and Ben shoulder to shoulder on the other side of the table. Joni was directly across from me, Ben across from Marc.

Over drinks and appetizers, we talked about Ben's early life, how he had grown up in Tuckerton, how for years he had thought our mother was his aunt and Marc his cousin, how before Alzheimer's had overtaken our grandfather, he had asked Ben to take care of our grandmother, Loretta. It was a promise Ben had kept. Our grandmother had actually served as Ben's accountant as he built a very successful career in sales.

Our conversation turned to Joseph Murphy, our grandfather. In his honor, our mother had given all four of her sons the middle name Joseph. Joe was the son of Irish immigrants and a member of what Tom Brokaw would later call the Greatest Generation. A veteran combat infantryman who had risen to the rank of sergeant, he had stormed the beaches at Normandy, was wounded in combat in France and Germany, and earned several commendations, including a Bronze Star and a Purple Heart, two of the military's highest honors. He also battled what the military termed a "mother hen" complex, a near-paralyzing reluctance to send the young men under his command to what he knew would be their deaths. In August of 1945, three days after the Japanese surrendered, Joe Murphy was honorably discharged from the United States military, his service to country complete.

Americans took to the streets to celebrate the end of the war, but very few fully understood the sacrifices that the war had required. As did many soldiers who returned from World War II, Joe struggled, haunted by the faces of the young men he had seen perish. Peaceful sleep rarely came, for he was often awakened by nightmares. He drank frequently and Loretta and he were nearly separated. When Loretta sought the advice of Joe's commanding officer, his counsel was simple and direct: "These men have seen horrors you can't even imagine. And you can't erase it from their memory. So, young lady, you're going to have to decide if this is what you want. Because this probably won't ever get better."

Adding to Joe's postwar struggles were the difficulties of his oldest daughter, Marian. Early on, she had shown a contrarian personality, and with Joe away at war, nobody was around to rein her in. Marian's mother, Joe's first wife (also named Marian), struggled with severe mental health issues and was likely an alcoholic. Joe was so distraught by his first wife's behavior that, late one evening, he whisked away his daughter Marian and her younger sister, Josie. They never lived with their biological mother again.

Ben's recounting of the Murphy family history was interrupted by the waitress who came over to get our drink orders. We decided on bottles of red wine, except for Joni, who wanted vodka. We raised our glasses with the simple word "family" and toasted our brother Bernard.

By the time the waitress came back to get our dinner orders, Joni was ready for another drink. She polished this off faster than the first. I saw Ben cast curious glances in her direction.

The restaurant was now bustling with patrons and in the full flush of summer activity. The once-audible roar of the ocean was now gone, drowned out by clinking glasses and fast-moving waiters. Ben was about to resume the story about our grandfather when Joni interrupted him to tell us that she and Mason were getting married. Congratulations echoed across the table.

"She's got brothers now, Mason, so you're going to have to get our permission," I said with a smile.

"You can't run, either," Marc said. "With Steve around, you know we'll find you."

We all laughed, and Joni was beaming.

"Dem big too," Mason said in response. He pointed at the three of us and struck a double-biceps muscleman pose. Another burst of laughter erupted from our table.

As entrees of chicken cacciatore and meatball marinara came to our table, so did a steady stream of vodka. Joni was becoming increasingly inebriated. Her movements became more exaggerated and violent; she didn't reach for her glass as much as she snatched at it. When some of it spilled, she grew furious. Her language coarsened and became laced with profanity. As her behavior declined, Ben became quieter and quieter. At one point, he physically picked up his chair and moved it a couple of feet away from her. Joni seemed not to notice. She slammed her empty glass down on the table and bellowed, "I want a drink! Somebody get me a drink—*now!*" Other patrons turned to stare.

"You've had enough, Joni," Marc said patiently. Our collective silence seconded his motion.

"Forget you," she spat back. She shot up from her chair, bumping the table hard. Liquid from our glasses splashed across the table. She nearly fell, reaching out at the last minute to steady herself on Ben's chair. Mason opened his mouth as if to say something, but Joni sent a time-stopping glare in his direction. "Forget all of you," she said, pointing at us one by one, her index finger making a small semicircle around the table. She backed away from the table like a bank robber exiting the crime scene, eyes shifting right to left, before staggering off toward the bathroom.

Ben leaned over to me. "You asked me what our mother was like, what I remember about her." He nodded in the direction Joni had gone. His voice was hard and cold: "That. That's what I remember."

Ben paid for our dinner, and we went to the reception area to wait for Joni to emerge from the restroom. She came out several minutes later, her voice loud and abrasive, announcing her arrival well before she actually came into view. "Let's go!" she barked at Mason. The two of them strode right past us, stepped outside, and vanished into the night. Marc simply shrugged his shoulders, and Ben shook his head in disbelief.

I shook hands with Ben and Marc, and the three of us agreed to stay in touch. I stared at the door Joni had just walked through, and it hit me: The four of us might never be together again. A long-sought connection had been found and lost all at once.

I drove back to New Bedford the following morning, unpacking all the events of our reunion. It had not been ideal, but at least I finally had answers to questions I'd had nearly all my life. When I returned home to my dark, empty apartment, memories of Joni lingered in my mind. Over the next two nights, I wondered how she was doing and whether she was safe. The woman I met was so fragile, mentally and physically. How long could she survive, living the way she did? On the third night after I returned from New Jersey, I called her. A mechanical voice answered, and I left a message.

A week later my phone rang.

"Yeah, hello, is Steve there?" a woman asked, rather brusquely.

"You've got me," I said.

"It's me, Joni."

"Oh, hey—"

She cut me off. "I can't talk to you no more. You're black, and I can't talk to you no more. Don't call me here again." And with that the line went dead.

I stared at the receiver until the incessant beeping began. Then I hung it up gently.

Twenty years later, it remains our last conversation.

CHAPTER 35

Expectation is the root of all heartache.

—AUTHOR UNKNOWN

Discovering my mother's family and meeting Kenny's during the summer of 1991 was both cathartic and sobering. I'd chased the mystery of my family and my origins for as long as I could remember, yet when I miraculously caught it, held it down, and wrested the truth from it, I found a Pandora's box of pain and loss and suffering. My mother's life had cast a long shadow over the Murphy family and they appeared to want to close the door on the past. The Pembertons seemed fractured and disconnected. The family had never recovered from the fire that destroyed their home and the loss of Kenny's mother at an early age. Kenny's tragic end seemed to further divide them.

On my mother's side, my grandmother seemed the only one among the Murphys interested in knowing me. Ben had been so shocked by my sister's appearance that he wanted as much distance as possible from the entire affair. Marc had simply disappeared. I tried to schedule several trips to meet my mother's sister, Josephine, but our schedules never seemed to align. My efforts to locate my youngest brother, Bernard, were thwarted time and time again. And Joni had disowned me.

I had grown tired of it all, and so during the early fall, I consciously decided that I should let the Murphys and Pembertons go. Flicking them away with a sweep of the hand, I'd simply move on. There was just one more thing I needed to do.

For my entire life, the name Klakowicz shadowed me, igniting questions I was no longer interested in answering. Later, the search for my roots had confirmed my long-standing suspicion that Klakowicz was not my real name. In September 1991, I petitioned the Probate and Family Court Department in New Bedford to change my last name to Pemberton. I met briefly with a judge in his chambers so he could establish that I was not a criminal trying to change my identity. A legal notice indicating that I desired to change my name would run in the newspaper for several weeks. Unless there was an objection, my petition would go through.

While the notice was running, I spent a lot of time thinking about this decision. Friends questioned why I wanted to assume Kenny's last name; after all, his lawless reputation had endured even years after his death. Strangers in New Bedford asked me which Pemberton brother I belonged to. When I told them, they would take a step back, eyeing me warily, trying to determine whether Kenny's darkness lived in me too. Yet I had already carved a life and made profoundly different choices than he had. I simply wanted what was rightfully mine. And I wanted the name Pemberton as a legacy that I could pass on to my own children someday.

The petition went unchallenged, and in October 1991, I fully assumed the last name Pemberton. Armed with this new identity, I moved on.

PART 3

THE JOURNEY HOME

CHAPTER 36

Years passed, and although I occasionally called the Pembertons and the Murphys, I did not actively pursue a relationship with either family. In the late summer of 1991, I had accepted a position as an assistant director of undergraduate admissions at Boston College. I was back at the university I adored, entrenched in the work of higher education that I thoroughly enjoyed. Boston College had become a highly sought-after institution with a national and international footprint. I had responsibility for parts of the West, and suddenly I found myself flying to states I'd previously only heard of. In addition, I became an adviser to several student organizations and an informal mentor to many students.

When I eventually did reconnect with my family, it was as a result of developments in my romantic life. During the summer of 1995, I found myself on Martha's Vineyard, an island long popular with African Americans. A large group of my college friends rented a house less than a block away from Circuit Avenue in Oak Bluffs, a popular gathering spot for the singles crowd. Early in our stay, we decided to take a walk down the avenue. A light rain had been falling all morning, rendering the beach out of the question. As we turned the corner, the crowd of people on the avenue amazed us. Cars were parked next to the quaint clothing shops and overflowing restaurants. That summer's anthem, "This Is How We Do It" by Montell Jordan, pumped from car stereos. A line of people staggered out the door of Mad Martha's, the popular ice cream shop, known for its vast array of choices.

We walked down the avenue, bopping our heads to the music,

when we saw three or four African American women walking in our direction. We stopped to talk, and I stood next to Tonya, a strikingly beautiful woman with chestnut hair pulled back into a bun. She had a caramel-colored complexion, high cheekbones descending to a small, delicate mouth, a radiant, genuine smile, and deep brown eyes. She was also engaged, a fact my friends made sure to point out. We chatted for a few minutes about my career in college admissions and hers as an elementary schoolteacher in New Jersey. We would have continued talking, but the rain had picked up, and her friends were calling her to join them.

As she walked away, pulling the hood of her blue sweatshirt over her head, I was struck by her aura of an almost angelic innocence. *What an amazing spirit,* I thought. *Whoever marries her is going to be one lucky man.*

I saw her one other time that weekend. She was standing on a crowded beach, ankle-deep in the surf, looking out to sea, her arms wrapped around her shoulders, seemingly unaware of the impromptu game of beach volleyball that had sprung up right behind her. Dark sunglasses rested on her head, and she removed them momentarily to wipe a strand of hair away from her face. She appeared to be deep in thought. It reminded me of how I felt on my bike rides along Horseneck Beach. I knew not to intrude.

The following summer found me back on Martha's Vineyard, looking forward to another July Fourth weekend with friends. We rented the same house, a tan two-story New England colonial, down the street from Circuit Avenue. The number of people on the island seemed to have doubled from the previous summer, and large, exciting crowds met us everywhere we went. Our first night there, we got dressed early and headed out to a popular nightspot, Cat on a Hot Tin Roof. It was unusually humid, even by summer standards. The line was long, but we managed to make it in right before they starting turning away patrons. I was leaning against a pole and watching the ebb and flow of nightlife, when I felt a pair of eyes on me. I turned to see a stunningly beautiful woman, dressed in a white shirt and red pants. Every time I glanced up, I found her staring back at me, keeping her gaze on me so long that I finally had to look away. *Who is she?* I wondered. Finally, she and her friend began walking in my direction. I nodded at her and smiled as she walked past.

"How are you?" I asked. Her chestnut hair was long and framed her features. Her skin was bronzed and flawless. She was even more striking up close, a natural and effortless beauty.

She smiled and said, "I know you." My first thought was: *Now I understand why she has been looking at me so intently.* My second one: *How in the world can someone this beautiful know me without my knowing her?* I couldn't say that, of course. I wound up saying something else, something worse: "You *do?*"

The minute I said it, I wanted to take it back. She recoiled, frowning and leaning away from me. I had come across as an arrogant playboy in constant pursuit of attention. My arched eyebrow didn't help my cause. "I must be mistaken," she said, turning to walk away. She moved with such grace and style that I felt even worse for not recognizing her. Then it hit me: *Circuit Avenue... a light rain... a teacher... her smile. This was the woman I had met last summer, although she appeared even more graceful now.*

I touched her arm. "Are you still teaching?"

"I am," she said, smiling again.

"I didn't recognize you at first because your hair was pulled back then. But now I do. We were standing on Circuit Avenue, right near Mad Martha's. You had on a blue sweatshirt and yellow shorts. Your friends were giving you a hard time because they wanted to get going. They called you T."

Her smile had grown even bigger. "You do remember, don't you?"

I laughed, surprised by my own recollection. "You were also engaged."

"I was," she said, "but it didn't work out."

We tried talking for a while, but the music was so loud we could barely hear each other. Coming in, I had noticed a small garden with a few chairs. We sat down, away from the pounding music, and spent the remainder of the evening talking about our college days, our careers, the importance of education, and her family. She hailed from New Jersey and had grown up knowing her grandparents and their siblings. She'd gone to the University of Maryland before transferring to Rutgers, largely because of the cost. She'd also been a model and competed in the regional Miss USA pageant during her college years, ending that career path because teaching was her passion and love. A biology major and premed student in college, she had returned to school to get her master's degree in teaching.

For my part I told her a bit about my own past but kept it as general as possible: I'd grown up in foster care, and after twenty-four years had finally managed to locate my biological family, changing my last name. It had long been my rule to offer people I met the shortened version of my life, deliberately stopping the conversation before it turned toward how my childhood trauma had affected me. To say more than that would have assumed, I thought, an extraordinary degree of understanding on the other person's part. But I sensed those rules did not apply when it came to this beautiful stranger. After listening to me, she asked something no one had ever asked: "Does it still bother you?" Something in her eyes told me she was asking the question about herself.

"Not really," I said, shrugging my shoulders but not entirely sure this was the truth. "What's done is done, and there really isn't anything I can do to change it. There comes a time you have to move on."

She was sitting right across from me at a black circular table. Moonlight filtered down on us through wisteria leaves hanging off the white trellis.

She was very quiet. The moment passed, and we spoke of other things. She glowed as she told me about her mother, Shirley, and her brother, Doug. The three of them were close, driven together by her father's sudden departure from the family. As we continued to talk, I realized that it was Tonya's inner beauty that made her so breathtaking. She didn't define life by what she had or whom she knew. She seemed to see the world through the eyes of possibility. She struck me as the type of person who took a moment to enjoy the smell of a springtime flower or the quiet rush of a peaceful river. I was surrounded by cynicism and hopelessness for much of my childhood, and the search for my origins brought fresh battles that had exhausted me. But Tonya possessed a certain peace, as if life's storms had barely touched her.

For years I had wondered when I would meet the person I'd share my life with. I'd had a few relationships over the years—five years with Alicia, my first girlfriend; a year with Liz, from New Bedford; and four years with Andrea, from Chicago. While each of these relationships had been important to me, none rose to the level of a lifetime love. Ultimately we each went our separate ways, feeling as if we had met a good friend but not a soul mate. I hadn't stopped searching, though. As I sat in the alcove across from a woman I had met briefly once before, the entire world seemed to shrink to this one small place, and I wondered if my search had come to an end.

During the summer of 1996, I traveled almost every weekend from Massachusetts to New Jersey to visit Tonya. Often we'd spend the day in the picturesque tourist village of New Hope, Pennsylvania, located along the banks of the Delaware River and overflowing with restaurants, art galleries, and playhouses. Its tree-lined streets, modest homes, and antique shops spoke of a simpler time and offered an escape into a more romantic past. We strolled arm in arm, peeking into the charming shops and having dinner by the river. Early in our relationship, we both sensed there was more here than two people simply passing time. It was as if we had been traveling the same road for years. We talked more seriously about the future.

"What matters most to you?" I would ask.

"I have to be first in your life," she'd say. "I wasn't first to my father. And you? What matters most to you?"

"I won't live in the shadows," I'd respond. "Don't try to control me or dictate my path."

I began to tell her a bit more about my childhood: the battles with the Robinsons and the improbable discovery of my parents and the distance between their families and me. She listened quietly, interrupting only to ask a question here or there. She was especially curious about my early years. "How did you survive?" she asked one night, as we drove back to New Jersey from New Hope. "When my father left, I still had my mother and my brother and a large family. I knew people loved me. But you had no one—no mother, no father. I can't even imagine that—to have no one at all."

"I'm not entirely sure," I said. "I prayed a lot. I read a lot. I always thought the next day would bring another chance for me. I'd be one day closer to freedom, to finally finding my family."

"Have you ever seen anybody about this—you know, talked it through?"

"No, not at all," I said. "And I never will. I was forced to see psychologists when I was younger. They always questioned me as if *I* were the one with the problem. None of them identified what was going on at my foster home. All I really needed was just one person to intervene. Maybe it was the times—people just didn't get involved. But, I've always found my strength in talking to God. He's been my counselor."

During these day trips to New Hope, I realized that beneath Tonya's gentle spirit resided a quiet resolve shaped by her own hardships. Her father—a New York firefighter—had been in a serious motorcycle accident, and it took him nearly a year to recover. He was placed on disability by the city, effectively retired at the age of thirty-three. The loss of his livelihood had been too much, and he turned to alcohol and drugs to cope. The deeper he sank into addiction, the more he vanished as a person, shattering the family. When Tonya talked about him, I saw an aching and longing in her eyes, a pain no one could heal. Yet that setback had steeled her, forging a desire for a new life not defined by loss and heartache—a life similar to the one I wanted. I think she saw in me someone similarly uncompromising: a resolute man bent on righting the wrongs he'd inherited.

As we dated, I attended large family gatherings, laughing as her mother, brother, grandparents, cousins, uncles, and aunts shared colorful stories of their childhoods. Despite her father's absence, they had managed to find a new happiness. Their stories led me to daydream about my own family and whether it was possible for the Murphys and me to find our way forward, despite my mother's troubles. *Why hadn't we connected? Maybe we hadn't tried hard enough*, I reasoned, *and I'd had responsibility for that as well.*

During the late summer of 1996, I reached out again to the Murphys. My timing couldn't have been better (or as it would turn out, worse). My aunt Josie; her husband, George; and their four children—Jane, Laura, Renee, and George; as well as my brother Ben were all going to be in Tuckerton in a few weeks time, a rarity given their hectic schedules. They asked if Tonya and I would like to come spend time with them.

I hadn't been back to Tuckerton since 1991, but I was eager to introduce Tonya to a part of my history. Driving again down Tuckerton's Main Street, I was struck by the peaceful nature of this seaport community. The blue sky was open and cloudless. I rolled down my window and took in the cool air, the hum of traffic, and the occasional boat parked casually on a lawn. On the right-hand side was Stewart's, a bright-orange drive-in eatery, and across from that was Lake Pohatcong. An old wooden bridge abutted the lake, and ducks and geese glided and landed in its waters. It seemed so at odds with my mother's turbulent life. *She once drove through here*, I thought, and that familiar longing to feel connected to her resurfaced stronger than ever. Again I searched my memory, trying to recall something—*anything*—of my time with her. Once again, I turned up nothing.

It was early afternoon when Tonya and I arrived at my grandmother's. Her neighborhood sat right in the middle of a marina. Boats of different sizes dotted the landscape, more commonplace than trees. Down one of the small side streets was her home, a charming single-level powder-blue ranch. White awnings hung over two of the front windows and azaleas sat beneath them. At the base of one of the azaleas was a small American flag, faded but still fluttering in the early afternoon breeze. Small stones bordered her wide walkway, some of them seashells.

Loretta, or Grandma Murphy as I had taken to calling her, greeted us at the door. She was petite with large green eyes. Her light auburn hair was cut short, and one curl fell perfectly across her forehead. I bent down to give her a long hug. "It's so good to finally meet you," she said, escorting us down a short, narrow hallway stacked with books and papers.

"You too," I said. "You were more helpful to me than you know."

Off a modest living room was a den, and I could hear several voices as we approached. I recognized my brother Ben immediately. His blond hair had darkened a bit, but other than that, he had not changed much since our meeting a few years before. My aunt Josie was tall and blond—similar in appearance, I imagined, to my mother.

We shook hands with Josie's husband, George, and her youngest child, George Jr., and introduced ourselves to her daughters—Jayne, Laura, and Renee. Our introductions were formal, and there was no sense that we shared a common bloodline. The den that abutted the living room was small and quaint, painted the same powder blue as the rest of the home. It had several windows, and I could see the marina that ran through the neighborhood. On the back wall hung a picture of several different kinds of birds. Overhead a white ceiling fan thumped and whirred.

We sat down at a small table covered in a bright blue, cross-stitched tablecloth. Tonya and I sat shoulder to shoulder, and the Murphys sat in front of us. On the table my grandmother had placed a bag of Starburst candy, several glasses, and a tall pitcher of iced tea. Josie's family was beautiful, almost as if they had appeared out of a Norman Rockwell painting. Physical similarities flowed easily between them, including a finely chiseled jawline that seemed sculpted from granite. Based on the pictures on the wall of my grandmother's home, these features seemed to have originated from my grandfather Joseph

Murphy. I'd not seen a resemblance between my mother and me in any
of the pictures my grandmother had sent. I'd never noticed my own
jawline and hadn't given any thought as to whether it linked me to my
mother or to the Murphys. I'll have to remind myself to take a look, I
thought.

Our conversation began the way so many social conversations do.
I could tell that Josie and her husband George were good people and
wonderful parents who had built a solid foundation for their children.
Updates about their children's careers and college plans flew across
the table. There was also a bond and an intimacy there, an understanding that if all else failed, you still had your family by your side. How
wonderful that must be, I thought, to have grown up knowing where
you've come from, or that you were loved, or where you belonged. A
momentary pang of sadness overcame me as I once again realized that
my opportunity to experience those things had long since passed.

Tonya and I regaled them with the story of how she and I met.
Soon, though, the conversation turned to my childhood and I shared
with them the difficulty of those early years; the Robinson's Rules,
the long but ultimately successful battle to be free, the unanswered
questions about my identity, the strange last name of Klakowicz. They
listened quietly but intently and I could tell from the subtle shakes of
their heads and nervous rubbing of their hands that they had not fully
understood what had happened to Marian's children. Despite their
obvious empathy, there was a distance between the Murphys and me.
A hundred questions floated through my mind as I tried to identify
the source of that distance. Was it the shock of seeing one of Marian's
children, after all these years? Was it because I was black and they
were white? Was it that they hadn't tried to find me? Did they feel
partly responsible for what unfolded? Did I hold them responsible?

Those questions hovered like a dark cloud around the powder blue
room and, to avoid them, we turned to more pedestrian things, including my career in college admissions. How the admissions process really
worked was a source of some curiosity to the Murphys given that my

cousin Jayne, who ultimately chose the University of Pennsylvania, had applied to some of the nation's most selective colleges.

But that conversation opened the door to the rather uncomfortable topic of affirmative action. Suddenly, Ben and I began sparring over the merits of this controversial issue. The Jesuits at Boston College had taught me there were good people who simply thought differently than you might on a particular matter, who are as wedded to their beliefs as you are to yours. Having a healthy debate was often the first step toward resolution. And in this brother I barely knew, I found a ready and enthusiastic opponent—one who seemed no more willing than I was to back away from a debate or a challenge.

Still, I was decidedly uneasy. Affirmative action was a deeply charged topic and the lines of demarcation were as clear as black and white—in this case literally. In another time and place, this debate would not have been any different from the political discussions that sail back and forth across many family dinner tables. But on this unique occasion—meeting most of the Murphy family for the first time—a this-or-that, us-versus-them, seemingly black-versus-white confrontation made me increasingly uncomfortable.

I thought I could convince Ben that there was more to the issue than was readily apparent. "Ben," I said, "I hear what you're saying, but I'm afraid it's a bit more complicated than that. In fact, I would—"

"Really," he said, raising an eyebrow. "Doesn't seem like it to me."

"It doesn't?" I asked, smiling. "And how would you know?" Ben was a very successful businessman whose career path had not taken him to college. As the debate between Ben and I went on, there was a silence in the room from the Murphys. Out of the corner of my eye, I saw Tonya lean back in her chair, surprised that our conversation had taken this direction.

The discussion was beginning to exhaust me and I folded an orange Starburst wrapper, hoping the conversation would simply fade away.

Tonya saw my retreat and laid her hand gently on the table. "I really don't think Steve came here to have this discussion."

"Why not?" Ben said, turning toward me. "Because I'm right?"

"No," I said quietly. "Because you've already formed your opinion, and you don't seem to have any interest in another point of view. As I told you, it's more complicated than that."

Across the marina, a boat horn sounded, breaking the quiet that had descended upon the small room. Tonya chimed in again showing that trademark grace and class I would come to know so well. "Well, I don't think we are going to solve that issue today, at least not with you two in the room." She gestured at Ben and me. We all laughed.

Josie rose from her seat and picked up her glass of iced tea from the table, nurturing it with both hands. "Now, Steve," she said sweetly, "these people who raised you, what were they?"

"They were African American."

"And is that what you consider yourself?"

"It is. That was the community I grew up in and even though I didn't look like many African Americans around me, I still knew that's what I was."

"But how is that? You do have Irish blood, too, you know. A little bit of German too."

The conversation about affirmative action had no sooner faded than another emotionally charged issue had sprung up—the issue of my identity. Like many biracial people, I had encountered the perception that because I identified with one race I was denying another. But this family reunion was about something a lot bigger than race, and I was frustrated that it had again entered the conversation, seemingly trumping family.

Growing up in New Bedford, I'd heard stories of how whalers stared down into the depths looking for any hint of the enormous creatures, trying to determine where they would surface next. When they spotted a whale, it appeared as little more than a speck, but as it exploded to the surface its massive volume often swamped boat and crew. As I now realized, the issue of race had been like these whales— a barely discernible presence beneath the surface of our relationship.

The Murphys recognized me and accepted my existence, but there was a distance there. And now, with my girlfriend at my side, that distance appeared to be about race, threatening to derail the very delicate balance we'd been nurturing.

I let out a long, slow breath of air, trying to disguise my growing agitation.

"Aunt Josie, you have to understand. There was no one there to tell me I had Irish blood. I went to Boston College, a Catholic university with Irish roots, and the entire time I didn't even know my mother was Irish."

The topic we'd all avoided—my mother, her children, what had happened to us—was now in the room, larger than life.

Tonya gently placed a hand on my forearm, and I knew what the gesture meant—tread carefully.

"It was very difficult not knowing where I came from, who I looked like, where my family was, and why they had left me in that terrible situation."

The statement hung there like an accusation and was answered only by an awkward silence.

Josie looked away. The room again grew quiet, except for the whirring of the fan. I didn't express the other thought that had nagged at me since I had found the Murphys: Why didn't you ever look for me? If I hadn't found you, I'm not sure you'd have tried to find me. Didn't you ever wonder where Marian's children were or what had happened to them?

I kept this to myself because I sensed it would dramatically change an already fragile relationship.

"All I can tell you is that I am very proud to be African American. This is who I am. And if I am comfortable with that, then everybody else should be as well."

Grandma Murphy suddenly rose to her feet.

"Steve, have you ever seen your mother's letters?"

"No, Grandma, I haven't."

"Well, I'll go get them for you. I think I know exactly where they are." Her voice trailed away as she went deeper into the house. "They are in a back closet, I think."

The next few minutes were awkward. The Murphys talked among themselves about their careers and college. Tonya and I compared notes on the picturesque marina right outside the window. Finally, Grandma returned with a single letter.

"Here," she said, handing it to me. "From your mother."

The Murphys continued talking among themselves. I was entirely focused on the letter. This was the first possession of my mother's I had ever touched. The pages were tinged a faint yellow; the letter had not been opened in years and their perfect creases snapped as I unfolded them. I'd expected to see the ragged handwriting of a woman in tremendous turmoil, but instead I saw an artist's elegant penmanship. The letters were perfectly formed, the loops of the g's finishing with a flourish, the i's dotted exactly above their stems. Teachers had often asked where I'd learned to craft letters and words so artistically. I'd never really known; it just seemed natural to me. Now it was clear: I'd gotten that from my mother. I smiled to myself, shaking my head at this amazing commonality.

Through the open window I could see a small sailboat heading out of the marina. I laid the envelope on the small dining table and held the letter close, wishing that somehow this item my mother had touched could fill the cavernous void I felt at not knowing her. Tonya leaned over my shoulder and began to read with me. I can't remember my mother's exact words, but her message is seared upon my memory. It was addressed to her father. She wrote that she was ready to straighten out her life, ready to get back on her feet—all she needed was some money. She was tired of being tired, and most of all she wanted to get her children back, especially my youngest brother, Bernard.

Where was my name?

This thought had barely registered when I read the children's names again: Ben, Marc, Joni, Bernard, all in chronological order. I looked again.

It wasn't there. My name was brutally and inexplicably absent.

I scanned the letter again and again, hoping I was wrong—that if I read it one more time, I would see my name written in her beautiful hand, with the kind of care parents take when penning their children's names. But I knew my first glance had not deceived me. Like my father, my mother, too, had written me right out of her life, this time literally.

I doubt the Murphys had any clue how much emotion I was feeling just then. They were still deep in conversation—their conversation about colleges and careers now no more than distant chatter to me. Sighing heavily, I let the letter drop to the table and watched as it folded back into its original form. There was nothing more I wanted to read, no explanation that would ease the sting. I closed my eyes and rubbed my hand over my forehead. Tonya touched my hand softly, and when I finally looked up at her, I could see tears welling in her eyes. Outside, the sailboat had moved even farther out of the marina, its sail billowing in the late afternoon breeze.

I had been warned several times about digging up the past. And I had ignored that counsel, even as the defeats piled up (and the victories too). Some of this defiance reflected my belief that nothing I learned would hurt more than the pain of the Robinson years or the even greater difficulty of not knowing where I had come from. And there was something else as well. As long as I kept pursuing the past, I could keep alive the hope of discovering and enjoying a family.

The Pembertons' disconnected family, Joni's unwillingness to accept me, and the distance between the Murphys and me had begun to close the door on that dream. Now the slightly yellowed, perfectly folded letter had slammed it shut. And yet, despite this crushing discovery, I didn't want anyone to know how much it hurt—not Tonya, and certainly not the Murphys.

"Steve, are you okay?" Tonya asked, searching my face.

"I am, T," I whispered, patting her hand. Jayne came over to talk to Tonya, and I got up from the table and went to find my grandmother. I found her in the kitchen filling up a pitcher of iced tea.

"Grandma, where is your bathroom?" I asked.

"Around the corner," she said politely.

Stepping into the small bathroom without windows, I flicked on the light, turned on the faucet, and splashed cold water on my face, letting the water run from my face into the sink. When I felt ready to go back out, I remembered that I had wanted to see if I had the same jawline as my relatives. Staring into the mirror, I saw that I did; it was the only physical resemblance I could discern. I lingered for a moment longer, and then turned out the bathroom light, ready to leave this lonely place, determined never to return.

CHAPTER 37

History, despite its wrenching pain,
Cannot be unlived, but if faced
With courage, need not be lived again.

—MAYA ANGELOU, "ON THE PULSE OF MORNING"

I can't say I remember much about the ride back to Tonya's home in central New Jersey. From time to time, Tonya reached over and laid her hand on mine. I sat in the passenger seat and looked out the window, watching the trees whipping by, still too stunned to talk. We did not return to her mother's house as we had planned but, instead, went to Colonial Park near her home in Somerset. With its gardens and arboretum, the park was a popular place at all times of the year but especially in summertime. Large, grassy fields and a vast open sky offered a freedom not easily found in the hectic pace of everyday life. People strolled slowly along the many walking paths to take in the fragrant irises, peonies, roses, and lilies. There was a peace and quiet here. We parked and walked over to the lake. Clouds were rolling in—a summer storm—and the staff was waving the paddleboats back to the small dock.

We didn't go to the gazebo but instead sat down at the base of one of four weeping willows that lined the banks. Tonya had pulled a blanket from the car, and I spread it out on the ground. She sat, legs crossed at the ankle, and patted the spot next to her. I shook my head no and stood a few feet away, tossing small pebbles into the water. "Steve, talk to me," she said gently. "Are you okay?"

That was a good question. Ordinarily my response would have been a quick, emphatic yes. But now I had to think about it. For years I had remained above my own story, soaring like a bird over a landscape, gazing down but unwilling to land. Perhaps this was nothing more than a survival mechanism, one now rendered useless by Marian's letter. A duck glided across the pond and then landed, sending little ripples toward us. The seas of gray clouds were now being blown away by a more ominous color of gray. The wind had picked up. "I know that I will be okay," I said, "because I always have been, but this . . ." I shook my head in a side-to-side motion.

I'd always been stubborn and willful, never more so than in pursuit of my origins. Even after I learned who my parents were, I kept asking questions because, maybe, I would find different answers. Perhaps somewhere I would learn that my parents had fought for me, that I had meant something to them. The revelation that I'd been an inconvenience, a child simply discarded, was the greatest disappointment of my life. All those years of longing and dreaming had represented little more than the naive quest of a boy who had stubbornly refused to let go of his one childhood wish. It was time for me to be done with it all, to stop playing the role of a time traveler trying to change the past. Although part of me would always long for what had been lost, I needed to end this fruitless task of trying to reclaim my history as if it were an antique capable of restoration.

I looked out over the nearly empty park. The big question now was what to do next. *How do you overcome something like this? How do you live a meaningful life when you know for sure that your mother and father didn't want you? How do you become a man?* As the crew locked up the last of the paddleboats, the sound of the heavy chains rattling, I realized that the answer to that question had been in front of me all along. Alongside my lifelong mission to find my family had been another, relentless quest. It had begun as a child, formed in the darkest of days in the basement of the house on Arnold Street, furthered as I plotted my escape during my teenage years, and solidified as I grew into manhood. It's a quest that continues to anchor me today. I could build. I could create a better life than the one I had inherited. *I can end this*, I thought. *All of it. I can make certain this never happens again. I can begin anew. Right now.* I extended my hand to Tonya and together we hurried toward the car to beat the storm.

The coming days and months would bring a realization of how fortunate I was, despite all that had been lost. My career in college admissions gave me as much pleasure as ever. One of the best parts of my job was the ongoing opportunity I had to read applicant essays. Out of those papers poured the unique life stories of thousands of students and their families: where they had been, where they were going, what they had overcome. For months on end, I sat by my fireplace in the dead of winter, the essays on my lap, logs cracking and popping, snow falling gently outside my window, marveling at these amazing tales of human resilience. Those stories helped me realize that, although tragedy and loss are regrettably commonplace, we aren't measured by what happens to us but rather by how we respond to it.

And that had not been my only blessing. Around this time I met Dierdre and Russell Jackson, a wonderful couple from Los Angeles; she was an aide to the lieutenant governor, and he was an anesthesiologist at Cedars-Sinai. They were deeply spiritual, caring, and loyal. While I was having dinner with them in Los Angeles one night, they made an announcement: they were going to adopt me. I laughed openly at their humor. I was then in my midtwenties—too old, I reasoned, to be adopted. But they did not return my laughter. "You are never too old to have parents. So, we are going to be your parents, and there really is nothing you can do about it. Pass the water, please."

Just before going back to New Jersey to meet Aunt Josie and her family, I had begun to share my own story. I had long been reluctant to talk about it publicly—not because I felt ashamed or embarrassed but because I wasn't sure that talking about it would help anyone. As it turned out, my tale seemed to enthrall my audiences, whether college students or professionals attending national conferences in their fields. They, too, were trying to help family members or were struggling to repair their own fractured pasts. After I spoke, they came up to me, grabbed me gently by the arm, looked deep into my eyes, and told me that I did not look like my story. I would respond by saying that none of us really do; it is impossible to tell, from a single glance, the journeys someone has traveled, the experiences that have made them who they are. Ultimately, I realized that what they were really asking was how I managed to survive.

Tonya had been asking me the same thing. For years I had never really known the answer to their questions. There had been a period in my late teens and early twenties when I had carried a hubris that bordered on arrogance, a belief that I had survived because of my own strength. But maturity had shown me that though willpower may have had something to do with it, it wasn't the sole reason or even the predominant one. Still, I groped for answers. *Why had I survived?*

Clarity came soon enough. I was speaking to a conference of foster parents and caregivers in Columbus, Ohio. Afterward, many members of the audience came up to share their appreciation of my remarks or to ask me a question. One particular woman caught my eye because she kept allowing others to cut in front of her. I realized she wanted to be the last one in the line. Nearly an hour passed, and still she waited. She was middle-aged and white, had long brown hair, and wore a pantsuit that matched the color of her hair.

The last person stepped away, and finally she walked up. The only people left were the conference organizers and the hotel staff breaking down the room for the next event.

"You've been really patient. I just hope I can answer your question," I said as she approached.

"Oh, I don't have a question," she said. "There is something I need to tell you. I was sitting there listening to you, and it just came over me, and I wanted to make sure I told you."

I folded my hands in front of me. There was a quiet intensity emanating from her dark green eyes.

"Yes, ma'am."

"What I want to tell you is . . . God is not done with you yet." And she quickly turned on her heel and exited the room.

In the most difficult times, I always found comfort in prayer. I first discovered this comfort as a small boy in the basement of the house on Arnold Street. I don't know how I knew to pray; the Robinsons rarely went to church. Still, I found that peace and quiet and strength often followed my humble requests. I talked to God the way one talked to a best friend. These petitions had changed from desperate pleas to lighten Willie Robinson's hand to earnest appeals to help me find my family.

The kind stranger had reminded me that God had been there all along—never more than in the last several years when I found my biological family and met Tonya.

I didn't realize it then, but God was about to really show up.

In the fall of 1996, several weeks after returning home from my ill-fated trip to visit the Murphys, I received a strange phone call. I was in my office packing for an admissions trip to California when Marci, my assistant, knocked on the door and said a caller was on the line. Usually she just put the call through. But standing there in the doorway, shifting her weight nervously from side to side, I could tell that this call was different.

"Who is it?" I asked.

"Well . . . he says he is your brother."

"Is it Ben or Marc?" I asked, smiling. This was a pleasant surprise. I had not heard from either of them in some time.

"Neither," she said. "At least, I don't think so. He says his name is Mr. Sanchez."

I stopped packing and looked up at Marci. "I don't have a brother named Sanchez."

"Well, he said you do. And he won't give his first name."

How strange. Neither Ben nor Marc had the last name Sanchez. Who could it be? A fraternity brother? A friend pulling a practical joke?

"Steve," she said, pulling me from my reverie. "What should I do? Put the call through?"

"Sure, sorry, Marci. Please, put it through."

She left my office, and I walked over to my desk, waiting for the call. My office overlooked the famed Quad at Boston College, an intersection of four of the university's oldest buildings. On this particular day I had my window open to allow the last vestiges of summer in. Students hustled in between classes while snippets of their conversation drifted up to me. I was too perplexed to sit, so I just stood there, staring down at the phone. When it finally rang, I picked it up slowly, taking advantage of the pause to try one last time to figure out who this caller might be.

"Hello? Hello?" someone on the other end of the line said.

"I'm here," I said, pulling the phone closer to my ear.

"Hi," a voice said. There was a long pause.

"Yes?" I asked.

"I'm looking for Steve Klakowicz." The voice was soft and quiet.

"This is he." It would take too long to explain to a stranger that Klakowicz was no longer my last name.

"You're my brother," this voice said emphatically, the softness replaced by conviction.

"I don't have a brother with the last name of Sanchez," I said. "My youngest brother's name is Bernard Klakowicz."

"Well," the voice said, "that *was* my name before my adopted family changed it."

I stood there, stunned, holding the receiver to my ear. Though I had spent considerable time and effort looking for him, it hadn't occurred to me that my youngest brother would have been adopted and assumed a different name. Nor had it dawned on me that he would also have been searching for *his* family. I thought I had been the only one yearning for a connection.

My brother sensed I needed more convincing. "Our mother's name is Marian," he said.

"Yes, it is," I said slowly. His use of the present tense told me he thought our mother was still alive. I knew what his next question was going to be. The bells from Gasson Tower had begun to ring loudly. I turned toward the sound, letting the breeze from the open window gently buffet my face. A lone student sauntered down the walkway toward the student center, her casual pace suggesting that her day of classes was over. "Bernard," I said, closing my eyes. "Our mother . . . we lost her . . . a long time ago."

There was a long silence on the other end. I didn't know much about his life, but I could imagine what he was going through, the pain he felt. *Take as much time as you need, brother,* I thought. I walked over and closed the door to my office. When he finally spoke, his voice was barely more than a whisper: "I was hoping that it wouldn't be true, but I already knew."

It took a few minutes for him to collect himself, but then we spent some time getting to know each other. He lived in Florida as a mortgage broker. He was married and was the proud father of a two-year-old girl. His adoptive family's name was Sanchez, so while he was growing up, everyone thought he was Hispanic. With olive skin and wavy hair, he certainly looked the part. "In truth," he said, "I don't really know what I am because I don't know who my father is."

"Believe me, I know how you feel," I said, nodding. I spent a few minutes describing my own quest to discover my father's identity and learn about his life. "So your name is Bernard Sanchez?" I asked.

He sighed. "Well, yes and no. You're not going to believe me."

"At this point, I can believe just about anything."

He cleared his throat, like an old man of the sea getting ready to spin a yarn. "Like I said, the family who adopted me already had the last name of Sanchez. But shortly after I went to live with them, I asked them if I could change my first name. I was adamant about it. I wanted to get away from the name Bernard and any other reminders of the past. So my new foster family agreed. At that time, I had no idea I had any siblings, let alone what their names were. It came down to James or Steven, and I decided to go with Steven as a name."

I whistled loudly. You couldn't make this up if you tried. My brother had no idea he had siblings yet had chosen the same name as the sibling closest to him in age. What were the chances?

"Now you know why I was afraid to tell your assistant my first name," he said. "I thought you'd hang up on me."

Outside my front door, I could hear the admissions office starting to shut down for the day.

"What do you remember of our mother?" I asked.

Again, a long silence followed. I sensed that if he had been standing in front of me, I would have noticed a faraway look in his eye, except that the emotions were not distant at all, nor perhaps ever would be. "I remember many things," he said. "Living in a house that was half burned down, men in and out of her life. One time, when I was about six years old, I watched a man beat her. And when I tried to stop him, he started to beat me too."

A searing image passed before my eyes, one of a little boy fighting to defend his mother. Tears welled.

"She was blond and was always focused on her hair," Steven continued, "and she loved vodka. I can still remember the smell. I remember always being hungry. I remember her leaving me in a lot of different places, with a lot of different people. She always promised she'd return. She usually did, too, but only when the police came looking for her. One day when I was seven years old, she left me at an orphanage in Springfield. I kept waiting for her to come back. Two weeks later, she still hadn't returned, but I still believed she was coming back, that this time wasn't going to be different from the others. Then one afternoon . . . I can't remember how it came up . . . I told one of the staff who worked at the orphanage that my mother was going to come back for me . . . he was mean, and I still remember when he snarled at me . . . 'You don't get it, do you? Nobody wants you'—and he smiled when he said it. But what I remember most is how much we were constantly on the move."

Outside my window the sun had begun to set, casting off a

beautiful arrangement of oranges and purples and pinks, the rich hues blending in with the magnificent trees and Gothic architecture that framed the campus. Sunsets, the sheer majesty of them, have often struck me as God's way of letting us know he is here. Some of them, like the one I saw that late summer day, are so majestic, so awe-inspiring, that it can only be God showing off.

But God does not show off just in sunsets. He appears in quiet whispers and coincidences that bring new beginnings that change the arc of your life, awakenings so powerful that you mark time by them. My brother's sudden arrival had brought such an awakening, so transformative and arresting that I had to lean against my office wall. For the first time, I fully understood that none of us had emerged unscathed from the storms that had engulfed our mother. My brother Steven had not. Nor had my older brothers, Ben and Marc. Joni certainly had not.

Our mother had failed at nearly everything, but her greatest failing was motherhood. She brought six lives into the world, and the five of us who survived would each crash through our childhoods like bumper cars at an amusement park, spinning in circles, slamming into one object and then another, desperately trying to find a clear path. We would make it to adulthood, scathed and scarred, trying to convince ourselves that we were not the accidental offspring of a tortured woman who had forsaken us.

My brother and I spoke for a few more minutes before hanging up. I gave him telephone numbers for Ben, Marc, Joni, Josie, and our grandmother, who I told him was actually our step-grandmother. I didn't have the heart to tell him what I knew about Joni. Much as I had, he had spent his life trying to find out what had become of his family. I knew well the joy of finally having answers, and I did not want to intrude on that happiness by sharing the tragedy that encircled us as children.

After we hung up, I sat in my office for a little while longer. During my conversation with Steven, Marci had slipped my itinerary under my doorstep. There was no one in the office save Mike, the elderly custodian. He knocked on my door, as he often did, looking for my trash barrel. I'd always made it a point to say hello and have a quick chat because he reminded me of the guys I'd worked with the summer after my freshman year of college. And I also loved his thick Irish brogue.

"Working late, eh?" he asked, his hand on the doorknob.

I came out from behind my desk. "I am. I have a trip to California tomorrow."

He turned to go.

"Hey, Mike," I asked. "Did I ever tell you I was half Irish?"

He smiled and pulled up a chair.

CHAPTER 38

In January 1997, a few months after meeting Steven and some six months after my visit with the Murphys, I proposed to Tonya. To the degree that any marriage proposal can be, mine was anticlimactic. I knew almost as soon as I met her that she was the person I wanted to spend the rest of my life with. I proposed to her from the top of Boston's Prudential Center, which offers a 360-degree view of this beautiful, historic city. Through tears of joy and much to my relief, she accepted. We set the date for late June and set about planning the wedding. Our relationship had been long distance, but as the date neared, I found myself often traveling back to New Jersey to assist with preparations.

A new peace was settling upon me. Talking with my brother Steven had given me a broader and deeper awareness of my mother's life. For the first time I began to feel for her and the long, hard road that had been her existence. Mother's Day had always been a day for others to celebrate; it carried no special meaning for me. But Marian was my mother, the woman who brought me into the world. I decided I would go to her grave and place flowers there. I suspected I would be her only visitor that day.

I needed to find out where she was buried, so I called my grandmother. After exchanging a few pleasantries, my grandmother told me my mother was buried in Greenwood Cemetery in Tuckerton. "Why do you want to know?" she asked, the rich tone of her voice crackling across the line.

"Well, I'm going to be in New Jersey, and I would like to go place flowers on her grave."

There was a long pause. "When will you be coming, Steve?"

"Around nine Sunday morning, Grandma. Tonya and I need to get back for a meeting in the afternoon."

There was a momentary pause. "Why don't we join you?" she said quietly. "Your aunt Josie and her husband will be here, and I know your brother Ben wants to see you as well."

"I'd like that, Grandma. By the way, where is Marc?"

She sighed. "Well, Marc is off again. Sometimes we hear from him, and sometimes we don't. But he'll turn back up. He always does."

Greenwood Cemetery is right off Route 529. There are several single-lane roads that serve as entrances to this nearly two-acre plot of land. A black wrought iron fence, no more than hip high, runs the entire length of the cemetery. Large maple trees stand like guardians at the entrances, and their branches, in the full bloom of summer, cast shadows over the entryway. This small quaint piece of earth is my mother's final resting place. I didn't need to look to find her gravestone. As soon as Tonya and I pulled into the cemetery, I could see my aunt Josie, her husband George, my grandmother Loretta, and my brother Ben huddled together.

I stepped from the car carrying a basket of flowers, and I held it in my hand as I gave everyone a hug. We stood there in silence for a moment, staring at my mother's gravestone. The sculpted stone sat above the earth, and it glimmered and shone in the early morning sunshine. Small blades of grass grew from the soil, and they cast small shadows on her marker. I pulled a few of them away, when Ben knelt down and began to remove the grass as well.

I placed the basket of flowers down next to her stone, deliberately obscuring the date of her passing. Above her name, in capital letters, was the word DAUGHTER. Below her name were her date of birth, October 12, 1937, and her date of passing, January 30, 1978. On the stone, the space between those dates was little more than a couple of inches wide. But in life, that space had been filled with so much loss and suffering.

Something else caught my eye: The last name I carried for nearly all my life—Klakowicz. Here, on my mother's gravestone, it had been misspelled: Klakowitz. Rudolph Klakowicz, Marian's first husband, had disappeared from the Murphys' view some twenty years before my mother passed, and I understood why they would not have recalled the spelling of such a complex name. I was certain that no one but me knew her name was spelled incorrectly.

Of her surviving children, I was the only one who had no memory of my mother. Absent those remembrances, this name had been the only thing connecting me to her. But it had not belonged to either of us. My relentless pursuit of my past had given me the opportunity to change my name, to finally shed that ill-fitting label. And that had given me a certain peace, a peace my mother never knew. The irony of my mother resting under a misspelled name, one that was never really hers, saddened me, and I felt anew all that had gone wrong for her.

I rubbed my finger over the letter *t*, as if doing so would remove it from the stone. Behind us, traffic hummed down the street. A flock of birds flew overhead and settled in a nearby pine tree.

Josie adjusted her sunglasses and began to talk in a low, hushed tone. I stood up so I could hear. "Your mother was my sister, and I loved her. But she was so very troubled. We tried everything we could to help her, but it was impossible because she fought us every step of the way. There were times when we thought we'd get her back, that she would come back to the family, but . . ." She choked out the last word and began to weep deep sobs of loss and regret. George rubbed her back, and she laid her head on his shoulder.

Out of the corner of my eye, I could see Tonya nodding in complete understanding, recalling her own father's battles with addiction. She, too, began to sob.

I was not a complete stranger to the damage of addiction; I had seen it in my sister Joni. Yet I'd never truly known what it was like to lose someone you've known and loved your entire life to addiction— the helplessness you felt as they turned into a complete stranger, the overwhelming despair as you watched, powerless to stop their descent into an abyss from which they could not emerge. I'd had no comprehension of what my mother's difficulties had done to her family, how they had forced brutal choices on them.

Josie removed her sunglasses to reveal red-rimmed eyes. "I was so young when Marian was having all her trouble. George and I had just gotten married, and we just wanted to get our life started. When I look at what happened to all of you, I wonder if we could have done more. Could we have done more?" She asked it again as if she were asking for the first time. "I don't know. I just don't know."

She raised a trembling hand to her mouth. "My father was never the same after she died. We had been through so much with Marian." She turned to Loretta. "You were a saint. You went through so much after my dad came back from the war and through all the trouble with Marian. You did a great job of raising Ben." She turned back toward me. "We wanted to put it all behind us, to just forget about what happened to her and to all of you. And I wanted to have a life that would be free of all those painful memories."

A gentle sun warmed us. Several cars had pulled into the cemetery since we'd arrived, but I'd barely noticed. Now as I turned to look, I saw families spilling out, flowers in hand, coming to pay their respects to their matriarchs.

For years, the Murphys and I had been on two completely different missions: I had been furiously chasing the past, believing it would bring me the perfect family I had envisioned as a little boy. The Murphys had been trying to forget that same past, for there appeared to be nothing there but painful reminders of lost children and a family fractured beyond repair. There had been no manual to deal with our divide, and in its absence we saw one another through the clouded lens of distance and difference. With no understanding of our common suffering, we had retreated to the worlds from which we'd come, staggering off to our respective corners like two spent fighters at the end of a final round.

But now I think we both realized that families are not always made up of faultless parents, magnificent homes, perfectly manicured lawns, and white picket fences. Behind these idealized pictures of American life are often other stories of hardship and loss, pain and suffering. That, too, is part of every family's history. Yet what makes a family is neither the absence of tragedy nor the ability to hide from misfortune, but the courage to overcome it and, from that broken past, write a new beginning.

"Steve," Josie said, "I thought a lot about what you said when you were here last, how difficult it was for you. You are a miracle; nobody should have survived what you did. But you've done so well for yourself. So have you, Ben. And knowing your mother as I did, she is probably looking down at both of you and saying, 'Look at my sons, Josie. Look at the men they have become. You see, I did do something right.'" And a fresh wave of tears overcame her.

We were all crying then. Tonya came to stand next to me and wrapped an arm around my waist. Ben came over and clapped me on the shoulder. We stood shoulder to shoulder, peering down at my mother's grave, quiet weeping the only sound among us, crying for ourselves and for Marian too. After a few moments, my grandmother turned toward me.

"Steve, when you were here last time, you seemed to think that we never looked for you. But that wasn't true. Your grandfather did look for you; he looked for all of you. He tried and tried." A soft breeze ruffled her beautiful auburn hair. "But the agency in Massachusetts wouldn't give us any information about you. They had a large case file, but they wouldn't let him see it. You have to understand, your grandfather was orphaned when he was a little boy, and he knew what it was like, the questions the three youngest children would always have. The last time he called was right after your mom passed."

She gazed off into the distant cluster of maple trees that framed the back of the cemetery. "I couldn't hear the other end of the conversation, but I remember he kept saying, 'You don't understand; these are my grandchildren.' After a while, he realized they weren't going to tell him. He got so angry that he hung up the phone right in the middle of the conversation. He walked out to the backyard and just leaned against the tree. It was a long while before he came back inside."

It was a stunning revelation, and I shook my head in amazement. My long-held perception that the Murphys had not looked for me was not true.

Joseph Murphy is buried right next to his daughter. A small, faded American flag accompanied his headstone; it had likely been there since the previous Memorial Day. Just a few feet away is another memorial, this one a shining bronze plaque commemorating his heroism in service to his country. Years before my grandmother had given me a picture of my grandfather standing outside an enlistment center, handsomely attired in his World War II uniform. He looked to me like a younger version of Ben: tall and erect, handsome and square jawed. That had always been my picture of Joseph Murphy, the grandfather I'd had no memory of. Now it had been replaced by the image of a once-orphaned, suspender-wearing grandfather, a World War II hero with a mother hen complex, engaged in a futile quest for his grandchildren.

We had been at Greenwood Cemetery for more than an hour, and it was time to leave. We exchanged long embraces and walked back to our cars. I reached for Tonya's hand and looked into her eyes. A wordless question passed from me to her. "Yes," she replied, "you should."

I turned toward the Murphys. "Before we go," I said, "we are getting married next month, right here in New Jersey. It would mean a lot to us if you could come."

We were suddenly swarmed with congratulations and well wishes.

"So we will see you, then?" I asked.

"Absolutely," Josie said, beaming. "We wouldn't miss it for the world."

CHAPTER 39

The readiness is all.

—WILLIAM SHAKESPEARE, *HAMLET*

For weeks Tonya and I had been reading almanacs, watching weather forecasts, desperately hoping it would not rain. As our wedding day neared, it became clear that it would not, and we finally breathed a sigh of relief. Wedding days planned for the outdoors don't lend themselves to last-minute changes in schedule. As the limousine carried my college friend and best man, Tim, and me over to Colonial Park, I smiled, thinking back to the night I had seen Tonya on Martha's Vineyard a year earlier. That weekend she had asked for my last name. "Pemberton," I had replied. "And one day that will be your name too." And now that day was here.

The limousine glided into the parking lot, and I stepped from it, breathing in the clean, fresh air. Suddenly I was overcome with emotion. Seated in front of the gazebo was everyone who was important to me: my brothers Ben and Steven; my grandmother Loretta; my uncle Greg, his wife, Sonie, and their three children; Aunt Josie, her husband, George, and their son, George III; John Sykes; Eddie Robinson; Tim's parents, Herbert and Cookie; my friends in admissions at Boston College; my fraternity brothers; Russell and Dierdre Jackson and their son, Perry; several of my students from Upward Bound. As I walked toward the gazebo, they formed an impromptu receiving line, drowning me in hugs, backslaps, and kisses.

As far as I am concerned, Colonial Park Arboretum and Gardens in central New Jersey has never had a day as beautiful as that late day in June 1997. A long, shimmering, white runway ran the length of the garden leading up to a small gazebo. Blooming soapwort and creeping thyme nestled alongside Japanese black pine and flowering hamamelis. To the right of the gazebo, a gilded white cage housed two doves that we would release at the ceremony's end. In the distance, the low drone of an airplane sounded. Geese flew overhead, honking their approval.

Steven and Ben escorted my grandmother Loretta up the aisle. Tonya stepped out of the long, white limousine (and from the pages of a bridal magazine, it seemed) and onto the lush grass of the garden. She walked up the runway toward me, escorted by her brother and her father, who had returned for her wedding. Halfway to me, she stopped to give her mother a yellow rose. A wonderful peace settled over me.

The wedding celebration continued at the reception hall at Bridgewater Manor. From time to time, I found myself looking around the reception hall, marveling at the sheer implausibility of this day. I had found my family after so many years, and we had all found it in our hearts to overcome our pain so as to create a new beginning. It occurred to me that never again would this group of people be assembled, and I wanted to savor this moment for as long as I could.

"Your father would be very proud of you," a voice suddenly said. I turned around to find my uncle Greg, a father of three and a successful physical therapist in Athens, Georgia. A broad smile framed the deep-set Pemberton eyes and prominent brow I had also come to see in myself. Several of my friends, who had never met another Pemberton, actually commented on the physical similarity between us. I had met Greg several years earlier, and over the years we had grown close, bonded by our common desire to write a different story for this generation of Pembertons.

Friends and family surrounded Tonya in the center of the dance floor, dancing around her as she laughed and smiled. "Can I make a confession?" I asked Greg.

"Sure," he said.

I took a deep breath. "Nearly everyone I have met has told me that Kenny would be proud of me. And to be honest, I've always felt he never had the right to be proud."

He thought for a moment. "I understand that. I really do. When the fire destroyed our home and scattered our family, most of my family was lost to me. And your grandfather was almost as distant to me as Kenny was to you. And Kenny was what he was, and wasn't what he wasn't. But he understood some things, even if he didn't live by them. Here's what you need to know: you are the man he could have been."

Off in the distance, the wedding coordinator was calling Tonya and all single women to the dance floor. I smiled as I watched my grandmother stand up and join the group. I extended my hand to Greg, and he took it warmly. "Thanks for coming and being part of our day. It wouldn't have been the same without you. I just hope I can build the family you have."

He winked. "I wouldn't bet against you, Steve."

Cheers and a rhythmic clapping erupted in the middle of the dance floor. My brother Steven was in the middle of the swaying crowd, dancing salsa with anyone brave enough to volunteer. There weren't many takers, since Steven was good, real good. His tie whirred and snapped, his feet chopped and glided as he spun his partner around the floor. I threw my head back in unbridled laughter. A short while later, I felt a tap on my shoulder. It was my aunt Josie, beautiful in a light-green blazer and matching skirt. Behind her were her husband, her son, my grandmother, and my brothers, Ben and Steven. Something was certainly up. Aunt Josie did not seem too pleased, either, a fact she confirmed as soon as she began to speak. "Now, Steve," she said sweetly, "we have something of a problem here." Her tone was pleasant enough, but there was the slightest hint of annoyance.

I glanced over at Ben. As soon as we made eye contact, he looked up, taking a sudden interest in the iridescent chandelier, nudging our cousin George. "Hey, Ben," I called. He ignored me, still looking up at the chandelier. I called him again, louder this time, "Ben, I know you hear me."

"Huh, what?" he asked, a sheepish grin spreading across his face.

"How much trouble am I in?" I asked.

He put a hand about twelve inches above his six-foot frame. "Oh, only about that much."

I put my hands out in mock indignation. "And you're not going to help me? I thought you were the oldest."

"Hey, bro, I've got to drive back with her," he said, laughing.

I pointed a menacing finger in his direction.

"That's enough, you two," Josie warned. Turning to me, she said, "I see this photographer running around taking all these pictures. And I am sure he is doing a wonderful job. And, of course, your friends are all such nice people. But we"—she gestured behind her—"we are your family, and you haven't taken a picture with us yet. And that," she said, folding her hands in front of her, "is why we have a problem."

I bowed my head and smiled. She was exactly right. In the hustle and bustle of the day, I had forgotten to take a picture with my mother's family.

Josie stepped away from the small entourage and adjusted my flower, which didn't need adjusting at all. "Isn't that nice?" she said lightly. "Your flower is the same color as my outfit. And you look so handsome today. A king if there ever was one." She lowered her voice so only she and I could hear. "Now, you know we really can't leave until you take a picture with *your* family. So can you be a dear and tell the photographer? We will be standing right here waiting for you." And with that she stepped back.

I went to find the photographer.

CHAPTER 40

I n July 1997, after our weeklong honeymoon in Cancun, we returned to New Jersey to pack up Tonya's things. We had decided to live in Massachusetts, where I would continue my career in undergraduate admissions and she would work as a teacher. We had a small one-bedroom apartment in Newton and a beat-up Oldsmobile Cutlass that would turn off when we went through a puddle. We also had more debt than both our salaries combined. Still, we had each other and went about enjoying our new life together.

One night a few weeks into our marriage, at about three in the morning, my eyes blinked open. There was an empty space beside me where Tonya should have been. I sat up and heard muffled sounds in the kitchen. I waited for a few minutes, expecting her to come back to bed. When she didn't, I got up and walked into our tiny kitchen. In the darkness, sitting on a stool at the island, was Tonya, head bowed and hands clasped. A soft moonlight came through one of the windows and lightly touched her shoulder.

"Hey," I asked, "what's going on?"

She looked up, and in a glance I could see that she was upset. She tried to speak, but each time, she couldn't get the words out. A thousand thoughts ran through my mind. *Does she think we made a mistake? Did we get married too soon? Is she having second thoughts?*

"What do we do now?" she asked.

We had been so busy planning the wedding, the honeymoon, and her move to Massachusetts that we hadn't thought much about the life that would follow. What was marriage supposed to be like? I think we both sensed the stakes were a bit higher for us than for many newlyweds, that we were not only trying to build a life for ourselves but also trying to repair the past. We didn't have a framework for this, and as a result, it seemed like such an overwhelming task for Tonya. We resolved that night that we would focus our energies on building our future as best we could and in the way that we thought best.

Scarcely had we begun that journey when we encountered an unexpected obstacle. A few months later, Tonya, who had always been a workout warrior, began to experience rapid, temporary accelerations of the heart. These episodes were frightening to watch; from a few feet away, I could see the pulse pounding in her neck. When I placed my hand over her heart, I could feel it thumping rapidly through her chest wall. She became dizzy and short of breath. On several occasions, we rushed her by ambulance to the hospital, certain her life was in danger. Eventually we learned she had atrial tachycardia but still were not able to get a clear idea of their origins. Our only comfort came as she began to have them less and less frequently.

But Tonya's health issues were not over yet. Tonya began to complain of extraordinary fatigue, muscle aches, and a level of exhaustion that seemed to take over her entire body. At first we thought this was the result of the pace of her kindergarten class and the demands it placed upon her. We saw one doctor after another, she underwent one test after another, but we could not arrive at a diagnosis. Finally, a specialist in Newton, Massachusetts, told us she had fibromyalgia, a chronic fatigue disorder with no known cause and little in the way of treatment. It was not fatal, and she could live a fairly normal life, but her symptoms would continue indefinitely and were likely to be permanent. It was a harsh diagnosis; neither of us had foreseen a chronic condition, and now two had suddenly appeared. Amazingly, Tonya was more concerned about me and would apologize for the illnesses that had taken over her life. "I know you didn't sign up for this," she'd say.

But she had brought me the greatest love I had ever known. I had found safety and peace with her by my side and I would remain by hers—without condition or qualification.

A week after her diagnosis, Tonya called my office in tears. She was not given to easy emotion; she rarely cried. But the doctor warned us that there would be times like this when she would have moments of sadness. I listened quietly and noticed there seemed to be something different about her tears, something I couldn't quite discern. Stammering, she told me she had gone that morning to see her general physician who decided to rerun another series of tests to be sure they hadn't received false negative results. She was openly laughing now. The diagnosis of fibromyalgia had been wrong. She was pregnant. I was going to be a father.

Over the next eight years, we had three children—Quinn, Vaughn, and Kennedy—raising them in a small, two-thousand-square-foot home in a working-class Boston suburb. Fatherhood brought me the greatest joy of my life. From the beginning, I embraced the responsibility of raising a baby—changing diapers, adjusting car seats, assembling cribs. I often rushed home from work to see what new skills my children had acquired. As soon as I hit the front door, the kids wrestled me to the ground, drowning me in kisses and hugs. They were a whirlwind of activity, and Tonya and I nicknamed them after weather occurrences: Quinn is Lightning, Vaughn is Thunder, and Kennedy is Tornado. What I treasured most was lying on the couch with a child resting on my chest, hearing his or her tiny breath deepen as we both slowly faded off to sleep.

In the evenings, long after baths were taken, nighttime stories were read, and bedtime prayers were said, I found myself standing at their bedsides, marveling at their deep and innocent sleep, their breaths rising and falling in perfect rhythm with the universe. I would lean over to kiss them and, despite the depth of their slumber, they sighed in response. There was so much I wanted them to know: that I loved them with all that I was; that I would travel this path a thousand times, knowing it would bring me to their bedsides; that

they had righted every wrong in my life; that being their father had
quieted my soul.

I had long felt that my own story would not be complete until I
became a father. What I hadn't expected, though, was that fatherhood
would cause me to rethink the stories of my own parents. I had discovered that my mother and father had left me to the winds of chance,
and it had been all I could do to connect with their families. Intent
on building my own family, I had moved forward with my life, but it
had always deeply puzzled me how any parent could so easily aban-
don a child. Fatherhood added to that mystery; I could imagine no
force alive that could separate me from Quinn, Vaughn, and Kennedy.
Their innocence, captured in the smallest of moments, told me just
how much they needed me—just as I had needed Kenny and Marian.
Because I couldn't understand their choices, my unwillingness to forgive my parents only deepened. My faith told me that I should forgive,
but for me that was far easier said than done.

Thoughts of my parents came to the fore as my children grew and
began to ask questions about my family. Tonya's mother, Shirley, often
traveled from New Jersey to Massachusetts to see us, and they would
ask when my mother was coming to see them too. They wanted to know
why there weren't any pictures of my family gatherings as there were
of Mommy's. They couldn't understand why I had a brother with the
same name as mine. As I handled their innocent queries, I found myself
answering the questions for myself as much as for them. Realizing that
their questioning would only intensify, and adamant that they have an
understanding of my early years, I began to write down the circumstances as I understood them to be. There had always been one loose
end—the information contained in my case file. I'd not pursued gain-
ing access to it largely because I thought the case file would tell me
nothing I hadn't already learned. I should have known better.

In January 2003, I called the Massachusetts Department of Social
Services requesting access to my case file.

Six months later, I came home to find a three-inch-thick manila envelope wedged in my front door. It had been too big to fit in our mailbox. It tumbled down to the porch as I opened the door. At first I didn't know what it was, but then I saw the official Commonwealth of Massachusetts seal. I recalled my caseworker Mike Silvia's warning that the file was large and that its contents were disturbing.

I dropped my briefcase at the front door, loosened my tie, sat down on the living room couch, and began to read. On the very first page, I received a shock. My mother was calling the Department of Social Services for help. She was eight months pregnant. In an entry dated March 13, 1962, a social worker provided the following account of my mother's appearance at her office: "[Marian] appeared to be recovering from a bruised right eye, had a fur coat on, which appeared to be sheared muskrat; it was dirty and stained. She had on a very dirty white blouse and [illegible] hair."

The stories I had been told about my mother had given me a picture of a woman who seemed contrarian and beyond help—someone who *wanted* to live on society's fringes. Only now did I realize the sheer desperation of her plight, as well as her own awareness of it. Here was a woman frightened and anxious and incapable of taking care of herself, not a determined wanderer.

As I read on, I understood for the first time just how tormented my mother had been over the loss of her children. In 1960, she lost Ben to her parents. In 1962, Marc was born, and after some vacillation she decided to keep him. She disappeared from the agency's view until 1964, again eight months pregnant, in a volatile relationship with the baby's father and with no idea of what to do. At the time, Massachusetts's law held that a mother on welfare had to appear before the court when she had her second illegitimate child. This worried her, and she asked the social worker: *Will I be committed to jail? Will it make any difference if I put the child up for adoption?* She didn't go to court at that time, but in October of that year, she found herself before the judge who gave her probation and a stern warning after Marc was found roaming the neighborhood. She had left Marc with a friend, and the friend's teenage son had left the three-year-old in the hallway of Marian's apartment building when Marian hadn't answered the door. Marc wasn't found until the next day.

Marian promised that the judge would never see her again and that she'd take good care of her children. She kept neither promise. A little more than a year later, in December 1965, exactly one day before her probation was up, she was arrested for disorderly conduct and sentenced to six months in jail. Marc and Joni were taken from her. The harsh confines of prison appeared to have a sobering effect on my mother.

Conversations with her new caseworker showed a mother desperate to recover her children. "I will get a job as soon as I get out," she said. "I want my children desperately, and I don't want to lose any more of their love to foster parents." She was paroled after several months, and her entire focus became getting Marc and Joni back, but the agency refused until she found a job. For nearly a year she looked for work without success, and her desperation grew deeper. "I miss [my children] terribly, and I will go off the deep end if I don't get them back."

In March 1967, my grandfather called the agency and my mother with his own plan. Although his house was too small for my mother and her two children, he'd secure an apartment nearby and provide her support money. Yet she was strangely undecided about taking advantage of her father's offer. Some time after that, her social worker went to visit my mother at her apartment. The place was in disarray. The social worker took one look at her, and suddenly everything made sense: the inability to find a job, the refusal of her father's offer to return home to New Jersey, the long coat she rarely took off. Marian was pregnant again, this time with me.

My mother knew this pregnancy meant she was going back to jail. She did the only thing she must have felt she could do: she lied. She said Rudolph Klakowicz, her first husband and Ben's father, was my father. She claimed that she had resumed her relationship with Klakowicz in the fall of 1966 because "it was the best way to get Marc and Joni back." This wasn't true. The real father was a rising fighter with an outlaw reputation: Kenny Pemberton.

The caseworker's conversation with my mother shortly before I was born showed another looming problem: "Mrs. Klakowicz has had a difficult pregnancy. She said this is the worst one yet. She will not have any more children. She said she would not be surprised if the doctor told her she couldn't have any more. She told the worker that this baby was going to be a boy. She had prophesized [sic] before and been right. Worker asked her how she was planning to get to the hospital to have the baby. He said that she could go in a taxi. The man downstairs on the second floor offered to take her, but she said that he is colored. She added that he is very nice, but she would not want anyone at the hospital to think that he was the father of the baby."

This was little more than a clever smoke screen, intended to hide my father's race, for she well knew the consequences of revealing his true identity.

There was no one to deny her story, unless, of course, Rudy showed up in New Bedford, a highly unlikely scenario given that she had not seen him in six years. But amazingly, Rudy *did* show up, and in the newspaper no less, when he and a friend were arrested for hitchhiking. Concerned that the agency officials would question Rudy, my mother went to the House of Corrections to visit him, and he told her what they both already knew: the unborn baby was not his. Agency officials never had the chance to speak with him, however. He appealed to the judge to let him go, and the judge granted his request, with the caveat that he leave town. He apparently never set foot in the city again. Now, in New Bedford, only Kenny and Marian knew my father's true identity.

Rudy's sudden arrival in New Bedford had been an unwelcome surprise to my mother, I am certain. His exile, though, was also a bonanza because now she could cite his banishment as a reason to get assistance. And she did. "I was simply trying to get my children back. We've separated for good, and the marriage is over. I have nowhere to go.

Please don't hold this pregnancy against me." The agency, convinced of her sincerity, responded with additional assistance. Her father sent her a baby carriage.

My mother had dealt in secrets and surprises for most of her adult life, but on June 15, 1967, it would be nature's turn to dole out the unexpected. At 7:19 a.m. I arrived, weighing five pounds twelve ounces. That was expected. What was not expected was the arrival, three minutes later, of my twin sister. The next day my mother called her caseworker, Deborah Chase, at her office to tell her of the twins' arrival. We did not arrive without complications, however. I was born with six digits on my left hand, and would need surgery to remove the extra finger. My sister would not be as fortunate.

From the moment she arrived, doctors at St. Luke's Hospital sensed that something was not right with Starla Louise Klakowicz. After a series of exams, they determined she had a heart condition, and she was immediately transported to Boston. My mother overheard the nurses talking about her baby girl and knew there was little hope. Several operations to save her failed. My sister clung to life for five days before dying of a brain hemorrhage on June 20, 1967. There is no record of a funeral being held for her nor an indication my mother received support of any kind to cope with my sister's passing.

My first year of life with my mother appeared to be a trial run to determine whether or not she could handle the demands of motherhood. From the agency's point of view, she appeared to be making some progress. Still, there was cause for concern. Her apartment was often in poor condition. A caseworker's unannounced visits in the afternoon would bring the sound of scurrying feet, and only after several long minutes would the door crack half-open, revealing a groggy, half-awake Marian. Random people appeared to be living with her; they hid in a back room when caseworkers came calling. I was still sleeping in a baby carriage, as my mother had not yet purchased a crib. All these factors contributed to the agency's refusal to grant her wish that Marc and Joni be returned to her.

By early 1968, however, my mother at least had a steady man in her life. Bernard Cruz, whose offer to take her to the hospital she had refused because of his race, seemed a good provider. Yet it appears that both the agency and my mother overlooked his volatile temper. At one point, when I suffered a broken collarbone, the agency and the police department suspected him of child abuse but declined to investigate further, citing a lack of evidence. The agency believed that Bernard provided enough support to warrant returning Marc and Joni to their mother. On the afternoon of May 10, 1968, after a three-and-a-half-year separation, Marc and Joni were returned to our mother. Later that fall, Marian announced that she and Bernard were expecting a baby, due right around the holidays.

For the first time ever, my mother appeared to have her life on track. Christmas Eve 1968 was, I imagine, the happiest she had ever been. She had a boyfriend who loved her and whom she loved in return. She was in a clean, new apartment with hardwood floors and central heating. She had furniture, linens, pots and pans, and even a new washing machine. She had been able to buy an artificial Christmas tree that she adorned with ornaments. Wrapped in presents under the tree were new clothes for all three of her children. Her caseworker brought gifts from the agency, as did Marc's and Joni's former foster parents, who had kept their old stockings and filled them with toys. Most important, she was prepared for the arrival of this baby.

Though I was too young to remember, history has taught me there were heady events in 1968: the assassinations of Martin Luther King and Robert Kennedy, racial protests and demonstrations, riotous anti–Vietnam War confrontations at the Democratic National Convention in Chicago, and as the year drew to a close, the first manned spaceflight to leave Earth's orbit, *Apollo 8*. The spaceflight had given the country hope after the tumultuous events earlier in the year, and it was fitting that it would be launched just a few days before Christmas.

My grandfather worked for NASA as a technical writer, and

I imagine my mother sat us down to watch the broadcast. I can see us huddled around the television, staring at those grainy, black-and-white images, as close to a family as we had ever been, listening to the Christmas Eve message from the crew of *Apollo 8*: "In the beginning God created the heaven and the earth. And the earth was without form, and void; and darkness was upon the face of the deep. And the Spirit of God moved upon the face of the waters. And God said, Let there be light: and there was light. And God saw the light, that it was good: and God divided the light from the darkness."

Four days after Christmas, a healthy baby boy arrived. They named him Bernard, after his father. His middle name was Joseph, after Marian's father, as she had done for her other three sons. In February 1969, the agency closed my mother's case. They believed she had turned her life around. This turned out to be a disastrous decision, one that would have consequences and repercussions for decades to come.

A year and a half passed. In July 1970, race riots erupted in New Bedford, in a series of events that would capture national attention. On July 22, 1970, in the midst of the heat and swelter of the riots, the Department of Child Guardianship, now named Department of Social Services, received a telephone call from an irate babysitter. Our mother had paid a babysitter to take care of us for the day. But five days later, she had still not returned. On the fifth day, the babysitter called our mother's apartment and found her there but with little interest in coming to get us. Instead, she suggested to the babysitter that her children—ages eight, six, three, and two—walk the nearly two miles back to the apartment.

The Department of Social Services immediately assigned an investigator to the case. When he visited a week later, he found the apartment in deplorable condition. Broken furniture, clothes in trash bags, writing on the walls, and mattresses scattered about the floor all greeted him upon his arrival. I had six stitches on my left foot that appeared to be swollen and infected. Her boyfriend Bernard was nowhere to be found.

My mother argued with the investigator. "I've been out looking for a new home."

"Stop using the excuse of wanting to move as the reason for neglecting the house and the children," he shot back.

"I'm not neglecting the children," she retorted. And on they argued. The investigator told her he would be back, and when she asked why, he told her it was to be sure he gave the family "a fair assessment." My mother could read in between the lines of that statement and knew what he was really suggesting: she would lose the children—again. "If you try to take the children, I will move with them out of the state," she threatened.

The investigator's surprise visit and subsequent threats to take her children had little effect. Two weeks after his visit, the agency received another call from a different babysitter, describing a frighteningly similar scenario: she had dropped the children off for the day and then had not returned for five days. Despite the dangers, the agency did not come back for another visit until the first week in October. In detailed notes, the caseworker described what he saw:

The house was cluttered with dirty clothing. There was a strong unpleasant odor in the house as well as in the hallway. Dirty dishes were piled up on the counters and in the sink. There were eggshells and other undistinguishable [sic] pieces of food remnants cluttered on the table top and on the floor. During this conversation, Mrs. Klakowicz was very defensive in her attitude . . . She held Steve to her side while she leaned on the gas heater. At one point, he turned his back to both workers, exposing a burn about six inches in length, running horizontally between his two shoulders . . . Mrs. Klakowicz expressed hope that all this nonsense of coming to check up on her would stop.

The shock from reading about our living conditions had barely registered before I received another. Our address was listed in the case file as 11 Lincoln Street. The familiarity of the street had nagged at me when suddenly it hit me—Lincoln Street was in the same neighborhood as Arnold Street, four short blocks away. I had walked past the house countless times, unaware that it was the very place where I had spent my early years with my mother.

During the next month, the agency tried contacting my mother several times, to no avail. Though they apparently understood the severity of the situation, they did not react with the urgency one might expect. That would all change with a single phone call from a school nurse to the agency on November 6, 1970. My sister, Joni, had been fainting in class for no apparent reason, and my mother did not seem in the least bit concerned by this, claiming that Joni "always passed out before she got sick." Their concern grew when the school nurse visited the apartment on Lincoln Street and was overcome by the living conditions.

At the school's request, the caseworker went to visit that same day. Though he didn't think it possible, he found the living conditions even more deplorable than on his visit a month before. Though summer was a distant echo, an army of flies swarmed over everything, including my brother Steven and me. Both of us were barefoot and covered in dirt and old food. Dirty clothes, old cans, and used disposable diapers were strewn about the floor. A garbage stench permeated the small apartment. Several times the caseworker was overcome by the terrible smell and had to step outside to get air.

Equally concerning was my mother's attitude. Defensive and belligerent, she had an excuse for everything. Whatever was wrong with Joni had nothing to do with her but with the foster family she had lived with before. The terrible condition of the apartment? It didn't matter since she was getting evicted anyway. The policewoman who had stopped by a few days before, expressing concern? She was harassing her.

For years the agency had failed to take decisive action, largely because the prevailing wisdom of the time was that children were best served by staying with their biological mothers. But now teachers, nurses, school officials, neighbors, other tenants, and the police had all weighed in with their concerns. Anyone who came in contact with Marian and her children could see how this was going to end. A phone call from the owner of the house on Lincoln Street to the agency encapsulated what everyone else seemed unwilling to say: if these children stay with their mother much longer, they are going to die.

The agency had a very clear plan when they came to our apartment that cold December afternoon in 1970. Joni and I were to be signed into foster care, and Marc was to go to New Jersey to live with our grandparents. The department seemed to grasp the traumatic effect such a move would have on our mother and decided to let Steven stay with her for the time being. The movers struggled to remove items from the apartment, hampered by the trash and debris that cluttered the floor. My mother was not prepared for our departure. She scurried around looking for clothing for me but could find nothing. Finally, the caseworker took me out to the car in what I had on: shoes and a sweater. I had no socks, no jacket, no pants. The temperature was in the thirties.

I was wrapped in a blanket, and the caseworker gave me a jar of candy. I proceeded to eat the entire contents, stuffing three and four candies into my mouth at one time. It was the first time I had eaten that day. I asked a lot of questions about where I was going, but my backseat companion never said a word.

As I read further in the report, I suddenly bolted from my seat. My first memory, the one I had retained all those years, the one that seemed so disconnected from everything else in my life, was of my final day with my mother. And the identity of the child in the backseat, the one I did not want them to take away? That was my sister, Joni.

Today I have no recollection of the moments before I got into the car. I would like to remember because it would give me something I long for and that no one else can give me—a memory of my mother. Right before I climbed into the car, I was with her, near her, close to her. Though I close my eyes and scour my memory, impose my will on it, desperately try to recall something of her—her voice, her smile, the color of her hair—I cannot. Though others describe these things to me, those are *their* memories, and I cannot make them mine, try as I might.

We left Joni that day at an orphanage, St. Mary's Home. A wonderful family from Taunton, Massachusetts, eventually adopted her, but she would be haunted by the memories of those early years with our mother. My grandfather, Joseph Murphy, picked up Marc the following day. Within a year, largely driven by finances, he made the gut-wrenching decision to return his grandson to foster care. But unbeknown to Joe, Marc would be taken in by New Jersey foster families who treated him terribly. Like Marc, I would fall into the clutches of cruel foster families: first the abandoning Andrades and later the ruthless Robinsons, arriving at their home shortly after my father's murder in August 1972. Though Betty Robinson knew who my father was and could have brought me to the Pemberton family, she never did. The case file told me that Betty and Willie Robinson were fully aware of the horrors of my initial years with my mother. Yet this would not stop them from unleashing more devastation. My brother Steven stayed with our mother for another three years and lived the life of a transient before he, too, was placed in foster care. Twenty years would pass before we would see one another. At no point in our lives have the five of us been together at one time.

I have no idea how my mother reacted the day the agency came to take her children. I do know that Marian Klakowicz fought on, battling the courts and the agency to have her children returned. The agency pleaded with her to release custody of us but she refused, driven by her belief that "all children belong with their mother." At one point, she told the caseworker that she would consider adoption, but only for me—because of my mixed race, she believed I would be better off in a different family setting. As I read this, I couldn't help but think back to the letter I'd read at my grandmother's and my mother's stinging failure to mention my name. For years that letter had been her final legacy to me, but now the case file had painted a different picture: a mother who wrestled with the idea that she could best love her son by letting him go.

But no matter what her hopes were or how desperate her pleas, the agency refused her requests. In fact, the agency implored her to sign the necessary papers to release us for adoption. Each time she angrily rebuffed them, exercising the last remaining legal right she had. It was a stalemate between a recalcitrant mother who desperately wanted her children and an intractable agency that had seen first-hand the torment her children had suffered in her care. Ultimately the agency would win. My mother, I suspect, would have found some victory in knowing that she had never willingly signed us away.

On occasion she apparently felt the tug of motherhood and called the agency to see how her children were doing or to make another attempt to have us returned. The calls came from all over the Northeast: Rhode Island, Maine, New York City, Connecticut. In more than one instance she called from a detoxification center, but when the agency called back a few days later looking for her, they were informed she had left—against the center's wishes. She continued to rebuff her family's repeated attempts to help her.

Soon the calls to the agency became less and less frequent, and they stopped altogether in January 1975. In October that same year, the Department of Social Services determined that "any contact with Ms. Klakowicz, or her family, would cause an unnecessary uproar in the case." The long reach of this judgment would span across time, erecting bureaucratic barriers that, for the next twenty years, would thwart the efforts of Marian's children to find her—and one another. This was the same obstacle Joseph Murphy had run into when he tried to find his grandchildren. My mother was notified by form letter, at her last known address, that the agency petitioned the court to termi-nate her parental rights, the law of man trumping the law of nature.

Her children scattered, with no possibility of return, my mother sank even further into despair and depression. Her family would hear from her from time to time, usually when she needed money or someone to bail her out. Our mother's story could have ended right there, relegated to little more than a footnote in some future genealogical tree, and perhaps a question (Marian, now wasn't she the one who had some trouble?), if not for her children's quests to find out what had become of her. But when we did find her, we had little understanding of what she had endured. We had been so immersed in our own battles to survive, to make some sense of what fate had dealt us, that we'd reserved no room to understand our mother's futile struggle to keep us in her life.

I could now see that Marian Klakowicz née Murphy was a tortured, lonely, and desperate soul, constantly in search of someone or something that could bring a sense of normalcy to her life. She was almost certainly afflicted with some form of depressive condition that had gone undiagnosed and untreated, a condition made worse because she was an alcoholic. The agency had taken Joni and Marc from her. It would be three years before she got them back only to lose them again two years later. She had lost a baby, my twin sister Starla, shortly after we were born. She sought rescue in a number of relationships, but they were all fleeting. She had been imprisoned for nearly a year, was estranged from her family, condemned to a nomadic lifestyle, and frequently preyed upon by sadistic and violent men. Most damaging of all, she had lost the only thing anchoring her to this world—her children. No one would have willingly chosen that life.

When the superintendent had broken down the door of the apartment to find my mother collapsed and unresponsive in the chair, smoke billowing around her, he had no idea she'd predicted this very day: "I will not be able to live without my children." Less than three years after losing the last of her six children, my mother slipped away. No one was by her side.

CHAPTER 41

For of all sad words of tongue and pen
The saddest are these: "It might have been."

—JOHN GREENLEAF WHITTIER, *"MAUD MULLER"* (1856)

In December 2010, four small letters, tightly sealed in a FedEx envelope, arrived at our home. The envelopes that contained the letters were tinged a light yellow, corners frayed, the black ink of the mail stamps now ghostly apparitions of letters and numbers. They were dated from June 1969 and were addressed to George Carmo of New Bedford, whose love for the author had never allowed him to throw the letters away. The writer was corresponding from prison, where he had been incarcerated since November of the previous year. He was on trial for murder. The author of the letters was Kenny Pemberton.

Over the years, I have been sought out by many of his old friends who want to meet his son. The heroes of our childhood never really die and death further mythologizes them, turning these once corporeal figures into timeless icons. So it is with this once "golden boy" of New Bedford. Kenny's friends are tough, seasoned men but none of them can talk about him without weeping. They want to share a story or two about him, about the man he was, his love and loyalty to those he cared about. Though he was not those things to me, I politely listen, appreciating their genuine desire to connect a son to a father he never knew, to convince the boy that his father was more than he appeared to be.

These accounts are important to me but they are not the same as the voice of a father. And as I opened the first of the four letters, the forty-year-old paper crackling, I realized that I had never heard from Kenny directly. And the story he told of his own life was very different than any I had heard.

The same week Richard Nixon was elected president of the United States, a seventy-seven-year-old man from Rochester, Massachusetts, named Manuel DeSylvia Jr. was discovered lying in a pool of blood in his home. He had been brutally assaulted, beaten around his head and face, and the police concluded that he'd been beaten to death by someone's fists. Only a trained fighter, the police and criminal investigators said, could have inflicted such damage. Kenny Pemberton immediately became a suspect. They also had evidence that Kenny, on horseback, had been on the man's property. An all-points bulletin was immediately issued, and within a couple of days Kenny turned himself in to the New Bedford police. The story of his arrest ran on the front pages of the *New Bedford Standard-Times*, showing a picture of a defiant Kenny being taken into custody. For eight months Kenny languished in prison awaiting trial.

In his letters he proclaimed his innocence while remaining uncertain what would become of him. Reading the letters, it was clear to me that the Carmo family—Charlie, George, and their mother—had become his family after his own had disintegrated. He referred to Mrs. Carmo as "Mother" and told George he thought of him as a younger brother. He revisited childhood memories, recalling previous summers of fun while riding double on a scooter.

He referred to Louie Carmo—George and Charlie's younger brother and Kenny's best friend—as his "twin." Recalling Louie must have pained him, for three years earlier Louie had been allegedly murdered, poisoned by well-connected men who were brought in for questioning. While they were being questioned, an enraged Kenny stood across the street from the New Bedford police station firing bottles at the building in an unsuccessful attempt to get arrested so he could get inside to deliver his own version of justice. The men were never charged with Louie's death. During Louie's funeral services, Kenny had been so distraught that he had to be dragged away from his friend's grave site. But that is not the only heartbreak the letters reveal.

Kenny wrote of more disappointment, saying that the only love he had ever known was "the destructive kind," that he'd had one shot at true love and had lost her. "Guess it's something I'll just have to live with," he wrote. And the way he lived with it was by believing that love and family were for other men but not for him. Heartbroken over his losses, he said he would never marry any woman, let alone a white woman.

The letters reveal glimpses of the Kenny who still commands the loyalty and love of those who knew him. He seems more concerned about the plight of others than about himself. He was happy for George and proud of him that he was getting married: "I believe a man should do what he feels in his heart . . . the heart is the way to happiness." He told him to take care of his wife and new baby. His last words to George are telling, a fatherly bit of advice that speaks to me now, more than forty years later: "Keep family safe."

Kenny was painfully aware of the precariousness of his situation. "Jail is not a place fit for a dog to stay," he wrote. He knew life in prison awaited him if he were found guilty, a fate that he said was the equivalent of death. In each of the four letters, he insisted on his innocence, saying that he did nothing wrong and was confident he would be acquitted. In none of them did he mention boxing.

The trial took place in the Plymouth County Courthouse in July 1969. Without air-conditioning in the ancient courtroom, even the proximity to Plymouth Harbor just outside the open windows did little to ameliorate the intense summer heat. The all-white jury listened to the state's evidence that established Kenny's horse was stabled near DeSylvia's home and that Kenny had the boxing skills to inflict the kind of damage that killed the victim. But his attorney, Malcolm Jones, deftly countered the state's evidence and made a mockery of the state medical examiner's shabby handling of the body and the timeline of the alleged murder. Jones chose to keep Kenny off the witness stand, deciding that the state would be unable to prove guilt beyond a reasonable doubt.

Late in the afternoon of July 16, after less than a day of deliberation, the jury came back with a verdict of not guilty. Kenny embraced Jones and Charlie Carmo, who had been a daily fixture in the courtroom throughout the trial. Back in New Bedford, the newly freed Kenny returned to the place that had always been his sanctuary, the boxing gym. He reconnected with one of his former trainers, Jerry Huston, and decided to make another run at boxing glory. Jerry was happy to take Kenny back. He knew of Kenny's checkered past, but he had great personal affection for the young fighter. A year away from the ring did little to dull Kenny's boxing skills. He was just twenty-three years old and was back in the ring within weeks of his release, fighting a national AAU middleweight champion to a draw, though the decision went to his opponent.

By February 1970, Kenny was back in Lowell fighting once more in the finals of the New England Golden Gloves tournament. He won the tournament for the third time, and in the aftermath, Kenny and Huston prepared for a spot in the National Golden Gloves championships in Las Vegas. Kenny had returned to New Bedford in triumph after the Lowell match and was interviewed by a local television sportscaster. In the video, he and Huston appeared on the broadcast together, and Kenny, in soft, barely audible tones, talked about turning pro that summer. Huston predicted a huge win for Kenny at the nationals. But Huston had a full-time job and could not leave to accompany Kenny to Las Vegas.

The Golden Gloves provided cornermen for each fighter, and Kenny easily won his first two bouts to advance to the finals. In the championship fight, Kenny apparently soundly defeated a white middleweight from Grand Rapids, Michigan, named Larry Woods, but Woods was awarded the decision by a tenth of a point. The crowd booed the decision and threw bottles and chairs into the ring.

Kenny believed the decision had been racially motivated. And as it turned out, the New Bedford he returned to from Las Vegas was about to explode in the racial violence of the riots of the summer of 1970. Though he hadn't been politically active, Kenny could no longer ignore the growing rage in the West End streets. Kenny's change in physical appearance reflected the changing times. Pictures of Kenny while in Las Vegas show a clean-shaven young man who had maintained the processed hairstyle in deference to his idol, Sugar Ray Robinson. But a few months later, he had grown a beard, grown his hair into an Afro, and had taken to wearing a red bandanna around his head.

Unemployment had sapped the African American community in New Bedford of pride and hope. The Black Panthers had established a base in the city, and confrontations with the police and the white community began to occur more frequently as a hot, tense summer began. The riots that had raged around the country in 1968 finally arrived at New Bedford's doorstep. This waterfront city, its long ties to liberty a distant memory, suddenly became reacquainted with the struggle for access and opportunity.

On Wednesday, July 8, a routine traffic stop and the arrest of a black man in the West End ignited a night of clashes with police and firefighters. Groups of angry youths shouted "Off the pig!" amid fires, gunshots, and arrests. On the next night, violence escalated and then spread to the South End. Abandoned buildings were firebombed in an attempt to draw police away from Kempton Street, where the action was centered. Eventually, the police erected barricades around the West End to seal off the area.

On Saturday a group of West Enders, including African Americans, Cape Verdeans, and Hispanics, were gathered outside a club when a car screeched to a halt on the street. The car had swerved around the barricades and came tearing into the area. Three white men jumped from the car, and the driver leaned over the hood with a shotgun and fired wildly into the group. A seventeen-year-old Cape Verdean youth was struck, along with three others. The white men peeled away in their car, and the crowd grew into an angry mob.

Kenny emerged from the crowd and leaned down over the youth who was most seriously hurt and was stunned to see his cousin, Lester Lima, a gentle, nonviolent boy who was affectionately nicknamed Shoobie. Kenny, his brother Bobby, and another friend loaded Lester into a car and took him to St. Luke's Hospital several blocks away, passing right by the house on Arnold Street. It was too late. Later that night, Lester died. The city exploded into full-scale riots and several days of shooting, looting, burning, and rage. State leaders, such as U.S. Senator Ed Brooke, came to New Bedford to try to quell the violence, and Senator Brooke asked Kenny and Charlie Carmo to be members of an ad hoc committee to help calm the community. Kenny's stature as a local boxing hero made him an ironic figure in the quest for nonviolence, but with his arm in a sling as a result of a motorcycle accident, he grabbed a bullhorn and helped bring the city under a tense control. Less than two blocks away, my brothers Steven and Marc, our sister, Joni, and I were in a life-and-death struggle with our mother.

In one of the letters he wrote while imprisoned, Kenny, dejected and sullen over his circumstances, had said, "I've learned a lot about life." And he had. By the age of twenty-three, Kenny had suffered an extraordinary series of crushing disappointments and losses, heartbreaks I don't think he ever recovered from: the disintegration of his family after the fire that consumed their home; the early death of his mother when he was just fifteen; the tragic deaths of two siblings, Gordon and Elaine; the alleged murder of his best friend, Louie Carmo; his almost yearlong imprisonment; the riots that had taken the life of his cousin; his failed relationships.

For some men, losing that which you love can ignite a relentless search to find those things fate and circumstances have denied you. There is boldness in that mission, a confidence that it's not possible to lose more than you already have. Hope is your companion in that search; a belief that those things which you yearn for can one day—someday—come to pass. And when you find that place, you will also find peace. I had recognized that quest in my own life and now I could see it in my father's life as well.

For a time boxing appeared to offer Kenny that sanctuary, but the sweet science can also be a harsh mistress, and so it was with my father. The controversial decision in Las Vegas denied him a national title and could well have altered the arc of his life. Boxing had also blurred the lines between friends and acquaintances; Kenny couldn't discern who was a friend and who was a flatterer, more interested in hanging onto his coattails.

I was born during this time, making Kenny something he was not ready to be: a father. Lois Gibbs believes Kenny knew of my existence, as does Kenny's friend Ray Mott. And somehow Betty Robinson knew as well. It appears that while living with another woman—possibly his on-again, off-again girlfriend Evelyn Brown—Kenny had carried on a secretive relationship with my mother for several months. When my mother confronted him about the pregnancy, he initially denied it, claiming that the baby could not be his. But my mother, who knew the identity of each of her children's fathers, had insisted. Kenny, who at least knew that it was possible for my mother to be pregnant with his child, adopted the conventional street wisdom of the time—the baby was my mother's problem to solve.

As his losses racked up, and he searched in vain for some type of connection, Kenny muted his pain by turning to the harsh and unforgiving world of drugs, although his addiction wasn't immediately apparent to those who knew him. For many, he was still Kenny the promising fighter, the fiercely devoted friend. But Kenny's vices were winning over his virtues. In time he abandoned the ring, and his family and friends watched helplessly as their champion slid away from his pedestal into a heroin-induced darkness. Fate would soon deal Kenny yet another unkind blow.

In March 1971, Kenny and his brothers planned a get-together with their father. Kenny still maintained strong ties to his father and had actually lived with him for a time. Joseph Pemberton had been a fighter, and the two of them often discussed the sweet science and Kenny's promising boxing career. Right before Kenny went to Las Vegas, Kenny and his father took a playful picture in which his father is throwing a right cross to Kenny's jaw and Kenny is pretending to be knocked out. This get-together with Joe Pemberton was to be extra-special; the "fight of the century" between Muhammad Ali and Joe Frazier was to be fought in Madison Square Garden, and the Pemberton sons planned to take their father to a closed-circuit venue at nearby Lincoln Park to see the fight. They would never make it.

That afternoon, while resting in his favorite chair at his daughter Gerri's home, Joseph Pemberton died of a massive heart attack. Kenny took his father's death hard, nearly suffocating Gerri in a grief-stricken hug. Her brothers had to pull him away. A few days later, Kenny once again found himself standing at a grave site, devastated by the loss of someone he loved. He fell shuddering and trembling upon his father's grave with such force that family members backed away from him. He stopped only when Gerri gently told him that their mother would not want to see him carrying on like he was.

With Joe Pemberton's passing went any hope that those things Kenny wished for could one day come to pass. And in the absence of a deep and abiding faith, that hopelessness turned into recklessness. Kenny now plunged fully into the chaos of the drug culture. Hooked on heroin, he became a legend of another kind on New Bedford's and Fall River's streets: a ruthless enforcer with little regard for the thorny code of the streets. He began to accost drug dealers, beat them mercilessly, and steal their money and drugs. At some point, several local drug dealers sat down with Kenny to try to convince him that he had to stop this activity; that if he were not who he was, the matter would have been handled very differently. But Kenny, ever the warrior and certain no one would dare challenge him directly, refused to yield: he laughed at them and walked out.

Yet for all his bravado, it appears the consequences of the life-style he led had begun to sink in. One afternoon in the summer of 1972, Kenny stopped by the home of Eddie Casey. Casey was an accomplished boxer in his own right, and the two had developed a genuine friendship. Their relationship had been cemented when Kenny came to Casey's mother's home to help her with several odd jobs. Casey had been out of town, and so his mother wanted to pay Kenny for the work he did. But Kenny refused to accept the money.

His visit to Casey's home in New Bedford was a surprise; Casey had not been expecting him. He was even further puzzled when he saw Kenny standing there holding the huge trophy he'd received as runner-up at the National Golden Gloves finals in 1970. "It was beautiful and must have weighed one hundred pounds," Casey recalled. "Kenny said, 'I want you to hold this for me' and handed it over to me."

Casey knew how important the trophy was to Kenny and knew what Kenny's giving it away meant. Casey also knew how stubborn and forceful Kenny could be, but he refused to accept this good-bye from a man he loved and respected. "Kenny had a sense that something was going to happen. I looked at Kenny and said, 'You gotta cut this out . . . you gotta stop using.'

"'Eddie, listen,' he said. 'Nobody . . . nobody can talk to me about this. It's gotta be me. I have to do it myself. It's not that I'm not listening, but I gotta do it myself.'"

On July 30, 1972, four gunmen followed Kenny and his friend Carl Matthews for several miles before unloading their weapons on their vehicle. Matthews ran from the car, taking a bullet in the arm. Kenny stayed in the car and was somehow uninjured. The drive-by was not his last warning. On the night of August 2, Kenny bumped into one of his former trainers, Frank Brito, at a local New Bedford nightclub. Frank was a gentle man who had trained him as a young fighter. Some years earlier, a fellow trainer, Angelo Dundee, had invited Kenny and Frank to come to Muhammad Ali's training camp. Ali was training in Boston, preparing to defend his heavyweight title against Sonny

Liston, the man he had taken the belt from a year prior. During their visit, the ever-brash Ali had insulted Brito, and in a flash Kenny was flying across the room to take on the heavyweight champion of the world. The two were separated before any blows were thrown, but Frank never forgot Kenny's unwavering devotion.

But now Frank took one look at Kenny's half-closed eyes and teetering balance and realized that he was high. He motioned him over to a small table. "You know I don't get into your personal business, Kenny. Never have," Brito said. Kenny slowly nodded his head in agreement. "But I'm hearing some bad things out here in the streets. There are people looking for you, and they don't wanna talk. You gotta stay out of Fall River."

Frank Brito was not the only person Kenny saw that day. Earlier he had stopped by Jerry Huston's boxing gym in downtown New Bedford. Kenny had been strangely affectionate, clapping Jerry on the back while loudly proclaiming, "My man!" He soon became a distraction, and Jerry asked him to leave. Desperate to connect with her, he also appeared at his sister Geraldine's job, something he had never done before. Kenny's previous visits that day may have been the last pleas of a person looking for help or a man consigned to his fate. During their conversations, Kenny had appeared disoriented.

To Frank he had initially seemed unaware of the danger he was in. But on hearing Frank's advice, he turned clearheaded, his steely gaze boring holes through Frank. What he said next put the matter to rest. Placing a reassuring hand on Frank's shoulder, he told his trainer, "Anybody who is looking for me knows where to find me." Chills ran down Frank's spine. Kenny got up to leave and then turned back to offer one final comment.

"And if they don't know, you can tell 'em."

"Please, Kenny," Frank said. "Go home!"

He pleaded further with Kenny but to no avail. When he last saw his former prize pupil, Kenny was climbing into a car with Matthews, but not before looking cautiously up and down the darkened street checking for danger. Frank did not know it at the time, but they were headed for Fall River.

It doesn't take long to get from New Bedford to Fall River. It's about twenty minutes, fastest if you take Route 195. This is likely the route Kenny and Carl Matthews took that humid night of August 2, 1972. The official police investigation indicated that the two men went to the Massasoit Cafe, a popular nightspot on the corner of Pleasant and Rocliffe streets in Fall River. While inside, Kenny reportedly hit his head on a table and walked outside to "get some air." Matthews followed him outside with an ice pack, catching up to him a few feet past the Rocliffe Street entrance. As the pair walked up the street a bit farther, a man five feet six inches tall and wearing a white T-shirt and blue jeans strode past them, turned around, and opened fire. The first two shots from the small-caliber pistol struck Kenny squarely in the chest. The next two bullets ripped into his side as Matthews pulled him to the ground.

Kenny, who had made his living and his reputation with his hands, never had the chance to raise them in his own defense. Although a police cruiser was only a block away and several patrolmen came to his aid, there was little they could do. Kenny was pronounced dead on arrival at Union Hospital. Just as he had predicted, his killer had approached from behind. Kenny was twenty-six years old.

Relying on reports from eyewitnesses, police set up a dragnet over a thirteen-street radius, but the assailant managed to escape, fleeing through backyards behind the cafe. Matthews told investigators that he could not provide a description of the suspect. Police were initially optimistic that "several leads would pan out," but rumors began to fly across the two cities that Kenny had been set up, that he had been lured to the cafe and then gunned down. Kenny's grieving supporters in New Bedford, including members of his own family, had no intention of waiting to find out if this was true. Newspaper accounts indicate that a wave of retaliatory brawls and shootings erupted between New Bedford and Fall River during the next two days, and in each instance

Kenny's death was cited as a motivating factor. One of the incidents involved my uncle Warren, who was arrested after threatening two men with a gun.

With tensions high, the proprietor of the Colonial Funeral Chapel called the New Bedford Police Department requesting a police guard. He had been receiving threatening phone calls, he said. His request was too late. On the following Friday night, in the early morning hours, one or more perpetrators broke into the funeral home and set Kenny's body aflame, using a can of lighter fluid from a nearby storage cabinet. Only a falling plastic fluorescent light shade, likely the result of immense heat, extinguished the blaze. No one was ever charged with Kenny's murder, although rumors still abound that his death was avenged by the barbed scale of street justice.

Kenny, the sixth child of Joseph and Mary, was buried under heavy police guard in the southern end of New Bedford's St. John's Cemetery. Just one row away lay his beloved father. On the funeral stanchion, Kenny's casket was closed, a necessity given the events that had unfolded at the funeral home. Off to the side stood a large boulder that would be rolled over his grave to prevent further attacks. The only consolation came from knowing that Mary and Joseph were not alive to bury their son.

The section of the cemetery to which the mourners had come to say their final good-byes was named St. Matthews—the same name as the companion with whom Kenny spent his last hours. If you know the story, before following the invitation of Jesus to join his disciples, St. Matthew was a tax collector. I read a hard lesson in that: for the life you, Kenny, have chosen, the bill is now due. Etched on the grieving faces of his family and friends was another hard lesson: the ones who love you, Kenny, must also pay a price for the life you have chosen. Those who loved him could only lament—not just for Kenny and his eternal soul but also for the loss of that part of themselves Kenny had taken with him. Had they known what was to unfold, I suspect they would have cried some for me too.

CHAPTER 42

Cause and effect, means and ends, seed and fruit cannot be sev-
ered; for the effect already blooms in the cause, the end preexists
in the means, the fruit in the seed.

—RALPH WALDO EMERSON

After all these years, I have only dreamed of my father once. In my dream I'm standing across the street from the house on Arnold, and Kenny stands on the other side, directly in front of the house, his arms folded across his chest. His back is to me, and he stares up at the three-decker that had been my house of horrors. He senses I am there and turns around, unfurling his arms and letting them fall to his waist. Even from a distance, I perceive that he has a presence about him. For a moment I understand why those in his generation still talk about him as if he were still here. But he is not. He is gone now, and I am what remains.

We meet in the middle of the street. He shakes my hand quickly and emphatically, his grip every bit as strong as I expect. "It's good to see you," he says, with a smile intended to make up for lost time. An uncomfortable silence prevails. There is a long row of maple trees running down both sides of the street, and they buck and sway as if listening to our conversation.

"It's good to see you too," I finally say. We were both fighters whose lives had been marked by loss, defiance, and a desperate search for some sense of family. But our response to life's tragedies had been profoundly

250

different. In another time and place, I would have asked him about this, but I have more pressing questions to ask, answers I need to have. Here, in this dream, I get the chance. "So, you knew about me?"

"Yes, I knew."

I look away, trying to fight the surge of anger that is suddenly coursing through me. I point a finger at him and then at the house on Arnold. "You could have saved me from all this! You were the only one who could have. You were my only chance."

He has no answer. Now it is he who looks away, down past the corridor of trees, a soul forever tormented by regret.

I glance up at the house again, remembering all that unfolded here, feeling anew the loss of my childhood. "I needed you," I say. It is a confession that surprises me. And now my voice drops, and urgently and fiercely, my voice breaking slightly, I ask, "Why didn't you ever come for me?"

His shoulders slump and his head drops; perhaps he wishes I had not asked him *that* question. Yet it seems he already knew it was coming, because his answer is ready. He sighs deeply, the type of exhalation that unburdens a soul. Now it is he who confesses, his voice low and soft: "I thought I had more time."

I have not dreamed of my dad since.

CHAPTER 43

In the early hours of a summer Saturday morning, on the second floor of a small house in a western Boston suburb, I am awakened by the pitter-patter of feet walking into our bedroom. It can only be our six-year-old son, Quinn. He is often the first one to arise and usually makes a beeline right to me, demanding that I wake up. He does not see fit to bestow this privilege on his mother, who lies deep in the comfort of morning slumber.

"Dad, Dad," he whispers. I feign sleep, but the playful smile dancing across my face betrays me.

"I know you're awake, Dad. You're not a very good fooler."

Laughing quietly, I sit up. He is wearing his Buzz Lightyear pajamas, clutching his favorite book, *The Lion and the Mouse*. I drink in his light complexion, curly brown hair with blond tints at the crowns, and bright-blue eyes.

"I wanna go downstairs and read the story," he says, pushing the book into my hands.

"Gotcha," I say, swinging my feet out of the bed and into the plush cool of the carpet. The rest of the house is quiet. "Let's go check on your brother and sister first," I whisper to him. I take his hand, so small in mine. We walk down the hall and open the door to each of the bedrooms. His brother, Vaughn, younger by two years, is fast asleep, light-brown hair peeking above his burgundy comforter. The boys look so similar they are often mistaken for twins. I smile at the tiny hump under the blanket. Even at the tender age of four, Vaughn carries himself with certainty and purpose, as if he has been in this world before

252

and knows how it is all supposed to unfold. His sister, Kennedy, a year old and a near spitting image of her mother, with the spirit to match, is also deep in slumber, arm wrapped around her large Raggedy Ann doll, the one made for all new children who come into the congregation at Myrtle Baptist Church in Newton, Massachusetts.

"They're still sleepy," Quinn announces.

We walk to the top of the staircase, and here we stop. "Airplane ride, Daddy?" he says.

"Absolutely," I say, sitting on the top step. He climbs aboard my back, clinging to my neck, those tiny arms holding on for dear life. This is a morning ritual of ours, one that I will also enjoy with his brother and sister in time.

"Don't drop me, Daddy," he pleads. *Never, son,* I think. *I will never drop you.*

"I gotcha, buddy. Now let's start 'er up." He plants a wet kiss on my cheek, and off we go. We glide down the stairs, past picture frames of Pembertons and Murphys and of Tonya's family, the Bushes and Kees. Our laughter is joyous, bouncing off the walls. I take a particularly hard turn that I know will delight him, and he grabs on to my neck even tighter. We land gently in the living room, and again he takes my hand in his, pulling me to the deep brown leather chair near the fireplace. I sit down, and he climbs onto my lap, his head snuggled perfectly against my shoulder. The sun has already risen, its soft, yellow rays poking through the half-open blinds behind us. A small flock of house sparrows whisper by, banking and gliding, before landing on the banister of the back porch. We open the book and begin our story. Ten seconds later, he interrupts me. "Don't forget to use the lion voice," he says. "Got it," I say, shooting him a thumbs-up.

He settles back onto my shoulder, and I dive into the story with gusto. All is quiet, save the voice of the lion and the kitchen clock ticking gently in the background. Abruptly, he wheels around to face me again.

"Daddy?" he asks, his eyes searching the ceiling.

"Yes," I say. I am ready for a question as to how the mouse knew to save the lion. Though we have read the story many times, he never tires of hearing the answer. But this is not the question he has for me.

"When you were a little boy, did you have a daddy?"

I stare at him for a long time. I thought this question would come years from now, perhaps as a final father-son chat before he went off to college. But it was not in the future; it was right here, right now. I had long ago decided that, when the time came, I would tell my children the truth. "No, son," I say softly. "When I was a little boy, I did not have a daddy."

His brow furrowed, little lines of confusion marking his usually serene features. He searches my eyes, looking for an explanation, then looks skyward as he usually does when he is thinking.

Looking up, his troubled eyes now clear, he says, as only a child can say, "Maybe next time you will have a daddy."

ACKNOWLEDGMENTS

T he living and telling of this story is not possible without the intervening of a thousand angels. I am indebted to my dear friends Doug Hardy, who would not let this story fade, and Ron Sullivan, who set about the task of helping bring it to fruition; my phenomenal agent, Helen Rees, who stood beside me through all the perils and possibilities of a first-time author and in the process became my dear friend; my early collaborator Glenn Rifkin; my personal editor Seth Schulman, whose guidance and steady hand was always present; the good people of Thomas Nelson—Kristie Henson, Janene MacIvor, Jason Jones, and lastly Joel Miller, who saw the promise of this story at the outset.

That I am here to tell this at all is the reflection of so many whose kindnesses, big and small, propelled me forward in the most difficult of times. Their importance to me is reflected in these pages. I have also been blessed with an extraordinary group of friends who awed me with their support. There are far too many of them to list here but they know who they are. And so do I. To Jim Kirsch, Stephanie Robinson, Joan Wallace-Benjamin: there is no word available to me to describe your giving hearts and spirits. And I also want to thank my Fellow Travelers, those truly wonderful people I encounter in my professional life who continually inspire me.

I am eternally grateful to the Murphy and Pemberton families who took me down the often difficult path of their family's past and were brave enough to face it with me. My heroes and heroines will always be my brothers and sisters whose stories of courage also unfold in these pages.

ACKNOWLEDGMENTS

My wife Tonya always understood this was a story about home and family and of reconciliation and redemption. Her support and spirit never wavered and I will forever remember the way I saw her on so many nights—feet curled under legs, cup of tea in hand, listening intently as this story poured forth from me. T, your spirit has always been my safe harbor. To walk alongside you and share this life with you has been another of God's gifts to me.

To my darling children Quinn, Vaughn, and Kennedy: you have given me the gift of fatherhood and in the process also gave me a childhood. Someday, in the not-so-distant future, the beautiful sound of your own children's laughter will enter your universe. And when it does, you will finally understand why my first waking thought of each morning is you. But until that blessed day, may this story give you some hint of the depth of my love for you.

About the Author

STEVE PEMBERTON was born and raised in New Bedford, Massachusetts. After graduating from Boston College with a degree in political science, Steve worked in higher education for several years before moving to the private sector. Today he is Divisional Vice-President and Chief Diversity Officer for Walgreen's. He currently resides in Chicago with his wife and three children. This is his first book.

www.achanceintheworld.com